DEMAND
the IMPOSSIBLE

DEMAND
the IMPOSSIBLE

Science fiction and
the utopian imagination

TOM MOYLAN

METHUEN
New York and London

First published in 1986 by
Methuen, Inc.
29 West 35th Street, New York NY 10001

Published in Great Britain by
Methuen & Co. Ltd
11 New Fetter Lane, London EC4P 4EE

© 1986 Tom Moylan

Photoset by Rowland Phototypesetting Ltd
Bury St Edmunds, Suffolk
Printed in Great Britain by Richard Clay (The Chaucer Press),
Bungay, Suffolk

British Library Cataloguing in Publication Data
Moylan, Tom
Demand the impossible: science fiction and the utopian imagination.
1. Science fiction, American – History and criticism 2. American
fiction – 20th century – History and criticism
I. Title
813′.0876′09   PS374.S35

ISBN 0 416 00012 6
     0 416 00022 3 Pbk

Library of Congress Cataloging in Publication Data
Moylan, Tom, 1943–
Demand the impossible.
Bibliography: p.
Includes index.
1. Science fiction, American – History and criticism.
2. American fiction – 20th century – History and criticism.
3. Utopias in literature. I. Title.
PS374.U8M69   1986   813′.0876′09372   86–12542

ISBN 0 416 00012 6
     0 416 00022 3 (pbk.)

Contents

| | Acknowledgments | vii |
| 1 | Introduction: the critical utopia | 1 |

Part One: Theory

| 2 | The utopian imagination | 15 |
| 3 | The literary utopia | 29 |

Part Two: Texts

4	Joanna Russ, *The Female Man*	55
5	Ursula K. LeGuin, *The Dispossessed*	91
6	Marge Piercy, *Woman on the Edge of Time*	121
7	Samuel R. Delany, *Triton*	156
8	Conclusion	196
	Notes	214
	Bibliography	224
	Index	237

Acknowledgments

Many have helped me in my work on this book. Jack Zipes's encouragement and criticism have been there since the beginning. Others who read and made suggestions on parts of the book include Tom Anderson, Stanley Aronowitz, Mary Kenny Badami, Janice Bogstad, Samuel R. Delany, Teresa de Lauretis, Catherine McClenahan, and Lyman Tower Sargent. The errors and shortcomings are my own.

I thank the University of Wisconsin for the sabbatical grant which allowed me to complete the work, and I thank my colleagues, department chairpersons, and deans in the University of Wisconsin Center System for their support. I am appreciative of my students whose response to the novels discussed here taught me more than I found on my own. Typists Gunnar Lutz, Betty Gygax, Bonnie Siedlewski, and Claire Wroblewski deserve particular recognition. And Janice Price, Jane Armstrong, and Sarah Pearsall, of Methuen, deserve to know how grateful I am for their commitment to this project.

I thank my friends, especially those in Milwaukee, Wisconsin and Youghal, County Cork and those who participated in the Summer Institutes on Culture and Society and in the discussions on science fiction that developed over several years of Wiscon: the annual science fiction convention held in Madison, Wisconsin.

Special thanks go to my father, Thomas Michael Moylan, Chris Christie, Jim Cheney, Bernie Gendron, Ian Harris, Fredric Jameson, Sean Keane, Mark McCraw, John A. Murphy, Basil O'Leary, Alan Prim. And, to Áine O Brien.

I hope that this book will honor the memory of Judith Clark, Tom Donovan, and my mother, Hannah Fenton Moylan.

Last but not least, I thank my daughters, Kate and Sarah Moylan, for their patience and support. I hope they will know a world closer to the ones described in these novels.

Earlier versions of parts of this book appeared in *Science-Fiction Studies* and *Extrapolation*.

1 Introduction: the critical utopia

For in struggling with new structures never before experienced, people also struggle with the old images and make
new images: to distinguish that which has now become
possible, to show the disappearance of that which is unten-
able as already accomplished. Thus, in great models they
show themselves the New, which is difficult to imagine,
already functioning. Now since these new models were
already made from the old, were formed from the given, the
old appear to be false, but they aren't. They only became
that way.   (Bertolt Brecht)

Images of desire. Figures of hope. Utopian writing in its many
manifestations is complex and contradictory. It is, at heart,
rooted in the unfulfilled needs and wants of specific classes,
groups, and individuals in their unique historical contexts. Produced through the fantasizing powers of the imagination, utopia
opposes the affirmative culture maintained by dominant ideology. Utopia negates the contradictions in a social system by
forging visions of what is not yet realized either in theory or

1

practice. In generating such figures of hope, utopia contributes to the open space of opposition.

The phenomenon of utopian discourse is world-wide. Although it has ancient roots – including the Garden of Eden, the Buddhist Western Paradise, the Native American Happy Hunting Ground, Plato's Republic, the Celtic Hy Brasil, and popular songs from "The Land of Cokaygne" to Joni Mitchell's "Dreamland" – the specific western tradition of the literary utopia is generally agreed to have originated with Thomas More's *Utopia* in 1516 and has continued down to the "critical utopias" considered here: namely Joanna Russ's *The Female Man*, Ursula K. LeGuin's *The Dispossessed*, Marge Piercy's *Woman on the Edge of Time*, and Samuel R. Delany's *Triton*. Developed within the context of early capitalism and the European exploration of the new world, the literary utopia has functioned within the dominant ideology that has shaped the capitalist dream and within the oppositional ideologies that have pushed beyond the limits of that dream.[1]

Utopia, capitalism, and the new world

In *The English Utopia*, A. L. Morton discusses the connections between utopian writing and the growth of a new social-economic system. As the subsistence economy and self-contained social relations of feudal society gave way to more fluid social relations and an economy of expanding production and consumption for the accumulation of profit, the old cultural order was also giving way to new cultural forms. People's lives and the way they understood them were being altered. Morton describes the world in which Thomas More wrote as one of

> despair and hope, of conflict and contrast, of increasing wealth and increasing poverty, of idealism and corruption, of the decline at once of the local and international societies in the face of the national state which was to provide the frame within which bourgeois society could develop.[2]

The ideological paradigm by which the emerging society understood itself changed, and institutions, norms, symbols, and narrative forms developed that were either compatible with the rising classes which dominated the new systems of production and nation, or compatible with those subordinated to that economy and law, or contradictorily responsive to both, as in the case of a literary text such as *Utopia*. More welcomed the new paradigm and described his ideal commonwealth in humanist terms current to his day; but he also attempted to imagine a way to secure justice and a good life for those peasants, unattached serfs, and craft workers who were being displaced from land recently enclosed by profit-oriented landlords. Whereas the fourteenth-century "Land of Cokaygne" celebrated the desires of the peasantry for an easy life without indicating how such ease could be delivered within historical possibility, *Utopia*, written at a time of rapid social change two hundred years later, provided images of alternatives to the given situation which, while not yet existing in history, drew on the contradictions of the time and anticipated a response to the conflicting needs of dominant and subordinate classes. The images were not blueprints to be imposed directly on everyday reality, but they were the beginnings, at the level of imagination, of actual solutions to current problems.

The literary utopia developed as a narrative form in times of deep change, and it has continued to thrive in tumultuous moments since the sixteenth century. This is not to say that utopias are written only in times of crisis, but the form itself is suited to the sort of discourse which considers both what is and what is not yet achieved. However, it was not only a changing social and economic order that inspired such a literary development. For a utopian society to be imagined it must be located somewhere other than the author's own society. In More's day, alternative societies would not be located at the beginning or end of time, as many ancient visions were, or in a historical future, where utopian societies since the 1890s generally have been sited. Rather, they were situated elsewhere on the globe that was then being explored. The "discovery" of the non-European continents and islands provided visionaries of the fifteenth and sixteenth centuries with actual and imaginary space in which to create both practicing and literary experiments. The new space in the world reinforced the sensibility found in the landscape painting and pastoral poetry of the time that effused the presence of an arcadian locale in which dreams could be lived. The newly explored and reported-upon lands gave an air of possibility to

3

dreams which had until then been restricted to the frame of the painting or the end of the poem.

The European image of the "new world," then, was that of a "landscape untouched by history," as Leo Marx has called it, where the known evils of European life could be set aside and a redeemed or at least remunerative existence in an unspoiled land could be realized.[3] For social experimenters such as the Puritans, for entrepreneurs such as fur trappers and slavers and merchants, and for writers of travel narratives and utopian novels, the Americas especially offered space in which the imagination could work out alternatives that broke the bounds of the historical status quo. Exploiters and exploited infused the new area with a symbolic value that transcended the prevailing confusion, weariness, and frustration which marked the end of the medieval world. Various and competing schemes were expressed in the promotional literature which recruited Europeans to the new continents by means of alluring descriptions of an idealized land. The formal treatises on the colonies, travel narratives, requests for land patents, personal letters, and sermons given at the time of departing ships all focused on the imagined benefits of the new space. They gave a sense of refuge and room for a people to achieve their utopia: whether it was a "city on a hill" subject to the laws of God and justice rather than to pope or king, or the source of cities of gold or passages to the orient that met the needs of the capital-accumulating princes and absolute monarchs, or quite simply a way out for convicted criminals, debtors, or other social outcasts from the increasingly restrictive life in the new Europe. As More and others penned their utopian narratives, the idealized reports common to "new world" writing were taken into the texts as they filled in the geographical locus of hope. The brave new world provided a sense of alternative space for the emerging utopian form just as the developing capitalist and national structures supplied a sense of an alternative system.

Utopian narrative since the time of More has been linked with the broad changes at work in the modern social order and with the dreams and desires set in motion by the opening up of human existence promised in a growth- and profit-oriented economy. Utopia grew up with capitalism and the new world as its godparents while the underlying social and personal yearnings and

4

sufferings were its immediate progenitors. Midwifed by authors of many persuasions and abilities, utopia has both reinforced the emerging economic order and attacked it as the official promises failed to meet the real needs of people's lives. From the promotional broadsheets of More's period to the most recent piece of advertising, utopian dissatisfaction and imagery has been enlisted into the process of the creation of needs subordinated to the demands of production and profit; while, on the other hand, the very dream-making activity of the utopian imagination continually resists the limitation of human desire to the economic and bureaucratic demands of the given system. Unfortunately, utopian visions of alternatives to the prevailing economic or national structures all too often served to absorb the oppositional impulse by removing it to the plane of an interesting but unattainable other. From Gerard Winstanley's designs of a democratic and just society in the seventeenth century to the elaborate systems of the utopian socialists in the nineteenth, great alternate systems in print did little to generate fundamental social change. This is the point of Friedrich Engels's critique in "Socialism: Utopian or Scientific," as he charged system builders such as Saint-Simon, Owen, and Fourier with not sufficiently taking actual historical conditions or the process of revolutionary change into account.[4] What Engels did not realize in his otherwise useful critique was the more mediated effects that the utopian imagination can have on a set of readers at the level of ideological formation.

Utopias after 1850

The subversive side of utopian writing developed a bit further when in the mid-nineteenth century the dominant classes consolidated their power and occupied even more of the space on the globe and in people's everyday lives. By 1850, the system of profit and control had become more pervasive. M. H. Abendsour has identified the subsequent change in utopian narrative as one from the "systematic building of alternative organizational models to a more open and heuristic discourse of alternative values."[5] For example, the organizationally oriented *Staatsroman* of eighteenth-century Germany which plotted out the perfect state was no longer a useful sort of text at a time when the structures of domination were firmly set in place. Instead, utopias from 1850 on tended to adopt a stance more concerned with teaching and exposing for the reader the still unrealized potential of the human project of consciously being in the world – as does a novel such as William Morris's *News from Nowhere*. Generally speaking, the post-1850 utopia stressed neither the confidence of the rising classes nor the social longings of the declining classes. Rather, it portrayed a society in which change is happening, but because of and in reaction to the already established economic/political/ideological order. As Raymond Williams notes, this new situation is "always a fertile moment for what is, in effect, an anarchism: positive in its fierce rejection of domination, repression, and manipulation; negative in its willed neglect of structures, of continuity, and of material constraints."[6] Before the capitalist consolidation of 1848–50, the systematic utopia offered at least a hope that the world as it was could be structurally different. Whereas after 1850, the heuristic utopia offered a strength of vision that sought to subvert or at least reform the modern economic and political arrangement from within. The works of Morris, Edward Bellamy (*Looking Backward*), H. G. Wells (*A Modern Utopia*), Charlotte Perkins Gilman (*Herland*), Jack London (*The Iron Heel*), and others opposed what existed, but they could no longer look to an alternative located in the present time. Utopia on one island would not work. That there was simply no more room on the present social terrain was marked by such phenomena as the closing of the American frontier and the enclosing of desire and need in the mechanisms of commodity consumption located in the new "utopian" department stores. Consequently, in late nineteenth-century utopias, subversive visions were relocated in a future time when the process of revolutionary, historical change brought about the utopian society. At this point in the development of the genre, history more directly entered the texts, and utopian novels more regularly provided accounts of the required transition from the present to utopia. System building in some abstracted other place no longer suited the demands put on the utopian narrative: the process of change itself had to be included in the literary operations of the text. It is no accident that in *News from Nowhere* the chapter entitled

"How the Change Came" is one of the more compelling and readable in the book.

Faced with this shift to a concern for everyday values and to consideration of the revolutionary process, utopia was at its most subversive at the turn of the century. The number and influence of utopian novels increased immensely at this time when a variety of social movements were forging a common opposition to the fast developing power of industrial capitalism and imperialism.[7] Farmers, industrial workers, women, racial and ethnic minorities, intellectuals, feminists, socialists, communists, anarchists, syndicalists, populists, free love and temperance advocates, spiritualists, and many others shared a general rejection of the dominant system. Between 1888 and the 1920s, there were diverse expressions of resistance to capital's increasing power. Various oppositional strategies and goals for preserving self-determination and justice in an industrialized and rationalized age were articulated by activists and utopian writers alike. However, by the 1920s the corporate power structure had succeeded in securing control over industrial society and in repressing or coopting most forms of opposition. Socialist opposition, on the other hand, had narrowed to those strategies of the Soviet state, the social democratic compromise, limited reformism, or isolated intellectualizing. Radical utopian visions and political practice failed in the battle to control the direction of developing economic, political, and ideological systems. Whether this failure dates from the United States presidential election victory of William McKinley representing corporate interests over William Jennings Bryan representing the amalgam of radical and reformist opposition movements, or from the narrowing of the socialist vision either by the Soviet state or social democracy, or from the "red purges" of the period, or other such historical watermarks, the twentieth century saw the victory of a system that manipulated human activity for the sake of capital accumulation and power consolidation in the hands of a few. That victory foreclosed alternative possibilities which served human autonomy and authentic needs based on principles of social justice and freedom.[8]

Utopia in the twentieth century

In the twentieth century, utopian writing came upon hard times. Given world war, totalitarian rule, genocide, economic depression, nuclear destruction, massive famine, and disease, as well as the more subtle manipulations of mass industrial/consumer society, utopian discourse has, to say the least, been muted. On one hand, utopia has been absorbed into the affirmative ideologies of the totalizing systems of Stalinist Russia, Nazi Germany, and the corporate United States. Each of these formations has contained and coopted utopia into the maintenance of the given system. Stimulated but unfulfilled desires are effaced and channeled into the service of the state or the consumer paradise. In western industrial societies, utopian longing can be discovered as the underlying stimulus to the machinery of advertising or, perhaps most strikingly, in those living maps of restrictive pleasure which carry the passive consuming audience along in a totally managed environment, Disneyland and Disneyworld.

In his study of the social dynamics of advertising, Stuart Ewen traces the development of that industry and its tapping of human desire from the 1920s to the present.[9] Work became less meaningful as it was subjected to a process of deskilling wherein the worker loses conceptual control of production to "scientific management." Accordingly, non-working time became the terrain of satisfaction. The market penetrated into every area of private daily life from housework to education to sexuality and psychological wellbeing. Advertising, drawing on a simplified Freudian model of human motivation, created an image of the ideal life filled with material goods and proceeded to sell a steady line of products to those whose lives were shaped by that limited image. In the commodity society, then, utopia was reduced to the consumption of pleasurable weekends, Christmas dreams, and goods purchased weekly in the pleasure-dome shopping malls of suburbia. The system as it existed provided all the satisfaction that passive consumers were encouraged to want. Longing beyond those commodity-defined needs was suppressed and indeed questioned as being psychologically or socially aberrant.

On the other hand, as the socialist state or the consumer society claimed to have achieved utopia, the more radical critique that the genre is capable of escaped into the mountains of negativity and re-emerged as the dystopia, the narrative that images a society worse than the existing one. In the great narrative works of Zamyatin (*We*), Huxley (*Brave New World*), Orwell (*1984*), and others, utopian figures of hope were transmuted into an attack on present social systems which claim to be already existing utopias. Images of massification, identity by number, bureaucratic and technocratic control of behavior and desire, portrayal of daily life in a lustreless collectivity or in endless consumption – perhaps most gruesomely presented in that filmic dystopia of life in the land of shopping centres and hungry consumers, George Romero's *Dawn of the Dead* – fill these dystopian texts and reject the imposed limits of consumer capitalism or state socialism. Unfortunately, the dystopian narrative itself has all too easily been recruited into the ideological attack on authentic utopian expression: commentators cite the dystopia as a sign of the very failure of utopia and consequently urge uneasy readers to settle for what is and cease their frustrating dreams of a better life. Furthermore, the minority utopian societies in texts such as Huxley's *Brave New World* or Ira Levin's *This Perfect Day* are no more than reservations for unsatisfied misfits and not models for a transformed society; they serve as an artificially negative utopian zone employed by the hegemonic system to absorb resistance.[10]

Even though bibliographer Lyman Tower Sargent has demonstrated that utopian novels have been published in every year of this century, the general impression, especially in postwar industrial societies, is that utopia is now unnecessary either because it has already arrived in daily life or because it represents a dream incapable of attainment. The open pastures of alternative possibilities were enclosed by the steady encroachment of state and corporate control. Utopia became a residual literary form, and the dystopia was recontained and enlisted as proof of the uselessness of utopian desire. However, this neutralizing cooptation and inversion of utopia – this static conflict between toothless utopia and bleak dystopia – was itself negated in the revival of the literary utopia that occurred after the social upheavals of the 1960s.

The critical utopia

"I have a dream."   (Martin Luther King)

The deep conflicts of the 1960s, rooted in an affluence that hinted at the end of scarcity and in an experience of the repression and exploitation of nature and humanity needed to achieve such affluence, significantly awakened a subversive utopianism. As much as those uprisings, coded around the year 1968 but springing from the oppositions of the 1950s and late 1940s, might have been defeated by state suppression or contained by ideological reduction to individual narcissism, hip-capitalism, or even "Clean for Gene [McCarthy]" reformism, their spirit survived in a continuing activism that marked a return to the human agenda of the categories of cooperation, equality, mutual aid, liberation, ecological wisdom, and peaceful and creative living. This revived longing for the not yet realized potential of the human community was expressed in many ways in the emerging oppositional culture of the late 1960s and the 1970s.

Within this context, stimulated by the influence of science fiction and experimental fiction, utopian writing was given new life in the novels of Russ, LeGuin, Piercy, Delany, and others. The new novels negated the negation of utopia by the forces of twentieth century history: the subversive imaging of utopian society and the radical negativity of dystopian perception is preserved; while the systematizing boredom of the traditional utopia and the cooptation of utopia by modern structures is destroyed. Thus, utopian writing in the 1970s was saved by its own destruction and transformation into the "critical utopia." "Critical" in the Enlightenment sense of *critique* – that is expressions of oppositional thought, unveiling, debunking, of both the genre itself and the historical situation. As well as "critical" in the nuclear sense of the *critical mass* required to make the necessary explosive reaction.

A central concern in the critical utopia is the awareness of the limitations of the utopian tradition, so that these texts reject utopia as blueprint while preserving it as dream. Furthermore, the novels dwell on the conflict between the originary world and the utopian society opposed to it so that the process of social change is more directly articulated. Finally, the novels focus on the continuing presence of difference and imperfection within utopian society itself and thus render more recognizable and dynamic alternatives.

Inspired by the movements of the 1960s and finding new imagery in the alternatives being explored in the 1970s, the critical utopia is part of the political practice and visions shared by a variety of autonomous oppositional movements that reject the domination of the emerging system of transnational corporations and post-industrial production and ideological structures. As industrial capitalism and the nation state give way to a world-wide automated production maintained by structures of power that no longer seem to be controlled by particular human beings, the ground of radical politics is shifting from the older strategies of class struggle at the point of production to broader and deeper challenges in the general name of autonomy and justice for humanity and nature. The new historical bloc of opposition is one that draws together an alliance of various groups and interests. As André Gorz puts it, the core of the new opposition is individual sovereignty and local community, a goal which signifies a freedom based

> upon activities unrelated to any economic goal which are an end in themselves: communication, giving, creating and aesthetic enjoyment, the production and reproduction of life, tenderness, the realization of physical, sensuous, and intellectual capacities, the creation of non-commodity use-values (shared goods and/or services) that could not be produced as commodities because of their unprofitability.[11]

This general oppositional vision is challenging corporate and allied state interests. On the terrain of the emerging automated, post-industrial, post-scarcity social order, the choice comes down to the use of that new set of structures and mechanisms for human need and fulfillment or for the profit and power of a dominant élite. The new opposition is deeply infused with the politics of autonomy, democratic socialism, ecology, and especially feminism. Profoundly shaped by the modern women's movement, the new historic bloc seeks to "eliminate the principle of performance, the ethic of competition, accumulation and the rat-race at

11

the level of both individual behavior and social relations, replacing them with the supremacy of the values of reciprocity, tenderness, spontaneity and love of life in all its forms."[12] It is the sensibility of this consensus that runs throughout the critical utopian texts under examination here. Whatever the particular set of social images each text sets forth, the shared quality in all of them is a rejection of hierarchy and domination and the celebration of emancipatory ways of being as well as the very possibility of utopian longing itself.

What follows is a consideration of the relationship between oppositional politics and utopian writing. After a theoretical section which sets forth an understanding of the utopian imagination in opposition to dominant ideology and an understanding as well of the literary genre of utopia and its recent transformation as critical utopia, there are chapters in which the four novels are discussed as examples of this oppositional cultural practice.

PART ONE:
Theory

2 The utopian imagination

The effectively ideological is also, at the same time, necessarily Utopian. (Fredric Jameson)

"Be realistic. Demand the impossible."
(Wall slogan, Paris, May 1968)

Utopia and ideology

The revival of the utopian impulse in the latter half of the twentieth century may seem useless in the face of the cooptation of utopia by consumer capitalism on one hand and the destruction of a hopeful future by the threat of nuclear holocaust on the other. In these days of false promises, hard times, and dire fears, utopia often is unable to find a place in people's imaginations or actions. Yet, since the 1960s especially, the utopian impulse has played an important role in the politics and culture of the many movements opposed to society as it is structured by the modern phallocratic capitalist system and the bureaucratic state. The power of subversive imagining to move people beyond the

15

present toward a more fulfilling future is now expressed and understood as a more complex mechanism than those writing and working for radical change during the last wave of utopian discourse in the 1890s might have experienced.

Modern society itself has enclosed utopian desire both externally, in nature and the Third World, and internally, in people's private lives and the unconscious. Utopia is used to sustain the domination of the present economic and political systems of the west. The "total system" achieved by postwar world capitalism appears to have almost eliminated the subversive utopian impulse as a negation of the present system. Whether that system is understood in terms of its ability to "colonize the last remnants and survivals of human freedom" and sell them back to the passive consumers of post-industrial society or in terms of the "*société de consommation* in favor of the glittering surface of an individualized counter-culture," it has – since the end of World War Two – shaped society into a "seamless web of media technology, multinational corporations, and international bureaucratic control."[1] This system functions primarily by means of reification and exploitation – that transformation of human relations and unrestricted nature into the appearance of relationships between things that can then be produced and consumed, bought and sold. As Jack Zipes puts it, human beings

> have become little more than tools, for as they were required to place their skills and thought at the service of a system which uses industry and technology to increase the profit and power of elite groups, they were prevented from pursuing their own interests and internalized the norms and values of capitalist commodity production.[2]

The affirmative culture of postwar capitalism has served to lull and deaden people and make them into obedient automatons and not autonomous human beings.[3]

This "totally administered society" is maintained by both the coercive power of the state – wherein people are kept in obedient line by the power of the police, the military, and the legal system – and of civil society – wherein the socializing, or ideological, apparatuses of church, school, law, culture, media, and so forth more quietly and less obtrusively channel people into appropriate

16

and productive behavior. Antonio Gramsci noted that one of the most important functions of every state is "to raise the great mass of the population to a particular cultural and moral level, a level which corresponds to the needs of the productive forces of development and hence to the interests of the ruling classes."[4] As the hegemony of the dominant class increases within the cultural apparatus of the society, the need for overt coercive power decreases. Michel Foucault demonstrated in his various studies of bourgeois structures such as prisons, schools, medical and mental institutions, and knowledge and sexual practices how such systems developed in order to lessen the need for authoritarian coercion by producing the sort of person necessary for the optimal functioning of the general mode of production and reproduction of the profit-making economy.[5] And the labor analyst Harry Braverman described how the independent knowledge and skills of working people were appropriated by the use of "scientific management" so that the control of the labor process itself was taken from those who did the work and made the property of those who managed and owned the means of production.[6]

In the late or transnational capitalist system the practices of reification and totalizing administration have themselves served to opaque, to mystify, the actual social relations and structures by which exploitation and domination are carried on. By reducing life to the status of commodity and communication to the transfer of surface images, and therefore by trying to remove autonomous human activity from the realm of real possibility, this dominant social formation threatens to remove the very threat of opposition and resistance by turning even negative and utopian actions into mere commodities or images. This social formation, as Louis Althusser reminds us, is a set of distinct yet interrelated practices at the economic, political, and ideological levels.[7] What of course interests us most here is the operation of the ideological level: it is there that the human subject is shaped into that properly functioning object needed by the overall structure.

Ideology, once understood as simply a set of illusions or as false consciousness, is thus seen to be a more general set of practices that shape the self-understanding of individuals. It is a representational system of values, opinions, knowledge, and images which articulates the individual's lived relationship to the transpersonal realities of the social structure as experienced by a particular social class. By means of these projected imaginary relationships that overlay the actual historical situation, ideology re-presents society in such a way that conceals contradictions and doubts in favor of a total picture within which the individual can live and carry out the needs of her or his class. As Tony Bennett puts it, individuals "are related, in ideology, to the conditions of their existence through the imaginary concept of their own selfhood and of the place they occupy within the order of things as governed over and given sense and coherence by the Absolute Subject of God, Man, Nation, etc."[8] All expression within a culture – whether ordinary language, slick advertising, hard science, devout prayer, or utopian writing – is embedded in ideology, sometimes entirely within the dominant ideology, sometimes within a subordinate or oppositional ideology, often hovering non-synchronously between the two. Ideology, then, is one of the three major mechanisms by which the present system of profit and power is maintained and expanded. Consequently, if that totality is to be broken open in the name of oppositional classes or groups, or in the general name of the autonomy of humanity and nature, there must be a "reinvention of possibilities of cognition and perception that allow social phenomena once again to become transparent."[9]

This understanding of the power of ideology and the need to oppose its totalizing tendency brings us back to the utopian impulse. Karl Mannheim's opposition of Ideology and Utopia suggests immediately the role played by utopian desire in the process of social change. Mannheim defines *ideology* as the complex of ideas directing activity toward the maintenance of the status quo and *utopia* as the complex of ideas directing activity toward the changing of the status quo.[10] Utopia is that unconquered power of the imagination which resists the closure of ideology. As Mannheim sees it, only failed utopias or historically surpassed ones become part of the ideological baggage of the dominant system. Although this notion of the oppositional power of utopia over against the dominant role of ideology is still valid, it over-simplifies and reduces utopia and ideology to simple binary opposites, neither being tainted nor compromised by the other. Armed with the knowledge of the immense power of the late capitalist formation to absorb negativity and to congeal unfulfilled desire into commodified objects, and with Althusser's sense of ideology as the representational structure which sets up the individual's lived relationship to the real, we come to an understanding of the relationship between utopia and ideology that goes beyond that of binary opposites. Indeed, we must look at these two mechanisms as dialectically opposed and unified within the more general structure of social representation and socialization. We must see the utopian impulse as operating *within* the ideological, both helping it along and pulling against it. This is the point of Jameson's statement that "the effectively ideological is also, at the same time, necessarily Utopian."[11] If an individual is to be motivated by a system of ideological practices, she or he must be offered at least the promise of specific gratifications in return for "willing" behavior consistent with the ideology in question. This "rhetorical persuasion in which substantial incentives are offered for ideological adherence" rather than the adherence brought on by the sheer brute force of state power is one that, first, taps the utopian impulse as the key motivation to cooperate and, then, manages, defuses, and channels that impulse into the limited satisfactions and range of behaviors offered by the dominant social formation.[12] Utopia is not simply a challenger to ideology, standing as an unsullied white knight outside the gates of the total system. At least in this century it has been seduced and enslaved into the service of the system itself. If utopia is to do its subversive and emancipatory work again, it must break out of its commodified chains and seize the freedom to tear down the walls of profit and power and help lead the way to a radically new future.

The utopian impulse moves between cooptation by a given system and explosion beyond it. Early on, the ideology of expanding capitalism tapped the utopian longing for a better life in the post-medieval world by projecting images, through its cultural creations, of a brave new world that promised utopian satisfaction but delivered a more limited mercantile, industrial, and national system. On the other hand, the continuous tapping of the utopian ensured the constant dissatisfaction of those in the population who were denied the benefits of the current system

19

and pushed oppositional thought and practice to challenge the given system in the name of one that was more suitable to their unfulfilled needs and wants. Movements for racial emancipation, women's rights, industrial democracy, world peace, ecological balance, and others constantly drew upon the utopian impulse embedded in the dominant ideology of America as Utopia. That impulse was part and parcel of the continuing process of promise/denial, cooptation/revolt at the heart of a system that required the stimulus of constant dissatisfaction for its mechanisms of reification, exploitation, profit, and growth. Within this deeper understanding of utopia lies the possibility for a revived and more radical use of that impulse to resist and move beyond the current system of transnational capitalism, state bureaucracy, and male-dominated hierarchy. In liberating utopia from its enclosure and collaboration within ideology, that subversive impulse can be re-appropriated as an instrument of opposition.

The utopian imagination

If Althusser and others deepened our sense of the operations of ideology in postwar society, Ernst Bloch revived and deepened our sense of the revolutionary potential of the utopian imagination. Bloch's understanding of the utopian impulse jarred oppositional thought loose from historically bound terms which "essentially prolong the categories of capitalism itself, whether by negation or adoption (terms like industrialization, centralization, progress, technology, and even production itself, which tend to impose their own social limitations and options on those who work with them)."[13] Bloch's work allows us to consider the process of radical opposition in terms of radical difference. The utopian impulse is at the center of the process of radical rupture that is necessary for the constant striving of humanity for a world free of oppression and full of satisfaction.

The lifelong project of this Marxist philosopher was the determination of the possibility of humanity changing the world in which it lives and becoming the maker of its own history. His major work, *The Principle of Hope*, is an important study of the steady and often imperceptible tending of human history towards utopia, toward the fulfillment of humanity in the not yet realized future, when humanity could be "at home" for the first time:

> Humankind still lives in prehistory everywhere, indeed everything awaits the creation of the world as a genuine one. The real genesis is not at the beginning, but at the end, and it only begins when society and existence become radical, that is, grasp themselves at the root. The root of history, however, is the human being, working, producing, reforming, and surpassing the givens around him or her. If human beings have grasped themselves and what is theirs, without depersonalization and alienation, founded in real democracy, then something comes into being in the world that shines into everyone's childhood and where no one has yet been home.[14]

What interests Bloch is not so much what is or what has been, but rather the "latency of being to come," seen in the "figures of hope" which foreshadow the human potential. He traces the unknown path of the future anticipated or longed for in fables, fairy tales, religion, literary utopias, and in the revolutionary events of history. To be sure, the "concrete utopia" is the most privileged bearer of future possibility. Concrete utopias are points in history where utopian possibilities are established in the concreteness and openness of the material of history. Examples include the Peasants' Revolt, the French Revolution, the Paris Commune, the October Revolution, and May 1968 in Paris. These are moments when "objective-real possibilities are acted out, if only for a while, and existing actuality is surrounded with tremendous latency, the times when the 'potency of human hope' links up with the potentiality within the world."[15] Concrete utopia prevents the discarding of the visions of the goals ahead and calls for the living out of those visions in whatever is to be done.

Present time is provincial and empty. If humanity becomes too much taken with the present, we lose the possibility of imagining a radically other future. We lose the ability to hope. We lose what Bloch identifies as the *novum*: the unexpectedly new, that which pushes humanity out of the present toward the not yet realized future. For humanity to develop, we must keep an open faith in the future and guard against the memory which draws us back into the past and the anxiety which consumes us in the present. The source of this yearning is in the human unconscious and its desires, but Bloch's theory of the unconscious differs from Freud's. As Jameson explains, the Freudian unconscious is

> a no-longer consciousness, an unconsciousness of a world and a self which have officially, in the eyes of the reality principle, ceased to be; and this formulation is in itself enough to suggest the lines along which Bloch corrects it. In this sense there is room, alongside this no-longer conscious-ness for a new and very different type of unconscious, a blankness or horizon of consciousness this time formed not by the past but by the future: what Bloch calls a not yet conscious ontological pull of the future, of a tidal influence exerted upon us by that which lies out of sight below the horizon, an unconscious of what is yet to come.[16]

In this way, Bloch locates the positive drive toward the future in the negative, in the radical insufficiency of the present, for even those concrete utopian moments of fulfillment are future-bearing only in their very finite and passing nature. With each victory of the human project there remains a specific type of hope which is not that of the present and which carries that victorious moment beyond itself, anticipating the next one. The dissatisfaction at the very core of hope drives human desire forward and transforms each wish into a figure of the utopian wish itself. Thus in the "tendency" of a certain dynamic or aesthetic potential in history and in the "latency" of perceptual or aesthetic potentials, utopian desire pulls the present forward. Art can be anticipatory, a stimulant for revolutionary praxis:

> And it is very much in our day and age that the poetically exact dream does not die from truth, for truth is not the reflection of facts, but of processes. In the final analysis it is the portrayal of tendency and latency of that which has not yet become and needs an activator. Moreover, meaningful literature brings us an accelerated current of action, an elucidated daydream of the essential to the consciousness of the world. In addition, it wants to be changed. Among other

things, the world correlate to the poetically suitable day-dream is precisely the latency of being.[17]

The utopian moment can never be directly articulated, for it does not yet exist. It must always speak in figures which call out structurally for completion and exegesis in theory and practice.

In myth and in fairy tale, the act of wishing is central. These genres express the longing of humanity for a better future. Even if such longing is displaced into another time, another place, long long ago, in a Golden Age, or once upon a time – underlying the displacement is the wish for what has not yet been. Bloch is more circumspect about the literary utopia. Certainly, he sees it as another example of "meaningful literature" expressing the day-dreams of humanity, and it seems to be particularly important around moments of historical conjuncture:

> Hence all critical points in the transition of a society from one stage to another are characterized by books of social expectation, dream landscapes of a better world, in short, social utopias. Augustine wrote *De Civitate Dei* in the transitional period from ancient to medieval-feudal society, Thomas More inaugurated a series of utopias in the bourgeois modern period, while Fourier marked the beginning of a trend to socialism as it became possible. All utopias, or nearly all, despite their feudal or bourgeois commission, predict communal ownership, in brief, have socialism in mind. To be sure, this is expressed in an abstract, imaginative manner, since the productive forces of the time were not ripe for socialism. Yet, in all these utopias, these social voyages to Cytherea, there came to expression the expectant tendency that permeates all human history. Only in Marxism, however, did it find concrete expression, precisely because Marxism disclosed the real possibilities. And Marxism also reveals totality again – which is the method and the subject matter of all authentic philosophy. But, for the first time this totality appears not as a static, as a finished principle of the whole, but rather as utopian, or more precisely, as a concrete utopian totality, as the process latency of a still unfinished world.[18]

Bloch, however, objects to the literary utopian form much as Engels did. That is, when a utopian system is directly imagined and delivered in the text there occurs an impoverishment which is due to the narrative reduction of the multiple levels of utopian desire to the single, relatively abstract, field of social planning. With the disguise stripped away, the utopian plan stands against history in a fashion too simple and too stark for the anxiety of hope to do much with it. While appreciating the caveat concerning narrative reduction, we should recognize here, in Bloch as well as Engels, the same trap which other utopian scholars and critics have fallen into: that is, the literary utopia is read by them as blueprint only and is judged on its direct realizability as written. Perhaps Bloch would have been better off to read the literary utopia just as he read myth, fairy tale, and fable – as "preconceptual philosophical explorations of the world."

Bloch does not go as far as Engels in his doubts about the literary utopia. He holds on to the essential subversive elements of the genre: the expression of unrealized ideals, of alternative social tendencies, and the sense of a utopian ending. "Ideal images," he says, "insofar as they are not exclusively subjective, quite legitimately – as the subjective ideal tendency – hasten ahead of and precede an objective historical tendency, which need not necessarily rush ahead to meet its precursory dreams."[19] The solution of the "riddle of the world" is not yet complete, and utopian literature is part of the project of moving in history toward greater emancipation. Thus Bloch situates utopian imagination in the historical process not as the source of blueprints but as preconceptual figures of that which is not yet attained.

For a fuller detailing of the operation of the human imagination and its fantastic or utopian production, we must look to Herbert Marcuse's work. Marcuse's discussion of the imagination and the operation of fantasy is also rooted in a critical reading of Freud. In *Eros and Civilization* he challenges the established reality principle – performance for the sake of the civilized order – by arguing its historical limits. Given the advance of civilization, particularly in technology and its potential to reduce the human labor process and to generate a post-scarcity economy, Marcuse argues that the possibility of a gradual decontrolling of the instinctual development must be taken seriously as a distinct alternative, if not a necessity, in the face of a failing capitalism. In such a non-repressive civilization, the new, historically determined, reality principle would be the pleasure principle. To be sure, this is a source of desire that can be exploited by the market, but it is also a force that can transcend the present system.

In the 1950s, while some were calling for the rebirth of utopia, however compromised, and others for the end of ideology, Marcuse cut through the ideological posturing by articulating a new reality principle based on pleasure. Of particular interest to us is his discussion of the function of fantasy and utopia. According to Freud, the mental forces opposed to the reality (performance) principle are located chiefly in the unconscious. Fantasy is the exception, located as it is in consciousness and yet able to operate with a high degree of freedom from the reality principle. The similarity to Bloch's concept of the emancipatory function of daydreams should be noted, for both Marcuse and Bloch locate this fantasizing operation primarily in the realm of art. Fantasy links the unconscious with consciousness, dreams with reality, and preserves the "tabooed images of freedom." Though often subject to instrumental reason in the "civilized" subject, fantasy tenaciously retains the structure and tendencies of consciousness prior to its organization by reality, prior to its becoming the core of a socialized individual set off against other individuals. Fantasy

> has a truth value of its own, which corresponds to an experience of its own – namely, the surmounting of the antagonistic human reality. Imagination envisions the re-conciliation of the individual with the whole, of desire with realization, of happiness with reason. While this harmony has been removed into utopia by the established reality principle, phantasy insists that it must and can become real.[20]

To be sure, the products of the imagination are usually relegated by the ideological apparatuses of the dominant culture to the realms of art and to surreal processes such as day-dreaming and play. But, against this affirmative culture of the dominant ideology, art which taps the fantastic or utopian can oppose the "image of humanity as a free subject" (Adorno) to institutional repression.

For Marcuse, art as opposition survives only where it denies its traditional form and thereby denies reconciliation: whether it becomes the anti-art of the avantgarde or the anti-art of popular culture or, in the present case, the negation of utopia/dystopia by the critical utopia. He argues for the impermanence of the performance principle and the historical possibility of a form of emancipatory society with a post-scarcity economy and a non-repressive reality principle. Given this historical possibility, the utopian images of the imagination as preconceptual figures of the negation of present reality contribute to the oppositional re-jection of the dominant capitalist relations of production and ideology. Art is allied with revolution as an uncompromising adherence to the strict truth value of the imagination com-prehends reality more fully. The products of the oppositional artistic imagination contradict the surface facts. This is the basis for the revolutionary stance of the "Great Refusal": the protest against unnecessary repression, the struggle for the ultimate form of freedom.

Utopia and oppositional culture

> We know that there is no "good" government, "good" state or "good" form of power, and that society can never be "good" in its own organization but only by virtue of the space for self-organization, autonomy, cooperation and voluntary exchange which that organization offers to indi-viduals. (André Gorz)

In restoring the utopian impulse to the revolutionary arsenal, Ernst Bloch anticipated the concept behind one of the driving forces of the opposition to domination and hierarchy that devel-oped in the late 1960s and continues in all its discontinuity to the present day. In generating preconceptual images of human fulfill-ment that radically break with the prevailing social system, utopian discourse articulates the possibility of other ways of living in the world. The strength of critical utopian expression lies not in the particular social structures it portrays but in the very act of portraying a utopian vision itself. The task of an opposi-tional utopian text is not to foreclose the agenda for the future in terms of a homogeneous revolutionary plan but rather to hold open the act of negating the present and to imagine any of several possible modes of adaptation to society and nature based generally upon principles of autonomy, mutual aid, and equality.

The opposition to contemporary capitalism and the hierarchical state is no longer to be found limited to that of a single vanguard party or, at the other pole, an expression of pure negation and terror. The political opposition, at least since the late 1960s, occurs on all three levels of the social structure – the economic, the political, and the ideological/cultural – and is made up of a variety of autonomous movements grouped loosely in an historical anti-hegemonic bloc. Despite the particular agendas of these movements, they all recognize the shared task of smashing through the established totality toward emancipation. Generally speaking, this new historic bloc can be divided into three areas: feminism, ecology, and self-management both of the workplace and of the sphere of daily life. Stanley Aronowitz describes the premises of these movements as (1) the demand for "an end to male supremacy and for the emancipation of sexuality from the thrall imposed upon it by social and material reproduction," (2) the demand for "a new relation between society and its external environment, for the restoration of the autonomy of nature, and thus for a strategy of negotiation rather than the domination of nature," (3) the demand for "the self-management of the workplace and living space," the critique of "the character of science and technologies that perpetuate hierarchy," and the achievement of "racial, ethnic, and linguistic autonomy within society." Given the present understanding of the tendency of any system, dominant or oppositional, ruling or revolutionary, to enclose autonomy and establish its own structural hegemony, this new historic bloc must "become anti-hegemonic as a political and social principle, recognizing the *permanence* of difference." The struggle for a new society must remain radically open both in the course of the oppositional struggle and in the creation of the new society itself.[21]

Under these conditions of opposition not only to economic and political exploitation and domination but also to the increasingly successful ideological hegemony of the prevailing system, the ideological or cultural terrain has become in our time crucial to

the process of historical change. The new historic bloc finds itself engaged in the task of opening up oppositional spaces in the
social fabric from which further subversion of the system can be
launched. The bourgeois public sphere, described by Jürgen
Habermas as the locus of rational discourse and democratic
decision-making, has collapsed under the rationalization and
instrumentalization of society serving a technocratic ruling élite.
Developed in the eighteenth century as the site of communicative
action between the private sphere and the state, this public sphere
has become an empty ideal. But, as Alexander Kluge and Oskar
Negt point out, the forces of opposition have revived the public
sphere as a repoliticized area for popular democratic action. This
"plebian public sphere" is constituted by the various strata of
people who oppose consciously or subconsciously the formation
of policy in the bourgeois public sphere by creating alternative
agencies to articulate and secure their interests. Similar to Bloch's
concrete utopia, the plebian public sphere is not an institution but
rather a contradictory and non-linear space which unites the
fragmented experiences of the opposition movements. It is a
liberated cultural and ideological zone seized from the totalized
society from which the anti-hegemonic forces can attack the
present and move openly toward an emancipated and radically
open future.[22]

The new movements of liberation insist on a multiplicity of
voices, autonomous from each other, but commonly rooted in
unfulfilled needs centering around the practice of autonomy. This
shared goal of fulfillment of desire for collective humanity informs the utopian impulse at the heart of the historic bloc of
opposition. The impulse, however, is one that must resist closure
and systematization both in the steps taken toward it and in the
vision that expresses it. For a specific, homogeneous utopian
vision would be a betrayal of radical utopian discourse and would
only end up serving the instrumentalization of desire carried on
by the present structures of power. There can be no *Utopia*, but
there *can* be utopian expressions that constantly shatter the
present achievements and compromises of society and point
to that which is not yet experienced in the human project of
fulfillment and creation.

28

3 The literary utopia

A map of the world that does not include Utopia is not worth even glancing at, for it leaves out the one country at which Humanity is always landing.   (Oscar Wilde)

Since these reflections are taking shape in an area just on the point of being discovered, they necessarily bear the mark of our time – a time during which the new breaks away from the old, and, more precisely the (feminine) new from the old (*la nouvelle de l'ancien*). Thus, as there are no grounds for establishing a discourse, but rather an arid millennial ground to break, what I say has at least two sides and two aims: to break up, to destroy; and to foresee the unforeseeable, to project.   (Hélène Cixous)

The utopian genre

The revival of the utopian impulse since the 1960s has taken many forms. From intentional communities in the streets of San Francisco and the hills of Tennessee; to the theoretical visions found in analytical works such as André Gorz's *Farewell to the*

Working Class, Wendell Berry's *The Unsettling of America*, or Shulamith Firestone's *The Dialectic of Sex*; to the utopian desires at the heart of the many activist projects from nuclear disarmament to decent housing – the forward pull of utopia has been pervasive within the broad movement of opposition and change. What concerns us here are the literary utopias that were produced during this period, roughly from 1968 to 1976. But before we can move on to a reading of the specific texts, we must consider the genre of literary utopia as it has traditionally existed and as it was revived, destroyed, and transformed in the critical utopias of Russ, LeGuin, Piercy, and Delany. These literary works are a significant part of the social process of discourse, debate, and conflict about power and social relations. The absent course of history is made sense of partly through the operations of the literary texts, for they are symbolic acts that provide imaginary resolutions to real social contradictions. Literary artifacts provide in narrative form articulations of what Jameson terms the "the political unconscious," the "repressed and buried reality" of the fundamental history of "the collective struggle to wrest a realm of Freedom from a realm of Necessity," perhaps more simply stated as the process of social revolution and historical change.[1] An analysis that seeks to understand and explain a particular set of literary works must come to terms with those works as socially symbolic acts rooted in and expressive of history and its motivating contradictions.

Discussing the literary utopia, we must begin with the notion of genre itself. Genres, as Jameson defines them, are

> essentially literary institutions, or social contracts between a writer and a specific public, whose function is to specify the proper use of a particular cultural artifact. The speech acts of daily life are themselves marked with indications and signals (intonations, gesturality, contextual deictics and pragmatics) which insure their appropriate reception. In the mediated situations of a more complicated social life – and the emergence of writing has often been taken as paradigmatic of such situations – perceptual signals must be replaced by conventions if the text in question is not to be abandoned to a drifting multiplicity of uses.[2]

Seeing the generic contract and institution in this light allows us to understand a given literary work not only as an individual text subject to immanent analysis but also as one which can be further understood historically in terms of the evolution of the particular form and of the societal events and contradictions of which it is a part. The historical perspective allows us to chart the changes and deviations that occur as texts free themselves more and more from an immediate performance situation, and − in our time especially − fall casualty to the gradual penetration of a market system and money economy. In terms of literary utopias, then, a sense of genre and history enables us to see the origin of this genre in the early years of western capitalism and its development from texts that emphasized system to ones that focus on values and social change. It further allows us to see the transformation of utopia after years of cooptation and denial. For the critical utopias of the 1960s and 1970s not only revive the generic form but also, more or less aware of the totalizing limitations of the form as well as its cooptation by market forces, destroy and change that form in such a way that, self-critical and wiser for the wear, it can give new life to the utopian impulse without falling into compromised abuse or negated disuse.

As a literary form that falls under the category of the fantastic rather than the realistic, utopia can be understood to be a development within the general paradigm of the romance, as dealt with by Northrop Frye. Free from narrative homogeneity and "that reality principle to which a now oppressive realistic representation is the hostage," romance in twentieth century writing again offers "the possibility of sensing other historical rhythms, and of demonic or Utopian transformations of a real now unshakably set in place."[3] The romantic mode is centered around a process of wish-fulfillment or utopian fantasy that aims at a *displacement and transfiguration* of the given historical world in such a way as to revive the conditions of a lost paradise or to anticipate a future kingdom in which suffering and limitations have been effaced. As Frye puts it, romance "is the search of the libido or desiring self for a fulfillment that will deliver it from the anxieties of reality but will still contain that reality."[4] The conflict in romance "takes place in, or at any rate, primarily concerns, *our* world, which is in the middle, and which is

31

characterized by the cyclical movements of nature," in the continuing opposition between good and evil, higher and lower, heaven and hell, angelic or demonic.[5] The hero of romance, furthermore, is one who generally comes from the "good world" and confronts the villain of the "evil" world on the terrain of the present world. Here then is the general mode of various genres of non-realist literature including the fairy tale, heroic fantasy, horror and the gothic, science fiction, and utopian fiction. For "realistic" as science fiction and utopian fiction may appear on the surface, they are forms of the romance which are meditations upon deep conflicts in the historical present that are displaced onto the terrain of an other-worldly locus so that the reader, consciously or unconsciously, can see her or his society and its contradictions in a fresh and perhaps motivating light.

The description of the literary genre of utopia by Glenn Negley and Max Patrick in the 1950s was an early step in the development of an analysis of utopian writing that approached it as a literary practice rather than as unmediated moral or political philosophy. Negley and Patrick identify three characteristics of the utopian text: (1) it is fictional; (2) it describes a particular state or community; (3) its theme is the *political* structure of that fictional state or community.[6] This description, however, fixed on the category of overt political structure and did not go as far as Frye in understanding the deeper ideological contest at the core of utopian expression.

In a move from the general mode of romance to utopian fiction in particular, Raymond Williams distinguishes four types of texts that have at one time or another been grouped as utopian: (1) the paradise, in which a happier life is described as simply existing elsewhere; (2) the externally altered world, in which a new kind of life has been made possible by an unlooked-for natural event; (3) the willed transformation, in which a new kind of life has been achieved by human effort: (4) the technological transformation, in which a new kind of life has been made possible by a technical discovery.[7] Williams excludes the first two categories: the paradise because it is merely there, often by supernatural agency, and has not been developed by human agenda – although the delights and rewards of a land of Cokaygne are latently utopian; and the externally altered world because it too is not humanly transformed but rather by a natural agency. The key that Williams uses, then, is *willed transformation*, either directly as in his third category or in the less direct, more mystified, category of technological transformation. Thus utopia can be linked historically with that time of the flowering of human agency to create its own world, free of subservience to nature or supernature. The rise of the bourgeoisie in Europe in the sixteenth century was a period of conscious human development, exploration of new lands, development of a new society, valorization of freedom of will and rationality of mind: a period of political, economic, and ideological struggle over the direction and form the brave new world of capitalism would take. Utopias from More on share in this motivation and literary form, often critiquing the genre in new ways, but all going back to the source of the genre in history, in form, and in title: *Utopia*.

Darko Suvin's definition of utopia specifies the genre as "the verbal construction of a particular quasi-human community where sociopolitical institutions, norms and individual relationships are organized according to a more perfect principle than in the author's community, this construction being based on estrangement arising out of an alternative historical hypothesis."[8] Negley and Patrick's notion of the political, Frye's sense of ideological contest, and Williams's sense of willed transformation are thus joined by Suvin's emphasis on the alternative community and especially on the operation of estrangement. *Estrangement*, the mechanism of the utopian text whereby it focuses on the given situation but in a displaced manner to create a fresh view, is identified as central to the subversive quality of the genre – and indeed of its cousins in the fantastic mode in general. The Russian Formalists and Bertolt Brecht demonstrated that estrangement is that device wherein the world of the author, and the contemporaneous readers, is distanced by means either of a disruption of the realist illusion of the text, or of an alternative world, or, as we will see in the critical utopia, by both. As Suvin puts it, utopia "is a formal inversion of significant and salient aspects of the author's world which has as its purpose or telos the recognition that the author (and reader) truly live in an axiologically inverted world."[9] Opposed to other fantastic forms, utopias and science fiction practice an estrangement that is cognitively consistent with nature as it is known or with the imagined natural laws in the particular text. That is, the estranged world of utopia must appear realistic, must not partake of the impossibilities of the supernatural or the naturally undoable. This textual game depends on the author's rhetorical ability to create a mode of discourse which allows her or him to exaggerate, intensify, and extend scientific, technological, and social conditions to their most extreme point while convincing the reader that everything which occurs in the fantasy world is feasible.

Jack Zipes explains the operation of estrangement in terms of the Freudian notion of the *uncanny*:

> In his essay on the uncanny, Freud remarks that the word *heimlich* means that which is familiar and agreeable *and* also that which is concealed and kept out of sight, and he concludes that *heimlich* is a word the meaning of which develops in the direction of ambivalence, until it finally coincides with its opposite, *unheimlich* or uncanny.[10]

Freud explains the uncanny as "something which is familiar and old-established in the mind and which has become alienated from it only through the process of repression," and Zipes extends this notion to explain that the act of reading a fairy tale, or by extension other forms of the fantastic, is an uncanny experience in that it separates the reader from the restrictions of reality and makes the repressed unfamiliar familiar again. An estrangement from the known world results from the uncanny feeling, the recognition of suppressed human fulfillment, that is both frightening and comforting. This echoes Frye's sense of the romance as a meditation on the cyclic confrontation of good and evil, or in more general and less moral terms of that which is narrow and limiting against what is expansive and emancipating.

Thus the romance or the fantastic, including utopia, focuses on a quest for what has been repressed or denied, for *Heimat*, as Ernst Bloch puts it – that sense of *home* which includes happiness and fulfillment and which the human collectivity has never known. The uncanny, the *unheimlich*, makes possible a regained sense of the familiar, *heimlich*, but also of that second meaning of *heimlich*, of home. The operation of the uncanny, of estrangement, in the fantastic genres opens readers up to what Freud calls "unfulfilled but possible futures to which we still like to cling in fantasy, all the strivings of the ego which adverse circumstances have crushed, and all our suppressed acts of volition which nourish in us the illusion of Free Will."[11] In its particular method of envisioning an alternative society to the present one, utopian fantasy generates a "dreaming ahead" (Bloch): an act which is capable of revolutionary awareness and which can enter the activity of history. With such wishes and dreams,

> virtually all human beings are futuristic; they transcend their past life, and to the degree that they are satisfied, they think they deserve a better life (even though this may be pictured in a banal and egoistic way), and regard the inadequacy of their lot as a barrier, and not just the way of the world.[12]

Utopian literature as a form of romance or fantasy serves to stimulate in its readers a desire for a better life and to motivate that desire toward action by conveying a sense that the world is not fixed once and for all. In the estranged vision of another society lie the seeds for changing the present society. Utopian writing that resists cooptation and limitation within the categories of the given system can offer a forward and emancipating look toward an autonomous existence in a non-alienating setting. To be sure, that forward-pulling vision also carries with it the necessity of willed transformation, of struggle against all types of exploitation and domination – that is, of revolution.

The utopian text

The literary genres of utopia and science fiction are forms of the romantic mode that appear to concern themselves realistically with the future. Simplistic readings of these genres speak of their "predicting" or "planning" the future as though they were the narrative tools of some futurological technocrat. On the contrary, utopia and science fiction are most concerned with the current moment of history, but they represent that moment in an estranged manner. They restructure and distance the present not to a misty past nor to an exotic other place but rather to that one place where some hope for a better life for all humanity still

35

lingers: the future. To be sure, history always requires some mediating narrative to articulate its absent and unreachable reality, but in our time the historical present has become opaqued and packaged by the reifying mechanisms of contemporary capitalism and ponderous bureaucracy, thus rendering the social situation even more resistant to being radically perceived and transformed. This enclosing of the present by transnational capital makes the estranged genres that critically apprehend that present and hold open the possibility of a different future all the more important in the continuing project of opposition and emancipation. In preserving the expression of otherness and radical difference, the critical utopias of recent years hold open the activity of the utopian imagination while also being fully aware that the figures of any one utopian society are doomed to ideological closure and compromise.

In examining the utopian text, three operations can be identified: the alternative society, the world, generated in what can be termed the iconic register of the text; the protagonist specific to utopias – that is, the visitor to the utopian society – dealt with in what can be termed the discrete register; and the ideological contestations in the text that brings the cultural artifact back to the contradictions of history.[13] The utopian text can be pictured as a fabric of iconic images of an alternative society through which the thread of the discrete travelogue of the visitor is stitched: within the weave of the fabric and the strands of the thread are the conflicts and antinomies that articulate the deep ideological engagement which relates the entire text to history itself.

Central to utopian fiction, and to the entire mode of romance, is the alternative world imaged by the author. What in the realist novel would be considered "mere" background setting becomes in traditional utopian writing the key element of the text. The society projected in such a complete manner as to include everything from political and economic structures to the practices and rituals of daily life has long been seen as what the utopian novel is "about." Indeed, as Suvin's definition suggests, the utopian setting becomes the primary place for the text's exploration and exposure of the historical situation. The world as we live it in history is revealed or manifested in the world as we read it. The alternative world tends to absorb many of the actions and causations normally reserved for characters in a realist narrative. Kingsley Amis spoke of science fiction as a literature in which the "idea" was the "hero." So too in utopia, the social structure, and what it represents and encourages, is traditionally seen as the main protagonist. As Jameson puts it, borrowing from Kenneth Burke's terminology,

> the category of Scene tends to capture and to appropriate the attributes of Agency and Act, making the "hero" over into something like a registering apparatus for transformed states of being, sudden alterations of temperature, mysterious heightenings, local intensities, sudden drops in quality, and alarming effluvia, in short, the whole semic range of transformation scenes whereby, in romance higher and lower worlds struggle to overcome each other.[14]

In the iconic register of the text, then, can be found the conflicting dialogue between the world as we know it and the better world that is not yet. This "outer discourse" of the text, as Samuel Delany calls it, produces a map of the other society that in its very creation acts as a neutralization of historical society. This manifesto of otherness, with its particular systems that mark the uniqueness of each utopian text and carry out the ideological contest in diverse forms, is the commonly accepted *raison d'être* of the utopian narrative.

The traditional way in which the author of a utopia conveys the alternative world to the reader is by the perambulations and confused, cynical, or excited questionings of the main protagonist of this genre, the visitor to utopia. More of an investigator or explorer than a hero who conquers villains and reaps rewards, the visitor serves to represent in the text the compelling advantages which the alternative society has over the visitor's own, usually coterminous with the one in which author and contemporary readers live. Along with the visitor are the guides from the utopian society who take the neophyte around town and comment on the workings of the society and how they do better what was poorly or unjustly done, or not done, in the visitor's home. Clearly these characters – guides and traveller – are in the traditional utopia secondary to the society itself. Through the discrete register, then, the fine points of the social alternative are brought out in the dialogue between guides and visitor. This "inner discourse," which in realist novels would be privileged as the site of plot and major characters, provides the itinerary across the iconic map and generates the fable which led to the discovery of the utopia, its exploration, and the visitor's return to the home world. By means of this trip, the alternative society is presented, and the contrast with the historical world is highlighted in the questions and actions of the visitor.

In the traditional utopian novel the tension occurs between the iconic description of the society and the discrete narrative of the visitor's journey. Utopia is imaged in the social structure and in the experience of that image recorded by the visitor. Underlying both registers, however, is the set of binary oppositions between what is and what is not, between the "evil" of the given world and the "good" of the alternative. In these oppositions which "ratify the centrality of a dominant term by means of the marginalization of an excluded or inessential" one can be found the ideological contest of antinomies that symbolically resolves the historical contradictions of the time. What can be identified by the analytical reader at this level is the *ideologeme*: the "historically determinate conceptual or semic complex which can project itself variously in the form of a 'value system' or 'philosophical concept,' or in the form of a protonarrative, a private or collective narrative fantasy."[15] Teased from the iconic images and discrete adventures, the ideologeme leads back to history. Here we are at the junction of text and larger society, where the text's discourse with the world confronts the process of historical change in the actual formal operation of utopian discourse itself, for the utopian form embodies "an ideological critique of ideology" (Marin) that outlines the empty places which will later be filled by concepts of social theory or by practices of social change. Utopian writing marks a distanced place of neutrality in which historical contradictions are allowed to play against one another rather than be reduced to ideal blueprints. Within this neutral space is opened an area of critique, of polemic, that can operate without premature closure. Such a "utopic practice," as Marin puts it,

38

introduces, in the report of history and the exposition of geography, the sudden distance by which the contiguities of space and time are broken and through which is discerned, in a flash, before immobilizing itself in the utopic figure and fixing itself in the "ideal" representation, the *other*, unlimited contradiction.[16]

To write utopia is to indicate what cannot yet be said within present conceptual language or achieved in current political action. To write utopia is to perform the most utopian of actions possible within literary discourse. The form is itself more significant than any of its content.

Having identified the three operations of the utopian text, we must now move to that connection between the practice of utopian discourse and the historical context. Here it must again be emphasized that utopian narrative is first and foremost a process. Utopia cannot be reduced to the society imaged, the "utopia" constructed by the author, or to the experience of the visitor in that society, or even to its basic ideological contestation with present society. That is, utopia cannot be reduced to its *content*. To do so would be to cut short the process and limit utopia to a closed set of images, character activities, or ideological expressions. Instead, the utopian process must be held open as a symbolic resolution of historical contradictions that finds its importance not in the particulars of those resolutions but in the very *act* of imagining them, in the *form* of utopia itself. Utopia is not to be regarded as an ideal blueprint or system. Rather, this particular type of romantic discourse should be seen as

> a determinate type of praxis rather than as a specific mode of representation, a praxis which has less to do with the construction and perfection of someone's "idea" of a "perfect society" than it does with a concrete set of mental operations to be performed on a determinate type of raw material given in advance which is contemporary society itself, or rather, what amounts to the same thing, to those collective representatives of contemporary society which inform our ideologies just as they order our experience of daily life.[17]

The "work" of utopian discourse by means of its social images, its visiting and guiding characters, and its deep ideological assertion is its response to history by way of neutralizing the historical contradictions that generate the text. Utopia is literally out of this world, a negation of reality. The reader's response to it is the negation of the negation or that playful action which dialectically explodes beyond the status quo of the enclosing ideological version of reality. Whereas myth resolves social contradictions, utopia neutralizes them by forcing open a consideration of what is not yet and creating a space as yet unoccupied by a transforming theory of material conditions that would lead to fundamental social change. Utopian figuration anticipates the historical moment which its critique of current reality urges. As Jameson puts it,

> it is less revealing to consider Utopian discourse as a mode of narrative comparable, say, with the novel or epic, than it is to grasp it as an object of meditation, analogous to the riddles or koan of the various mystical traditions, or the aporias of classical philosophy, whose function is to provoke a fruitful bewilderment, and to jar the mind into some heightened but unconceptualizable consciousness of its own powers, functions, aims, and structural limits. Utopian praxis, "is thus," to use Kantian terminology, "a schematizing activity of the social and political imagination which has not yet found its concept."[18]

Before a change in history, before theories and concepts that help motivate such a change, the "preconceptual thinking in images" that generates the utopian text stands in opposition to the status quo and to limiting ideology, even that of a fixed utopian society that would exist by being imposed on real human beings. In the absence of a radical theoretical discourse yet to be developed, this figural anticipation of what could not yet be conceptualized is the driving impulse of the genre itself. The operation of utopian narrative, dependent as it is on the radical insufficiency of solutions at hand, can offer no systematic solution of its own. It can only offer itself as an activity which opens human imagination beyond the present limits:

utopia's deepest subject, and the source of all that is most vibrantly political about it is precisely our inability to conceive it, our incapacity to produce it as a vision, our failure to project the other of what is, a failure that, as with fireworks dissolving back into the night sky, must once again leave us alone with *this* history.[19]

The critical utopia

In the 1960s, at the very time in which utopias appeared to be a literature of the last century with their radical impulse absorbed by consumer capital or smashed by heretofore unheard of repression, suffering, and destruction, a series of new utopian novels emerged from the ferment of opposition and creation in the United States. This new utopian phase began with Joanna Russ's *The Female Man* (written in 1968 but not published until 1974) and continued on through Ursula LeGuin's *The Dispossessed*, Marge Piercy's *Woman on the Edge of Time*, and Samuel Delany's *Triton* (the latter two, ironically, published in the bicentennial year of 1976). In addition to these, there were also Ernest Callenbach's *Ecotopia*, Sally Gearhardt's *Wanderground*, Suzy McKee Charnas's *Motherlines*, Dorothy Bryant's *The Kin of Ata*, as well as apparently non-fictional pieces such as *YV 88* – a utopian plan for the Yosemite Valley – or Gerald O'Neill's plan for a new society located in space colonies at fixed solar orbits. That this publishing phenomenon marked a revival of utopian writing is clear, but the revival was actually a transformation which involved the destruction of utopian writing as well as its preservation.

It is no accident that the major writers of this movement – Russ, LeGuin, Piercy, and Delany – began their careers in the so-called "sub-culture" of science fiction (SF). Beginning with the works of H. G. Wells and Jules Verne in the 1890s, expanding into a pulp fiction genre with the launching of Hugo Gernsbach's *Amazing Tales* in 1926, growing to maturity in the postwar 1950s under the noses of unsuspecting McCarthyite censors, and maturing in the 1960s with a generation of younger writers influenced by traditional science fiction as well as by modern experimental fiction, this genre has been a uniquely privileged symbolic response to the conditions of existence in this century.[20] While appearing to concern itself with the "future," science fiction actually gives a fresh look at the present as it is represented in the past of a fictionally extrapolated future. As Jameson puts it,

> it is this present moment – unavailable to us for contemplation in its own right because the sheer quantitative immensity of objects and individual lives it comprises is untotalizable and hence unimaginable, and also because it is occluded by the density of our private fantasies as well as of the proliferating stereotypes of a media culture that penetrates every remote zone of our existence – that upon our return from the imaginary constructs of SF is offered to us in the form of some future world's remote past, as if posthumous and as though collectively remembered.[21]

Science fiction demonstrates our incapacity to imagine the future and brings us down to earth to apprehend our present in all its limitations. Especially in the work of the 1960s that broke beyond the adventure narratives and clichéd stereotypes of the 1920s and 1930s to experiment with more open narrative strategies while retaining the deeply socially critical concerns of the 1950s, a critique of the present was developed in a literary form that proved especially capable of resisting the affirmative culture of contemporary capitalism even as much of science fiction was reabsorbed into that consumer culture in print and, especially, in film.

Thus, in the literary space opened up by the science fiction of the 1960s, the critical utopian novel could be written. Aware of the historical tendency of the utopian genre to limit the imagination to one particular ideal and also aware of the restriction of the utopian impulse to marketing mechanisms, the authors of the critical utopias assumed the risky task of reviving the emancipatory utopian imagination while simultaneously destroying the traditional utopia and yet preserving it in a transformed and liberated form that was critical both of utopian writing itself and of the prevailing social formation. We can recognize here the process whereby the generic specifications of a literary form fall casualty to the penetration and cooptation of the market system and undergo changes to keep alive the multidimensional symbolic act that is unique to the genre. In resisting the flattening out of utopian writing in modern society, the critical utopia has destroyed, preserved, and transformed that writing and marks the first important output of utopian discourse since the 1890s.

The ideologically confined utopian form has been refashioned in a new social and cultural context. While utopia persists at the core of these new works, it does so in a more complex and often discontinuous and self-aware manner than its predecessors. The works retain older elements of the utopia – the alternative society and the visitor – but work with those elements in a radically different way. The individual text now contains what Ernst Bloch termed a synchronic "uneven development" as the older utopian elements coexist and conflict with the contemporary elements.[22] In what Jameson calls "generic discontinuities," or the play between generic norm and deviation, can be found the symbolic activity that expresses the current tensions in the political unconscious:[23] the particular contradictions in the present historical moment are the limiting situations that cultural artifacts encounter and provide imaginary solutions for. The romance and the utopia practice a narrative figuration centered around social structure and conflict, between good and evil or what is and what is not yet, that is especially suited to transitional moments such as our own in which two distinct modes of production coexist and contend: for us, the shift from monopoly to transnational capitalism, from industrial/mechanical society to post-industrial/cybernetic society, from modern to post-modern culture, from democratic participation to bureaucratic management. Both modes are opposed by a radical critique which seeks human emancipation and fulfillment. The critical utopia in this time of transition, then, can in its symbolic activity help to restore a sense of the concrete historical situation and offer its own form – the self-aware, critical utopian activity – as a meaningful act on the ideological terrain.

Before moving on to an examination of the particular texts, we must in this last set of generalizations posit the specific reversals and deviations practiced by the recent critical utopias. Such deviations occur at the iconic level in the way in which the alternative society is presented, at the discrete level in the way in

43

which the protagonist is presented, and at the level of generic form in the way the text becomes self-aware and self-critical. In these moves against the limit of the traditional utopia on one hand and the current historical situation on the other, the ideologemes of these texts can be teased out and connected back with the historical process.

There are two major changes that occur in the critical utopia that mark a break with the general pattern of the traditional utopia. In most utopias since More, the narrative opens with the departure of the visitor from her or his own land, usually very similar to the author's own society, moves to the arrival, by choice or by accident, at the land of the utopia and the tour around the new society by guides who answer the visitor's questions and extoll the benefits of utopia, often at the expense of the visitor's homeland; it closes with the visitor's return to report on utopia to the people back home. Usually, the visitor is won over to the utopian way. Over against this admittedly schematic summary of the traditional utopia to which there are many exceptions, the critical utopia at the level of the iconic register, in which the image of the alternative society is generated, breaks with previous utopias by presenting in much greater, almost balanced, detail both the utopian society and the original society against which the utopia is pitted as a revolutionary alternative.

In addition to this binary opposition of old/dominant and new/oppositional societies, the critical utopia also deviates by presenting the utopian society in a more critical light. Utopia is seen as "ambiguous" (LeGuin) or, in a response partly to LeGuin, as "ambiguous heterotopia" (Delany). Furthermore, in each of the new utopias the society is shown with its faults, inconsistencies, problems, and even denials of the utopian impulse in the form of the persistence of exploitation and domination in the better place. Here, of course, is echoed the historic failure to achieve perfection, a false goal in the first place, of the revolutionary societies from the United States to the more recent flawed alternatives experienced in the Soviet Union, the People's Republic of China, Vietnam, Cuba, and Nicaragua. The critical utopian imagination seems to have learned from Mao Tse Tung's dictum that contradictions would persist in society even after the revolution or, indeed, from Derrida's arguments for continual deconstruction.

At the level of the discrete register which generates plot and character, there is even more change in the critical utopia. Whereas in the realist novel, discrete plot and character were primary and iconic setting was secondary, in utopian texts the opposite is generally true as the societal imagery takes precedence over character and especially over plot. However, as the realist novel has become compromised by mass culture and fragmented by modernist culture trapped within the limits of capitalism, its human subject has become effaced. Consequently, a way forward in human action to a better society has become blocked. As the utopian novel tended to valorize its social ideal only to see it become linked up in the limitations of the prevailing system so that it no longer allowed the radical imagination to look beyond the present, the sense of possible change of social systems was denied.

The critical utopia, however, moves beyond this formal blockage. In the new utopia, the primacy of societal alternative over character and plot is reversed, and the alternative society and indeed the original society fall back as settings for the foregrounded political quest of the protagonist. The visitor becomes the hero, or in some cases the anti-hero. The visitor in some of the novels – *The Dispossessed* especially – reverses directions and goes *from* utopia to explore and learn from the original society; or in the case of *Triton* the visitor is a non-utopian misfit trying to live in utopia. In this reversal, then, the static nature of the utopian novel as well as the dead-end encountered by the mainstream realist novel is overcome. Readers once again find a human subject in action, now no longer an isolated individual monad stuck in one social system but rather a part of the human collective in a time and place of deep historical change. The concerns of this revived, active subject are centered around the ideologeme of the strategy and tactics of revolutionary change at both the micro/personal and macro/societal levels. Furthermore, in the critical utopia the more collective heroes of social transformation are presented off-center and usually as characters who are not dominant, white, heterosexual, chauvinist males but female, gay, non-white, and generally operating collectively.

Finally, the form of the utopia itself is altered at the level of the self-reflexivity of the text. The apparently unified, illusionary, and representational text of the more traditional utopia is broken open and presented in a manner which is, first of all, much more fragmented – narratives intertwining present and future or past and present, single protagonists being divided into multiples, or into male and female versions of the same character. Secondly, the critical utopian text includes much more commentary on the operations of the text itself, from the subtle connection of temporal theory with the chapter structure in *The Dispossessed*, to the narrative ambiguity linked with the vagaries of time and causation in *Woman on the Edge of Time*, to the interpolations of an authorial voice and exhortations on the subversive work of the book in *The Female Man*, to the self-reflexive appendices on the modular calculus in *Triton*. More aware of the limits of traditional utopias and the totalizing tendencies of consumer capitalism and bureaucratic states, the critical utopias keep the utopian impulse alive by challenging it and deconstructing it within its very pages. To echo one of most arrogant and terrible phrases of the United States military in the Vietnam war: in the twentieth century it has become necessary to destroy utopia in order to save it.

Reading utopia

> Not only is utopia not "realizable," but it could not be realized without destroying itself.　　　　(Louis Marin)

The interpretation of the specific critical utopias carried out in the next section proceeds through three layers of analysis. We move from the individual text through the broader social dimension of ideology and on to the horizon of history itself. This particular re-reading works towards articulating those elements of the political unconscious in which the contradictions of history and the process of change carried on by the collectivity currently opposed to the prevailing system are registered, temporarily resolved, and opened up in the preconceptual figures of these literary artifacts.

46

At the first level, the individual work is examined as a symbolic act which provides an imaginary solution to present historical contradictions. What in history cannot yet be worked out in the realm of theory and practice is provisionally organized and unknotted in the antinomies, or binary oppositions, produced in the formal operations and figures of the text. In particular, the societies, utopian and originary, generated in the iconic register are described in terms of the deep contradiction which is the concern of so many utopias and which was faced by the United States in the 1960s: that is, the structure and institutions of society itself.

In so far as America has been conceived as utopia since the early European explorations, a critical question in the 1960s was the shape of the American Dream that was emerging, or being denied, in the period of postwar affluence – a period which also included the repression necessary to achieve that affluent society sought by the dominant powers. The growth of multinational corporations and the military hegemony of the United States, the development of mass society especially in terms of suburban living, the replacement of labor activism by well-paid consumerism, the return of women to the home and traditional roles, the creation of the market-oriented "teenager" after the openness of employment in the war years, the establishing of a common national patriotic mass culture at the expense of negation and dissent in the realm of more localized culture, politics, and art – all these contributed by the 1960s to the sense of promise and problem, to the confrontation of two societal ideals: generally, the development of society for human need or for profit.

Utopian desires for a just and free society were suppressed and redirected into the static products of consumer capital – perhaps best imaged in those twin architectural figures that signify affluent society: the shopping mall and Disneyland. Utopia is denied except for its reflected image in the shiny surface of the newly marketed American Dream. What we see reflected and reacted to in the binary opposite societies of original worlds and breakaway utopian societies in each of these novels is the symbolic resolution of this conflict of social agendas as experienced and felt in late 1960s America but not worked out in concrete economic, political, or social reality. Contending images of

America as utopia are recreated and examined in the iconic figures of social institutions and structures.

At this level of interpretation, the historical contradictions around the social forms to be developed out of postwar wealth are re-presented in the social systems imaged in the novels. Locked in the closed combat of binary opposites, utopian alternative and original world encode the deep conflict over the uses to which the wealth of developing postwar society will be put. A second iconic confrontation is identified in the debates and conflicts *within* the alternative utopian societies themselves. Again we encounter a prefigural working out of yet another debate: that of the shape and purpose of post-revolutionary societies, a debate that was being explored within the forces of opposition in the late 1960s and early 1970s. Here, questions of centralization and decentralization, continued industrial growth or ecological balance, the persistence of patriarchy, the needs of public society or personal fulfillment, party or autonomy, maintenance of the new society or expansion of the revolution, nationalism or internationalism, parliamentary politics or the gun, are – among others – also reproduced in the social imagery of the iconic register and offered in a series of binary oppositions that contain these contradictions within sets of textual antinomies.

At the second level of interpretation, the analysis moves beyond the symbolic acts of the individual text to the ideological contestations in the broader social order. The closed binary oppositions identified in the text are opened up to the larger motion of human perception and action in the society at large. This, as Jameson notes, is the moment when "the organizing categories of analysis become those of social class" and indeed of a broadly defined class struggle between those in power and those in opposition.[24] The binary closure is broken by the antagonistic dialogue between these opposing classes or groups contending for control over the historical project. As texts generally of the oppositional public sphere, the critical utopias at this level of analysis can be seen as cultural practices that seek to contest and to undermine dominant ideology. The novels become potential gestures of defiance and weapons of struggle.

At this level, the focus of analysis shifts from the imaginary oppositions carried in the iconic register around the societal structures to the specific ideological concerns expressed through the characters and their activities as generated in the discrete register. Here, the concept of *ideologeme* – the "smallest intelligible unit of the essentially antagonistic collective discourses of social classes" – comes into play.[25] Ideologeme carries with it the dual sense of *idea*, of conceptual or belief system, and of *action*, of a narrative of appropriate class action. In the novels at hand, the ideologeme at the heart of their response to the historical contradictions in both theory and practice in the late 1960s and 1970s is that of the question of the human subject and in particular that of the *activism* (and its strategies and tactics) to be engaged in by that human subject in opposition to the dominant system. This is the process identified by Raymond Williams as willed transformation.

In the figure of the individual protagonist of the critical utopia – the visitor revived as hero – is coded the much debated question of the sort of activism required by the collective forces of opposition. This is where the reversal in the critical utopia of the usual priority in utopian writing of the iconic society over the discrete character assumes an intelligibility that would not be apparent at the level of the social structures presented within the individual texts. To limit one's analysis to the particular utopian or anti-utopian social plan would be to immobilize the utopian impulse within one limited ideal system. Systemic alternatives in the critical utopia, then, give way to the exploration of the utopian impulse and the ensuing strategy and tactics taken by a human subject once again able to carry on anti-hegemonic tasks aimed at bringing down the prevailing system and moving toward a radically different way of being.

The critical utopia, read at the level of the ideologeme, becomes a meditation on action rather than on system. The false utopia created by postwar consumerism which required a passive consumer is deconstructed in favor of the more radical utopia that re-engages the gears of active human resistance and creation. Manipulated behavior and channeled choice limited to a shopping list of alternatives is no longer the only option for the contemporary human being. Rather, the active protagonist symbolizes the experiences of the civil rights, anti-war, women's, and other movements in the late 1960s that valorized militant human actions, individually chosen but in concert with a renewed community of activists. Where utopia as system can only be passively wished for, utopia as struggle can be taken on in a willed effort to transform the social system. The ideologeme identified in this reading expresses the question of activism both at the level of *idea*, in considerations of broad *strategies* – that is, social, political, economic, and indeed personal goals to be achieved by political practice – and at the level of *narrative* in considerations of specific *tactics* to be adopted for particular strategic goals – types of political, military, or cultural activity chosen to achieve specific ends. Finally, this second-level reading at the discrete register further examines the decentered subjects in these novels: the so-called "supporting" characters who are often the most active and politically engaged and who tend to be the most socially other in the novels.

At the third level of analysis, the discussion moves to the realm of history itself. Here, the ideology of the generic *form* of critical utopian writing is considered as a complex response to and articulation of the changes occurring in history from one mode of production – that is, the general social structure encompassing the economic, political, and ideological practices that comprise the social relations of that structure – to another. In the ideology of form, the contradictions which coexist within the formal processes of a given genre, in this case the utopia, can be grasped as "sedimented content in their own right, as carrying ideological messages of their own, distinct from the ostensible or manifest content of the works."[26] As the utopian genre has developed from the traditional form of the last century to the current critical utopia, the older ideological message of the genre – the ability to create and establish a given social system – persists in the more recent, more self-aware, and complex critical form and clashes with the new ideological message – which denies the primacy of system while holding open the radical act of utopian imagination. System persists in the iconic, societal images, but it is negated by the privileging of action that is generated in the discrete character activities and by the self-reflexive and open nature of the form. In these generic discontinuities, the mission of the critical utopia to break with the status quo and open up a radical path to a not yet realized future can be detected.

At this level, the critical utopia is seen as plotting the move from the utopian closure on a synchronic ideal system to the more subversive opening to a diachronic narrative of autonomous, yet collective, action. As such, the ideology of the critical utopian form serves as yet another act of opposition. At the level of modes of production this opposition marks the rejection of the "totalized system" of contemporary capitalism as it moves from its industrial and national to its post-industrial and world-wide phase. The globe-encircling activity by the always exploiting market is opposed by a literary genre that once celebrated system but now re-opens the place of opposition to all such enclosing systemic efforts. The critical utopia, in its formal operation, and especially in its self-reflexive comments on those operations in the text, negates static ideals, preserves radical action, and creates a neutral space in which opposition can be articulated and received. The critical utopia speaks in the name of the autonomy of nature and humanity over against the domination of post-industrial world capitalism and its accompanying bureaucratic state. As the content of utopia is rejected as too limiting and subject to compromise and cooptation, the open form of the new utopia becomes a subversive new content in its own right.

Oppositional cultural practices such as the critical utopias can be understood as part of a broader, ongoing cultural revolution as the dominant mode of production is challenged by the possibility of one that can redirect post-industrial reality toward the goal of human fulfillment. Even the content of the critical utopia, purged of its confining ideal system connotations, can be reappropriated as so many suggestive preconceptual figures of what could be done in an emancipated society of the future. Indeed, the emphasis in these texts on historical change via human activism is also a sign of the permanent process of change that would be part of a reality in which freedom rather than necessity has become the driving force.

With this final level of interpretation, we return to history itself and to the recognition of the importance of the utopian impulse in the ongoing social revolution. The importance of self-aware, deconstructive, collective activity by human beings intent on the emancipation of humanity and nature is what in the last instance

51

emerges from our reading of these critical utopias. What remains now is to take the step away from the abstractions of theory and get on to the examination of the specific texts.

PART TWO:

Texts

4 Joanna Russ, *The Female Man*

Live merrily, little daughter-book, even if I can't and we can't; recite yourself to all who will listen; stay hopeful and wise. . . . Do not complain when at last you become quaint and old-fashioned, when you grow as outworn as the crinolines of a generation ago and are classed with *Spicy Western Stories*, *Elsie Dinsmore*, and *The Son of the Sheik*; do not mutter angrily to yourself when young persons read you to hrooch and hrch and guffaw, wondering what the dickens you were all about. Do not get glum when you are no longer understood, little book. Do not curse your fate. Do not reach up from readers' laps and punch the readers' noses.

Rejoice, little book!

For on that day, we will be free.

(Joanna in *The Female Man*)

Joanna Russ appreciates the use value of utopia. For her, the utopian practice of imagining a better world is one means of transcending the barriers to concrete utopia, one way of rejecting and negating those aspects of our world which are not fulfilling for the great majority of humanity. In the forefront of the utopian

55

revival of the 1970s, Russ uses the literary utopia in new and creative ways compared to what had become the model of that genre's tradition. Not the static, reified object of a passively perfect society, but the engaged, open, critical utopia is found in the pages of *The Female Man*, and indeed in her other works of science fiction as well.[1] She uses utopia as a literary practice; she does not assert utopia as a literary object. For Russ, utopia is not the authoritarian guidance of the blueprint, but rather the emancipating possibilities of the dream. To keep the utopian impulse active she continually works against its tendency to lapse into a rigid system. She fragments it. She makes it incomplete. She nurtures the reader in little tastes as the first food is given to one who is starving. She gives us utopia in throwaway lines that at first might not seem so important to the drama at hand. She offers a disruptive, multiplex utopian practice that resists strict linear, systematic, totalized closure on a single alternative.

In *The Female Man*, Russ offers the reader not the plan of utopia but the ambience of it. Like Charlotte Perkins Gilman in *Herland* (1915), a significant early feminist-socialist utopia, her concern is not so much with the fixed structure of social institutions as it is with the fluid practice of everyday life and human consciousness in a society where those who have been oppressed, particularly women, live free of their oppression. Ann J. Lane's description of *Herland* echoes what Russ does in *The Female Man* – especially in the matter of transition from the old world to the new utopia:

> Gilman's transition rests with marginal people – women. Because women are nurturers of the young and bearers of the cultural values of love and cooperation, and because women have been excluded from the sources of power, they are in an ideal position to create an alternative social vision. By the early twentieth century, women also had decades of sophisticated collective action and a trained leadership to call upon. Most utopias neglect the central role of education in reconstructing their worlds. In Gilman's work education – not formal education but the process by which values permeate an entire social fabric – evolves as a natural device in the creation of a new people, especially the young.[2]

In Russ's novel, both the education of the person – from birth all through life – and the consciousness-raising of Joanna, Jeannine, and Laura are central to the utopian praxis described.

Furthermore, utopia for Russ is self-critical, conscious of itself and its history. Therefore, utopia can question itself, and not be so self-righteous or so arrogant as to hold that any one utopian society is the most important alternative world. Indeed, Whileaway is a dream that challenges our insufficient present, a dream that makes us less satisfied with our lives in that present if we are of the many who suffer in it. Whileaway is not the answer, but rather the vision that provokes change.

According to Marilyn Hacker, Russ began writing *The Female Man* in the spring of 1969 – the year in which the Joanna character lives – and completed it in 1971.[3] Unable to find a publisher because the feminist polemic and experimental narration put off editors in the male-dominated world of science fiction publishing, Russ's novel was nevertheless read in manuscript by several authors in the science fiction community before it reached print in 1975. Among those who read it were Ursula LeGuin and Samuel Delany – both were at that time, or shortly thereafter, writing their own utopian works.[4] *The Female Man* smuggled utopia into the dystopian world of the latter half of our century and initiated the revival and transformation of utopia in the 1970s.

To be sure, the social-political movements of the 1960s are the historical base for the vision of *The Female Man* – just as the dystopian novel, postmodern fiction, science fiction, and, especially, literature written by women comprise the aesthetic base. But more precisely it is the coming to consciousness of women in the 1960s that was the immediate stimulus. In her essay, "Creating Positive Images of Women: A Writer's Perspective," Russ details her painful struggle against male supremacy, from her days as a student of creative writing at Cornell University in the 1950s to the period just after the writing of *The Female Man*.

She describes her struggle for "*Lebensraum* in my own soul" in a world where women are not safe on the streets at night nor accepted in their own right and power as persons, and in her case as writers who choose not to create within the parameters of

57

male-dominated literature. She describes her first effort at writing a sword-and-sorcery story with a strong female protagonist:

> I cannot tell how hard writing that first story was. It was dropping the mask and stepping out in my own person. I felt hideously ashamed, and guilty of some unspeakable crime. People would point at me in the streets. People would say I wanted to be a man. Reviewers would howl in derision. By writing an adventure story with a female hero I was clearly breaking some basic taboo. It took weeks even to sit down to the typewriter, and even then I was so ashamed of perpetrating the ghastly thing that like Virginia Woolf's *Orlando*, who makes a deep obeisance to the spirit of the nineteenth century (while keeping certain thoughts to herself), I kept trying and trying to make my protagonist *beautiful*. You know, just to show that in spite of everything, I knew which priorities *really* came first. However, she refused to be falsified like that, and came into the world as a short, stocky, unremarkable looking peasant.[5]

Thus was born the hero of her Alyx stories and of her first novel, *Picnic on Paradise* (1968), and so began Russ's continuing effort to liberate her fiction by creating female characters who were not filtered through male consciousness.

After writing her second novel, *And Chaos Died* (1970) – with its egalitarian society, made possible by psychic powers and matter transportation, and with its concerns about "failed sex, miserable sex, the guilt, exploitation, nastiness, and plain apathy that so often accompany what we call 'making love,'"[6] but with a male protagonist – Russ says in her essay that

> feminism came to Cornell with an intersession conference which included Betty Friedan, Kate Millett, and all sorts of "neurotic, castrating bitches" (as I was told by a male colleague whose wife later left him). I was thrilled. I was elated. I was scared to death. Saying those things out loud (although we all knew they were true) was *absolutely forbidden*.[7]

Out of her own struggle to become a free woman, and supported and encouraged by the growing feminist movement about her, Russ began work on *The Female Man*. The conclusion of her essay conveys her strength and vision:

> I believe women writers create positive images of women by living them. I'm still trying and I don't really know what will come next. But I do know that the first step must be to become resolutely self-centred, that is, *centered in your Self*, not spread thin around your own inner horizon with some boob in the center pretending (or you pretending) that he's either Santa Claus or The Big Bad Wolf. It means writing about mothers and daughters, about women friends, about women who are like you and women who aren't. It means learning never to "trust men" in the abstract (or women, either) but that (rarely) you can trust particular men (and women) without making trust an either/or proposition. It means, above all, I think, valuing friendship far, far above "love," until the latter stops being the most exploitative and polluted word in the English language. We need, not "love" but community, fellowship, concern, solidarity, comradeship, friendship, affection, and affectionate emotional support. It means learning (to give only two examples) that Lesbians will not rape you and that celibacy can be an immensely liberating experience. It means beginning – only beginning to understand other kinds of oppression and how yours and ours and theirs (whoever "they" are) are related. It also means learning that you can't go it alone, as a writer or anything else I've been helped by so many people (some of them people I've never met). By helping myself, I've apparently helped many others (or so they tell me). By helping yourself, you can't avoid helping me. So please – go do it![8]

With this coming-to-consciousness Russ emerged as a major influence in the fields of science fiction and feminist literature. Indeed, she was a key figure in the network of writers, editors, and fans that developed around feminist science fiction. That network marked the development of an oppositional cultural movement which challenged the male-dominated science fiction establishment. Examples of its output include anthologies such as Pamela Sargent's *Women of Wonder* collections, Vonda McIntyre and

Susan Janice Anderson's *Aurora: Beyond Equality*; feminist fan-
zines such as Amanda Bankier's *The Witch and the Chameleon*
and Janice Bogstad's *Janus* and *New Moon*; conferences, such as
the annual Wiscon in Madison, Wisconsin, that address the
connection of feminism and science fiction. At the beginnings of
this movement, then, Russ and her manuscript stand lonely, but
influential and supportive.[9]

Utopias of the 1970s, then, appeared in increasing numbers as
new cultural space was forced open by Russ and others in the
feminist science fiction movement. Dorothy Bryant's *The Kin of
Ata Are Waiting for You* (published in 1971 as *The Comforter*),
Ursula LeGuin's *The Dispossessed* (1974), Mary Staton's *From
the Legend of Riel* (1975), Marge Piercy's *Woman on the Edge
of Time* (1976), Samuel Delany's *Triton* (1976), Suzy McKee
Charnas's *Motherlines* (1978), and Sally Miller Gearhart's *The
Wanderground* (1978) are but a few of the titles which can be
identified as feminist and utopian. These are works which in
general are

> explicit about economics and politics, sexually permissive,
> demystifying about biology, emphatic about the necessity
> for female bonding, concerned with children . . . non-urban,
> classless, communal, relatively peaceful while allowing
> room for female rage and female self-defense, and serious
> about the emotional and physical consequences of
> violence.[10]

They are, in short, expressive of the non-dogmatic, multi-
tendency, feminist, ecological and libertarian oppositional
consensus that developed in the United States in the 1970s.

The emergence of science fiction and utopian fiction as an
important arena for such critical literature is primarily due to the
ability of these estranged genres to provide an alternative to the
present world. In her essay on Russ, Marilyn Hacker notes that
mainstream fiction can deal with the present situation, suffering,
and struggles of a female protagonist – or by extension a non-
white or politically radical or otherwise alienated protagonist –
but because the solution to the oppressive situation experienced
by that character must be limited to the world as it is, such a
solution must be limited to an *individual* choice: to live in the

system as it is, to go mad, or to die. Given the world as it is, a collective solution and/or a radical change in the social structure is not possible in mainstream realist fiction. "If the individual solution is not describable in novelistic terms, the writer is left with a pessimistic conclusion."[11]

With the generic potential to posit a world other than this one, the ground of the narrative is shifted; options other than capitulation or defeat are made possible. The iconic mode of narrative allows it to move beyond the status quo. As Pamela Annas puts it, science fiction

> as a genre is more useful than "mainstream" fiction for exploring possibilities for social change precisely because it allows idea to become flesh, abstraction to become concrete, imaginative extrapolation to become aesthetic reality. It allows the writer to create and the reader to experience and recreate a new or transformed world based on a set of assumptions different from those we usually accept. It allows the reader, for a while, to be reborn in a reborn world. And, through working out in concrete terms philosophical and political assumptions, it allows the reader to take back into her or his own life new possibilities. There is a dialectical relationship between the world and its imaginative and ideational reconstructions in the creations of the mind. The artist says for us what we almost knew and defamiliarizes what we thought we knew.[12]

Indeed, the motivating narrative premise in *The Female Man* is rooted in the traditional science fictional gambit of alternative temporal probabilities – that is, alternative universes in which variations of history exist in pasts, futures, and presents that are those of the protagonist, or reader. Russ, of course, uses such an extrapolative premise to set the scene for her novel of multiple feminist alternatives to the present male-dominated world. It is worth quoting the entire passage which sets forth this premise to see how the speculative situation informs the ideology and form of the entire novel:

> Sometimes you bend down to tie your shoe, and then you either tie your shoe or you don't; you either straighten up

instantly or maybe you don't. Every choice begets at least two worlds of possibility, that is, one in which you do and one in which you don't; or very likely many more, one in which you do quickly, one in which you do slowly, one in which you don't, but hesitate, one in which you hesitate and frown, one in which you hesitate and sneeze, and so on. To carry this line of argument further, there must be an infinite number of possible universes (such is the fecundity of God) for there is no reason to imagine Nature as prejudiced in favor of every human action. Every displacement of every molecule, every change in orbit of every electron, every quantum of light that strikes here and not there – each of these must somewhere have its alternative. It's possible, too, that there is no such thing as one clear line or strand of probability, and that we live on a sort of twisted braid, blurring from one to the other without even knowing it, as long as we keep within the limits of a set of variations that really make no difference to us. Thus the paradox of time travel ceases to exist, for the Past one visits is never one's own Past but always somebody else's: or rather, one's visit to the Past instantly creates another Present (one in which the visit has already happened) and what you visit is the Past belonging to that Present – an entirely different matter from your own Past. And with each new decision you make (back there in the Past) that new probable universe itself branches, creating simultaneously a new Past and a new Present, or to put it plainly, a new universe. And when you come back to your own Present, you alone know what the other Past was like and what you did there.[13]

This is the basis for the action of the novel, but it also signifies Russ's rejection of single-minded, linear, authoritarian, totalized visions of reality or indeed of opposition to the present reality. The alternative probability premise is the basis for the open and fragmented form of the novel itself. That form resists simple closure and consistency yet allows a strong statement about the present situation in the world, especially for women, and offers a clear suggestion of the several means which, taken together, can form the oppositional politics of change.

The Female Man, then, is a complex text that disturbs the reader's expectations of form and challenges the reader to re-envision what is and what could be. The text makes use of many literary forms including the realist novel, science fiction, the polemic essay, the utopia, the lyric, the epic, the drama, the fable, the pastoral, indeed the medieval anatomy in its explorations of the current and possible histories of women. The novel is an extended encounter among four protagonists – Janet, Jeannine, Joanna, and Jael – who constitute various aspects of the female self. Episodic in construction, in a literary montage the work wends its way through nine parts, with each part divided into anywhere from five to seventeen sections. Through this narrative the four characters from four different time probabilities are drawn into closer contact with each other and deeper explorations of their own selves, each other, their respective worlds, and the choices of action they have available to them. As Catherine McClenahan puts it, "the text operates through *excess*: it isolates, exaggerates, reconnects, *plays* with certain features or components of the personality under varying conditions."[14] Indeed, as McClenahan points out, Russ shapes aspects of her own psyche into characters: one characterized by narcissism, fear, hatred, masochism, passivity, and dependence (Jeannine); one characterized by strength, intelligence, imagination, adaptability, and self-love (Janet); a third, characterized by fierce independence, cunning, power, savage wit, and anger (Jael). The fourth character, torn among these three, is Joanna. And it is Joanna, the "author" of the novel, who isolates each of these potential persons within herself and pushes them to excess by developing their world and the way they respond to it. Finally, the deliberations of the four come back to a collective response to Joanna's, our, world.

The novel begins in the iconic register with utopia as Janet Evason, the visitor from Whileaway, introduces herself in a first person narration. The utopian person and her utopian society confront the reader head on, without the usual narrative frame of a voyage to utopia or the mediation of a guide to show the non-utopian visitor around. Immediately, Russ breaks open the traditional literary genre of utopia and confronts the reader with utopia rather than couching the alternative within a safely distancing frame. The radical utopian other confronts the reader without mediation. As Janet reveals her society to the other Js, and to the reader, the iconic text of the novel unfurls a set of images of that alternative society which is post-industrial, social-ist, ecologically sound, libertarian, and occupied entirely by women. As a contrast, the iconic register also supplies the reader with images of the other three worlds as well: Jeannine's, of a 1969 in the United States wherein the Depression never ended, World War Two never occurred, and women are more openly repressed than they are in our own situation; Jael's, of a future in which, referring to both genitalia and power, the "haves and have-nots," the men of Manland and women of Womanland, have engaged in a life and death struggle; and Joanna's of our own 1969 with its contradictory, and usually false, promises of liberation to the individual female in a society still dominated by men for the satisfaction of men.

In the discrete register, in the braided narratives of the four protagonists, the ideological question common to these critical utopias, concerning the strategies and tactics necessary to over-turn the present oppressive and unfulfilling situation and move toward a just and emancipated society, is articulated as the four characters confront each other and move toward a common stand, though with continuing differences, against the status quo. Based on an overall strategy of a necessary separatism from men to avoid any chance of compromise or the relegation of "women's issues" to a secondary place in the political agenda, the choices of the four characters identify the necessity for collective, though diverse and not centralized, tactical activity at the levels of service of people's continuing needs and satisfactions, violence against the existing powers that resist change, and ideological contest-ation to destroy old ways of seeing the world and to articulate a new emancipatory consciousness. Only in such collective and diverse action can the dystopias of Jeannine, Jael, and Joanna be eliminated and the utopia of Whileaway be achieved.

Finally, the form of The Female Man is an ideological express-ion of the resistance to present day capitalist instrumentality, phallocratic authority, and bureaucratic hierarchy that render all people into one-dimensional servants of the forces of profit and power. By means of a style that cuts through the binary oppositions of now and not yet, that explores the present as a multiplex and contradictory assemblage of closures and possibilities, and sets forth a vision of a better future as well as the activism needed to reach that set of possibilities, Russ's text in its very form disrupts the limits of the present ideological system. It uses the expansive possibilities of science fiction to express a utopia as well as an agenda for getting there that resists the traditional closure of narrow utopian systems, and hence their cooptation by the historical systems that they criticize. The fragmented, disconcerting, deconstructing, multiplex text – with its equally outrageous anger and humor – is a critical expression of the politics of opposition and a vision of a not yet realized society.

Whileaway: utopia as liberated zone

Although it constitutes only a portion of *The Female Man*, Whileaway is a fully conceived utopian society that plays a major role in the text. The utopia occupies a privileged place in the narrative as the novel begins with Janet's first-person description of the world in which she herself is a police officer, married, mother of one child, and the chosen emissary in Whileaway's first exploration across time probabilities. After the initial presentation by Janet, the Whileawayan utopia is distributed throughout the novel, but these fragmentary bits of information can be gathered together to sum up the alternative society expressed in the preconceptual imagery of the iconic text. Whileaway is a female society that exists well over 900 years in the future, in another time probability. During an earlier Golden Age when men and women were still alive, the Earth was entirely "reformed" – physically, but the pun tells us something of Russ's ironic politics – into a North and South continent, which echoes the shape and climatological spread of present-day New Zealand. In the male/female Golden Age, humanity had blended the best of high technology with an ecological economy and collaboration with nature; it had also reached out to the moon and outer planets to populate those areas and form a non-terran contingent of people politically separate enough to form a "Selenic League" able to enter into treaties with the Earth. The pre-catastrophe world from which Whileaway emerged had developed a balanced

65

relationship with nature and a liberation of human energies. The situation resembles the reforms in modern capitalist states which make human existence apparently more just and happy but which do not fully address the continuing oppression of women. However, it also resembles the deep changes advocated by the all-male new left of the 1960s before the challenge and critique of feminism changed the scenario. Russ is clear here: while such reformist or "revolutionary" achievements are notable, and necessary, they are not sufficient for full revolutionary emancipation.

Two versions of the transition from the Golden Age to Whileaway are given. The first, by Janet, accounts for the change by means of a plague, a natural catastrophe, which suddenly killed all males. Afterward, women created their own society through nine centuries of labor that included the development of parthenogenesis, the merging of two ova from the mother and the "other mother," with one bearing the fetus to birth. Opposed to this organic, mythic, version of the change from within a post-struggle Whileaway ideology is Jael's account from the distanced viewpoint of her world embroiled in the continuing battle between Manland and Womanland. Jael, who has sought out the other three Js to enlist their help in that battle, tells Janet that the deliberate destruction of the men by Jael and her comrades ended their rule:

> that "plague" you talk of is a lie. *I know*. The world-lines around you are not so different from yours or mine or theirs and there is no plague in any of them, not any of them. Whileaway's plague is a big lie. Your ancestors lied about it. It is I who gave you your "plague," my dear, about which you can now pietize and moralize to your heart's content; I, I, I, I am the plague, Janet Evason. I and the war I fought built your world for you. I and those like me, we gave you a thousand years of peace and love and Whileaway flowers flourish themselves on the bones of the men we have slain.
>
> (TFM, 211)

As Janet's organic ideology is demystified by Jael's political analysis, the reader learns that utopia is the product not of natural creation but of willed human transformation of society. The four

Is Jael uses in sequence mirror the four Js of the plot and represent the active involvement of all women in the building of the best society.

Whileaway's economy is a decentralized combination of balanced agrarian and industrial production in a land with no true cities but with a sophisticated technology including matter-antimatter reactors, biological engineering, space travel, probability mechanics, and the induction helmet which allows human labor to control machinery by direct connection with the human brain and nervous system. Most of the population live on farms which are

> the only family units on Whileaway, not that Whileawayans think farm life is good for children (they don't) but because farm work is harder to schedule and demands more day-to-day continuity than any other kind of job. Farming on Whileaway is mainly caretaking and machine-tending; it is the emotional security of family life that provides the glamour. (TFM, 89)

With younger women doing repetitive and onerous work by means of the induction helmet; middle-aged women doing more careful management, repair, and service work; and older women doing advanced mental work of planning and creation by being directly connected to the main computer, "in a state they say can't be described but is most like a sneeze that never comes off' (TFM, 53), the labor force is divided by age. But in no case does any Whileawayan work more than a sixteen-hour week nor more than three hours on any one job. The economy and development of technology is aimed at a way of life that combines a post-industrial, cybernetic technology with a libertarian pastoral social system. Fulfillment of each person, not accumulation of profit and centralization of power, is the goal of the economy.

Politically, the government of Whileaway is as minimal and decentralized as possible. As Janet tells Jeannine who is used to big, centralized, bureaucratic government, "there is no government here in the sense that you mean . . . there is no one place from which to control the entire activity of Whileaway' (TFM, 91). What government there is is located in two bodies, the Geographical Parliament and the Professional Parliament, which decide on issues of economic development but do not legislate morality or attempt to direct people's personal lives. What social direction there is comes from established custom regulated through kinship structures centered around the child-bearing couple in large communal families. The only other significant social grouping is "that network of informal associations of the like-minded which is Whileaway's substitute for everything else but family' (TFM, 51).

In line with this decentralized economy and syndicalist political structure, the legal system on Whileaway is almost non-existent. Neither written constitutions and laws nor courts and prisons exist, for the rule of custom and the value system of a libertarian society that is tolerant of almost every action are so internalized that the only enforcement mechanism needed is the local person willing to act as the Safety and Peace Officer to carry out the punishment that the perpetrator already knows is coming. The taboos that do exist include "sexual relations with anybody considerably older or younger than oneself, waste, ignorance, offending others without intending to," as well as the "usual checks on murder and theft – both those crimes being actually difficult to commit" (TFM, 53). The other "crime," always punishable by death, is the decision by an individual to deny the reality of other persons, to drop out of the social network – that is, the individual who says "ha ha on you, you do not exist, go away" (TFM, 143). As Janet explains, Whileawayans are "so bloody cooperative" that they have a solipsistic underside which leads them to this denial. Such a person is in fact already dead to Whileawayan society and to her own self; so the execution of that person by the S&P Officer is the completion of the suicide begun by the solipsist herself. Other conflicts between persons or families are settled by direct argument, ranging from shouting to physical fighting to killing in sanctioned duels, a method of resolving conflicts that passes in and out of fashion. The overall tolerance of Whileawayan justice is best summed up in the following set of epigrams:

> If not me or mine . . . O.K.
> If me or mine – alas.
> If us and ours – *watch out*. (TFM, 55)

Whereas the economy, administration, and legal systems are minimal, social and personal life is complex and varied and is the real center of this utopia. Clans organized in kinship webs constitute the social basis of life in Whileaway: "You cannot fall out of the kinship web and become sexual prey for strangers, for there is no prey and there are no strangers – the web is world-wide" (TFM, 81). Non-biological family units number from twenty to thirty individuals: and though each person traces her own kin from her two mothers, she makes a separate decision to join the family of her choice by age 22. When a family gets too large or ages just as individuals do, some go off to start a new family: so that one-quarter of the families at any one time are new. Befitting the emphasis on the role of education, child-raising and socialization are described carefully. Whileawayans bear children around age 30. The childbearing mother is relieved by the rest of her family of all household tasks during pregnancy and until the child is 5 years old: this time is one of slowing down, of a leisure that will not be known again until age 60, of total involvement in the nurturing of the child.

"At the age of four or five, these independent, blooming, pampered, extremely intelligent little girls are torn weeping and arguing from their thirty relatives and sent to the regional school" (TFM, 50). From 5 to 12 years of age, the children are cared for in groups of five and taught in groups of differing sizes depending on the topic. "Their education at this point is heavily practical: how to run machines, how to get along without machines, law, transportation, physical theory, and so on. They learn gymnastics and mechanics. They learn practical medicine" (TFM, 50). They also learn to swim, shoot, dance, sing, paint, play, and "everything their Mommies did." Turned loose at puberty, the children receive the ritual identification of Middle Dignity and have the right to food and lodging wherever they wander. From puberty to 17, they do not go home but wander alone or in bands. During this time they work sporadically, get involved in political movements, go directly to their desired work, drift or play. "The more profound abandon all possessions and live off the land just above or below the forty-eighth parallel; they return with animal heads, scars, visions" (TFM, 50). From puberty on, they are free to be sexually active. No Whileawayan is monogamous unless she chooses; however, later in life "some restrict their sexual relations to one other person – at least while that other person is nearby – but there is no legal arrangement" (TFM, 53). Sexual relations may, but usually do not, occur with members of one's own family.

Three-Quarters Dignity is achieved at 17, and all 17-year-olds are taken into the labor force and sent where they are needed, not where they wish. They take care of cattle, run machinery, oversee food factories, lay pipe, fix machinery – all with the technological help of the induction helmet. At 22 they achieve Full Dignity: at this point they enter their formal apprenticeships, have their learning certified, marry into pre-existing families or form their own. "By now the typical Whileaway girl is able to do any job on the planet, except for specialities and extremely dangerous work. By twenty-five, she has entered a family, thus choosing her geographical home base (Whileawayans travel all the time)" (TFM, 52). From 25 to 60 women bear and raise one or two children, work at their principal jobs, and travel and enjoy life. From age 60 on, they move to sedentary and highly intellectual work. Provided with the direct mental link with the computer, the older women are the most intellectually creative members of the society. They

> can spend their time mapping, drawing, thinking, writing, collating, composing. In the libraries old hands come out from under the induction helmets and give you the reproductions of the books you want; old feet twinkle below the computer shelves, hanging down like Humpty Dumpty's; old ladies chuckle eerily while composing "The Blasphemous Cantata" (a great favorite of Ysaye's) or mad-moon city-scapes which turn out to be do-able after all; old brains use one part in fifty to run a city (with checkups made by two sulky youngsters) while the other forty-nine parts riot in a freedom they haven't had since adolescence. (TFM, 53)

With IQs around 200, genetically perfect bodies, and indulged happy lives, individuals experience a high quality of life. Whileawayans celebrate for almost any reason. Their dancing is unlike either the stylized dance of the orient or the romanticism of the ballet: "If Indian dancing says I Am, if ballet says I Wish, what does the dance of Whileaway say? It says I Guess" (TFM, 102). Their art is produced from childhood on. Their music is collective, improvisational, performed for hours on end. Old industrial areas are transformed into gardens, and across the planet are strewn "sceneries, mountains, glider preserves, culs-de-sac, comic nude statuary, artistic lists of tautologies and circular mathematical proofs (over which aficionados are moved to tears), and the best graffiti in this or any other world" (TFM, 54). Housing on Whileaway is abundant: "There are many more shelters than homes, many more homes than persons; as the saying goes, My home is in my shoes" (TFM, 99). Homes are self-contained units with their own ecologically suitable power sources – solar, wind, matter-anti-matter, even grain alcohol. There are caves, indoor gardens, places in the Arctic to sit and meditate, rafts on the sea, houses under the sea, eyries reached only by gliders; all available to everyone. To get around, Whileawayans generally walk, but there are also monorails, hover-cars, farm tractors, boats of several kinds, gliders, and community-owned powered bicycles with guiding radio-beacons.

In general, Whileaway is a woman's place that thrives on the pleasure principle in a post-scarcity, non-phallocratic, non-capitalist, ecologically sensitive, anarcho-communist society. Hard work, tidiness, privacy, community, freedom, creativity, and a love of nature emerge as the primary values in a society that is purposely shapeless, without the linear order imposed by a central government or male abstractions. The resultant psychology locates the Whileawayan

> character in the early indulgence, pleasure, and flowering which is drastically curtailed by the separation from the mothers. This (it says) gives Whileawayan life its characteristic independence, its dissatisfaction, its suspicion, and its tendency toward a rather irritable solipsism. "Without which" (said the same Dunyasha Bernadettson, q.v.) "we would all become contented slobs, nicht wahr?"
>
> (TFM, 52)

In optimism and health, Whileaway continues through the years, transforming and refining life. "Whileaway is so pastoral

71

that at times one wonders whether the ultimate sophistication may not take us all back to a kind of pre-Paleolithic dawn age, a garden without any artifacts except for what we would call miracles" (TFM, 14).

Russ's utopia is a forward-looking vision into the not yet that re-appropriates the Garden of Eden with a post-phallocratic and post-statist pastoral innocence maintained by the use of an advanced technology in the service of a female humanity free from external gods or men and able to live fully in an egalitarian society at peace with nature and with themselves. Working against the generic expectations of a dull tour through utopia at the mercy of a talkative guide, Russ gives the reader the utopian person's own narrative and activity as the primary means by which Whileaway is presented, in bits and pieces, with humor and whimsy.

Futhermore, this utopia does not dominate the text and confront the reader in static monumental arrogance as the most perfect of all social alternatives. Indeed, life on Whileaway is not always peaceful or perfect since the freedom the society encourages includes the freedom to fight and kill, to be jealous and argue and go separate ways, to change the status quo and be constantly open to new ways of being. And as the novel unfolds and the reader learns of Jael and the struggle in her world and across time boundaries for the ultimate freedom of women everywhere and everytime, Whileaway's certain existence is itself called into question. For only with Jeannine's and Joanna's changes in consciousness and contributions to the struggle and with Jael's victory in the battle against Manland will the temporal possibility that is Whileaway exist. As Jael reminds Janet, it is human effort not natural causation that created the conditions for the existence of utopia in the first place. On the other hand, it is the very possibility of a feminist utopia that inspires the other women to change their lives and to continue the effort. While Russ provides a fully imaged version of utopia, she places her utopia in a context of historical possibility and social change as both the inspiration for social revolution and the vision of what that revolution is aiming for. Utopia in this critical text is put in its place as part of the forces of change rather than as a static and perfect Other that stands in simple binary opposition to what is, without the dialectical energy of transformation that would move people toward the alternative.

To be sure, while the iconic register gives the reader a picture of life on Whileaway, it also provides well-drawn accounts of the other three, decidedly non-utopian, worlds of Jeannine, Joanna, and Jael. The presence of these worlds in the text further emphasizes the importance of the utopian world. Jeannine's is a world in which the Depression still lingers, where Hitler died in 1936, World War Two never happened, Japan is still an empire, the USSR actually a federation, and the US still economically and militarily weak. Hence the rapid economic growth and social change of the postwar world never took place. In this slow-changing society, Jeannine manages to work only three days a week in a sluggish economy, and her lifetime ambition is to find Mr Right and end her life in marital bliss. In this worst case world, women are most directly enslaved, subject to male rule and a prewar romantic consciousness unchanged by the affluent society and employment of our own 1960s. Jeannine is a typical woman of her time: passive, fearful, fantasizing her absorption and peaceful loss of personality within a male-oriented marriage, yet annoyed and depressed by the reality of the men in her life and always seeking refuge in her own apartment with her cat and her ailanthus plant – that is, with those aspects of a still viable nature that do not use her or oppress her.

Whereas oppression in Jeannine's world is direct and complete, the situation in Joanna's world, our "own" time of 1969, is more contradictory and complex, but in the final analysis still oppressive. Here, women such as Joanna can be college professors and writers living apparently independent lives, but their "freedom" is a surface one encouraged by the economic need for women in the workforce in an expanding economy, for that economy and social system is still controlled by men for the benefit of men. Successful as she may be, Joanna is seen by her male colleagues as a sex object, subject to male manipulation. The false promises of postwar capitalism and male supremacy end up being as oppressive and indeed more confusing than the denied possibilities of Jeannine's world.

These two worlds of worst case and false promise as well as the utopia of Whileaway are all confronted with the extreme dystopian world inhabited by the trained assassin, Jael. This time possibility in which Manland and Womanland are linked in direct battle between the completely separated genders is one of overt violence and war. In a social system echoed in Suzy McKee Charnas's dystopian and utopian novels, *Walk to the End of the World* and *Motherlines*, Manlanders, behind the scenes of battle, buy male infants from Womanlanders and bring them up in "batches," until they are five years old. The little boys are then sorted out into those that will become "real men" – five out of seven, who are the ruling caste of this male society – the "changed", who undergo complete sex-change surgery – one out of seven, who as transsexuals exist to serve the desires of the real men as women once did, only now the male race is "purified" of any contamination by organic women – and the "half-changed," who without surgery keep their genitalia but grow "slim, grow languid, grow emotional and feminine' (TFM, 167) – the last seventh, who as parodies of gay males serve the needs of the pseudo-male and pseudo-female genders as the most oppressed caste. Manland is an authoritarian, homophobic, masculinist dystopia: it is a militarized society striving for the final solution in which the freedom of women is eliminated and only a few are kept as breeders for the men who cannot give birth to their own selves.

Womanland, on the other hand, is the place of action and mediation between utopia and dystopia, the front line of female freedom and fighting. Women live communally in safe "underground" cities, except for those élite who after years of service to the cause have secured private housing in the countryside. Not a utopia, Womanland must negotiate with the enemy and sell off its surplus male babies to survive. It allows a caste system of leaders and experienced fighters such as Jael, and it is a society engaged in terror and warfare against the enemy who are by no means defeated. The anger and resistance generated out of Jael's world is the necessary step in the struggle, the necessary mediation between the oppression of Jeannine's and Joanna's "1969" and Janet's utopia.

Thus, the iconic register of *The Female Man* generates not only a utopian society and two versions of our own present, contrasting with each other to illustrate just what life in 1969 is like, but also a male dystopia and a battle camp of women who will, it is hoped, smash the world of the present 1969, eliminate the possibility of dystopia, and create the conditions in which the camp can be disbanded and the promised land entered. Russ offers a vision of the present opposed not simply by a utopian other but by the necessary social reality needed to get from one to the other. The conflicting series of worlds resists the pacification that an idealistic utopian narrative or a defeatist realist narrative would encourage. In the fragmented openness enabled by the science fiction narrative, the possibilities of the social revolution are symbolically explored and celebrated.

Multiplex activism: the four Js

The dynamic conflict among the four worlds generated in the iconic register of Russ's text is reflected in the discrete register as a dynamic cooperation among the four women. At this level of analysis, we can see how the characters and their interactions express an oppositional ideological discourse that brings us closer to the direct historical confrontation between women and the dominant male society. The antagonistic ideologeme which *The Female Man* shares with the other critical utopias provides a focus on the type of activism necessary to destroy and replace those economic, social, and ideological systems that dominate our present historical situation. In exploring the various strategies and tactics for change represented by the four Js, Russ indicates the way forward to the social alternative imaged in her picture of Whileaway. As suggested in the time travel premise of the novel, however, that way forward does not privilege a single clear line of political action. Indeed, it is in the diversity within the unity of this gang of four that Russ makes her strongest statement about the social activism needed.

The Female Man's clearest strategic position is one of separatism as the only way that the women's movement can achieve success in the face of the constant tendency of males, friend and foe, to subordinate women's issues and actions in favour of male-oriented positions. The novel asserts a revolution of women alone, for a revolution with men – at least in the early 1970s during the main period of separatism in the women's movement, seen earlier in many ethnic and minority movements – cannot be trusted to succeed. Furthermore, the novel articulates a strategy of collective and non-hierarchical effort rather than leaving the process of social change to enlightened individuals or a central committee of some vanguard party. Women must work together in all their diversity and disagreement, for alone woman will not break through the bonds of the present system. The complexity of the current situation also calls for diverse tactics of opposition since a single, approved approach would only be an ineffective imitation of linear, authoritarian, male politics.

Within this separatist and non-hierarchical collective strategy Russ's tactics of change begin with the process of consciousness raising as each woman becomes aware of her own oppression, that of other women, and the possibilities of change which lie in the common action of all women. That such consciousness does not automatically happen given the deep socialization as well as actual coercive power exercised by the dominant system is made clear as both Janet and Jael engage in the process of consciousness raising and political organizing of the other two Js. Given such awareness and enlistment to the cause, the tactics carried out by all four can be divided into three general approaches, with no one of them taking precedence over the others: (1) the education, socialization, and service required to create and continue the new social alternative are represented in the utopian Janet, especially in her care for Laura, but also in her life and work on Whileaway; (2) the anger and violence, the military resistance, required to strike back and destroy the coercive powers of the current system are represented in the fighter Jael, and in her new recruit Jeannine, especially in Jael's assassination of the male official in Manland; (3) the ideological resistance to the present dominant discourse as well as the revolutionary articulation of new values and visions required to break down the old ways of seeing and develop new, self-confident attitudes in the present oppressed population is represented in the writer Joanna, especially in her act of writing the very text in which she appears.

The development within the discrete register can be read as the politicization process involved in the coming together of these four women. As they seek out or are found by the others, their interdependent individual and collective development continues until the final dinner, ironically on Thanksgiving Day, at Schraft's restaurant, after which they each go off on their new revolutionary tasks. Symbolized in this alliance, as Hacker points out, "is the possibility of a woman whose wholeness and scope are indeed 'speculative,' a Joanna who acknowledges who she has been, who and where she is, and thus has knowledge and control of what she can become."[15] If this is said of the development of a single free and actualized female subject, it must also be said of the collectivity of women moving into awareness and action, diverse but united, against the dominant phallocratic, bureaucratic, capitalist power structure.

Among the four Js, the two active organizers are Janet Evason and Alice Jael Reasoner. Janet, the hope of the future, begins the novel in an unmediated utopian voice, and immediately asserts the existence, at least in the possibility of utopian imagination, of a free and fulfilled woman rather than the subjected object expected by modern society. She introduces herself straightforwardly to the reader:

> When I was thirteen I stalked and killed a wolf, alone, on the North Continent above the forty-eighth parallel, using only a rifle. . . . I've worked in the mines, on the radio network, on a milk farm, a vegetable farm, and for six weeks as a librarian after I broke my leg. At thirty I bore Yuriko Janetson. . . . I have been Safety Officer for the county. . . . I've supervised the digging of fire trails, delivered babies, fixed machinery, and milked more moo-cows than I wish I knew existed. . . . I love my daughter. I love my family (there are nineteen of us). I love my wife (Vittoria). I've fought four duels. I've killed four times.   (TFM, 1–2)

Here, then, is the potential for all women once the "North Continent Wolf" is killed, once male power is broken and women are free to establish their own society and become full persons. As Whileaway's first emissary across time boundaries – they could spare Janet since with an IQ of 187 and the routine job of Safety Officer she was less bright than the others and could be released from a job that required little work in utopia – Janet contacts two women in the alternative 1969s: Jeannine, passive and repressed, and Joanna, awakening but still questioning.

Janet's effect on Jeannine is generally overwhelming to this subject person who had never even imagined the possibility of free and self-motivated women, much less a whole planet full of them. Around Janet and in Whileaway, Jeannine's reaction is usually to want to fade away into the woodwork and return to the secure slavery of her own time, yet she does not run off, and she continues to absorb the image of this utopian woman. Janet's effect on Joanna is more immediate, for Joanna is already partially aware as an individual trying to find her own self in a society that reduces her to a sex object. Janet shows Joanna the possibilities of anger and violence against males and love and desire among women as well as the vision of an entire society of free women. In observing Janet toss the host of a cocktail party across the floor after he has persisted in making a pass at this woman trained in martial arts and in observing Janet make love with the teenage Laura Rose Wilding, Joanna is motivated to change, especially when she sees as well the contrasting enslavement of Jeannine.

Important as utopia is for Jeannine and Joanna, the move from oppression to freedom that must be made by them in direct, willed action cannot be taken without the mediation of anger and the violence, metaphoric and political, of revolutionary change. That anger is provided by the fourth J who makes a brief appearance, in italics, on page 19, but who then backs off and lets the other three interact until she comes out once and for all on page 157.

Jael – Alice Reasoner is her cover name in her job as an employee of the Bureau of Comparative Ethnology – is the woman without a brand name, the fighter who is the one that brought the other three women into contact with each other. On assignment as one of the leaders of Womanland, Jael sought her "other selves" as they existed in other time probabilities to recruit them into the movement. She is the fighting force of change that provides the catalyst of action to reach the utopian possibility. At her estate in the Vermont hills, with its computerized house, ecologically balanced beauty, and live-in male android, the "sex-object" Davy who is the "most beautiful man in the world," Jael tells the other three about herself. She describes her move from the underground sentimental Arcadian communes, in a rejection of simple utopian escape, to her role as a guerilla fighter, now privileged to live in her own palace and gardens. She describes her commitment to revolutionary violence as a gradual one: "it took me years to throw off the last of my Pussy-fetters, to stop being (however brutalized) vestigially Pussy-cat-ified. But at last I did and now I am the rosy, wholesome, single-minded assassin you see before you today" (TFM, 187). Rather than find refuge in a pastoral escape that might satisfy herself, she realized that such an escape was still capitulation to the power structure and made a commitment to fight for the complete defeat of male power.

Jael demonstrates her tactical violence when she takes the three along on an assassination mission to Manland. There, with her steel teeth and retractable claws, spurred by her voluntary hysterical strength, she kills the male official by raking open his neck, chin, and back. This is yet another act in the war that will continue "until the beautiful, bloody moment that we fire these stranglers, these murderers, these unnatural and atavistic nature's bastards, off the face of the earth" (TFM, 173). At her home, she demonstrates the freedom of her desire as the three watch her make love with Davy, who exists only to serve her. After showing her anger and her desire, as Janet did earlier, Jael tells the three what she wants of them:

> We want bases on your worlds: we want raw materials if you've got them. We want places to recuperate and places to hide an army; we want places to store our machines. Above all, we want places to move from – bases that the other side doesn't know about. (TFM, 200)

Unlike Janet who offers a vision of a better place but no clear way to get there, Jael offers a way to resist the present domination so that the path toward utopia can be opened.

Jeannine is the one most directly affected by Jael. A childish, dependent, frightened woman of 29, she has bought romantic love so thoroughly that she feels that only by meeting a tall, dark, handsome, domineering myth can she ever be rescued from her worthlessness, the boredom of her bare-subsistence job, and the fantasies of romance and marriage that are her sole escape. She is frightened by the possibilities suggested by Janet and, while briefly back in her own time, tries to escape her self-fulfillment by capitulating and marrying Cal and thus pleasing her family and burying herself. In an extended tête-à-tête with Jael, Jeannine's resistance to change is finally broken, not by utopian fulfillment, but by the chance violently to destroy the male society that has so totally restricted her. When Jael kills the Manlander, Joanna is ashamed, Janet weeps, and Jeannine is calm in the revelation of the power of women to do their masters in. She has seen a way to be herself at last and decides to join Jael's movement. At the final dinner in Schraft's, Jeannine, the former slave in a peripheral "undeveloped" society, is the one who wholeheartedly joins in Jael's plan to extend the war into other time zones: "You can bring in all the soldiers you want. You can take the whole place over: I wish you would" (TFM, 211).

Compared to the revolutionary violence which the totally denied Jeannine chooses, the activism adopted by Joanna requires more time to develop and is of a more complex variety. For Joanna lives in the "developed" metropolis of postwar affluent society. Caught between Janet's self-realization which occurred in Whileaway and Jeannine's self-suppression which occurred in the dark ages of prewar, Depression America, Joanna has achieved a certain amount of freedom but is still constantly reminded that she is a second-class citizen whose main role in life is to serve The Man. She sees in Janet's violence and love-making and in her sisterhood and self-confidence, a role model that inspires her. She decides to throw off her old self, rejecting the brand name that reduces her to a sexual commodity, and become a "female man," that is a self-actualized and free person in her own right:

> What I learned late in life, under my rain of love, under my kill-or-cure, unhappily, slowly, stubbornly, barely, and in really dreadful pain, was that there is one and only one way to possess that in which we are defective, therefore that which we need, therefore that which we want. Become it.
> (TFM, 139)

Joanna's slow and painful process of consciousness raising is helped on by the utopian Janet and the worst case Jeannine.

However, the step from awareness to action is only taken after she returns from Jael's world having seen the power of direct action, as described in Part Eight. Thus Jael provides the negation of the negation that breaks through the binary opposition of Janet-Jeannine for Joanna; she is the catalyst that moves Joanna from awareness to action.

In Part Nine, Joanna becomes an active agent for change in her own right. She begins with her own microstructural violence:

> I committed my first revolutionary act yesterday. I shut the door on a man's thumb. I did it for no reason at all and I didn't warn him; I just slammed the door shut in a rapture of hatred and imagined the bone breaking and the edges grinding into his skin. (TFM, 203)

Two sections later, she commits "the crime of creating one's own Reality" by making love with Laura: "I can't describe to you how reality itself tore wide open at that moment" (TFM, 208). Finally acting on the anger and desire that she observed in Janet and Jael and then found in herself, Joanna is initiated into the movement and sets off on her own method of resistance: she writes the novel we are reading. She becomes the fifth, intrusive "I" in the text that calls attention to her activity of creating the characters, the aspects of her own self, that motivated her to act in the first place. Rather than choosing utopian service or dystopian violence, she chooses to work in her own present and create an oppositional literature that draws on utopian dreams and dystopian destruction to move people in her own time to awareness and action. At the final dinner, when Janet and Laura go off toward utopian bliss and Jael and Jeannine go off to fight, Joanna turns to the text and to the reader. She says goodbye to the other three women: "to Alice Reasoner, who says tragedy makes her sick, who says never give in but always go down fighting, who says take them with you, who says die if you must but loop your own intestines around the neck of your strangling enemy," "to Janet, whom we don't believe in and whom we deride but who is in secret our savior from utter despair," to Jeannine "poor soul, poor girl, poor as-I-once-was" (TFM, 213). All four now are changed. All four are free once the text ends.

Russ's ideological expression of activism as developed in the four Js is antagonistic, uncompromising, and aware of the deep awareness, commitment, and multiplex actions required even to begin to open up the status quo to a new way of being. In 1969, utopia was a long way off, for although the utopian dream is an important element in the overall consciousness of opposition, much more has to be accomplished before such simple dreams can be indulged in unrelated to the process of social revolution. As Russ herself put it,

> to insist on reconciliation before the conflict even occurs – certainly before it has clarified itself and run its course – is to put yourself in the wildly unbalanced position of that famous quotation about Dante: "With one foot he stood planted in the Middle Ages and with the other hailed the coming of a new age".[16]

Not one for halfway measures or reformist collaboration, Russ refuses the imbalance of such a temporizing position. She militantly insists on the necessity of struggle, with her sisters, to cast off the slavery of the Jeannines with the violence and actions of the Jaels and the Joannas before any Janet can exist. As the earliest of the critical utopias, *The Female Man* broke the new utopian ground with a deep cut into the prevailing system and made the strongest and least compromising of all the expressions on activism found in these utopian works.

"Go little book": utopia as praxis

> I would say the politics of montage is that there is no pretense to make all bits fit into a neat, seamless whole. I would say that montage is concerned with bits as bits, not as fragments broken from some original whole, nor as special detachments, representations of some greater whole. I would say that the politics of montage concerns the way in which we negotiate heterogeneity and multiplicity.
>
> (Yves Lomax)

Joanna Russ's novel lends itself to many readings, many views of its complex and open form. Basically written in the science fiction genre, it draws on the techniques and sensibility of the postmodern, experimental novel, uses literary modes from the drama to the essay, from jokes and puns to manifestos and fables. But as we shift this present reading from the ideological message of engagement developed in the discrete register, we will consider how *The Female Man* as the first of the critical utopias revives the utopian genre and enlists the future-bearing form into the service of the oppositional politics of the early 1970s. From considering the content of the novel especially in terms of the political activism that ends with the fictional author sending her completed manuscript out into the world as a subversive child, we can now move to a consideration of the utopian form as yet another, even more radical, ideological act of opposition to both the present power structure and to the centralist opposition of the old left, as both camps are characterized by male-dominated politics and discourse. The form of the novel negates the rigid instrumental fetishism and the authoritarian and hierarchical efficiency of modern capitalism and phallocentrism as much as it negates the complementary linear, dogmatic politics of vanguard parties. This "shapeless" text – granting it the one necessary, survival-based, limitation of feminist separatism – resists reduction to any single totality. The form further radicalizes the content developed in the iconic and discrete registers of the text. It deconstructs utopia as a static blueprint of the perfect post-revolutionary society and holds it open as a pre-figurative practice whose primary subject is the act of utopian imagination itself. It challenges the strategies and tactics of oppositional politics to resist restriction to a party line or single mode of revolt, and it embraces the multiplicity of actions that can be engaged in by an aroused people. Central to this reading is the observation of how the formal operations valorize utopian literary practice as an ideological rejection of the present situation by avoiding closure on any one reading – including the present one – and by calling attention to itself in self-reflexive commentary.

Yves Lomax's comments on photographic montage are pertinent to an understanding of *The Female Man*, for this novel is a literary montage that expresses a radically open negativity which includes the entire spectrum of anti-hegemonic activity from utopian desires to realistic perception of oppression to dystopian counter-attack.[17] The horizontal connection between the parts of

the novel and between the characters eliminates the usual instrumentally rational craving for vertical, hierarchical order. The
text is a crossroads of worlds and actions, of histories and futures,
that is far from the present overwhelming metropolitan totalities.
It maps a new ground of diverse behavior, personal and political,
motivated by the uncontainable energy generated in the risings of
the late 1960s but most recognized by Russ in the growing
women's liberation movement. The world as we know it is
broken up into utopian possibility, present suffering, and emer-
gent battles. Women are divided into separate, autonomous
persons resisting the present system in their own way yet part of
an overall sisterhood.

The montage effect in the text is achieved by its division into
nine parts, each of which is further subdivided into segments,
some of which are only a phrase or a sentence long. A few
segments connect directly with the one following, as in the shift
from Part One, IX which deals with Jeannine's attitude toward
work to Part One, X which describes the alternative attitude on
Whileaway. Many of the segments are set in sharp juxtapositions
that require the reader to connect them, as in Part Five, IX which
is a series of lists and short dramatic exchanges illustrating the
differences between female and male perception, followed by Part
Five, X which is a short essay on how "this book is written in
blood" that includes a fable illustrating the power of revenge
using the animal characters from the comic strip *Pogo*, followed
by Part Five, XI which is a first-person narration by Joanna
describing her visit with Janet's wife and others in a Whileawayan
kitchen.

The montage effect is further carried out in the non-linear
structure which lacks a consistent chronology or a clear "plot,"
for the sequence of events makes sudden and disorienting leaps,
back and forth, across time probabilities wherein some of the
events never happened or happened differently. For example, the
infamous cocktail party where Janet tosses the host to the floor
occurs once in Manhattan, another time in Los Angeles – encod-
ing a coast to coast uprising; and in one time reality Janet and
Laura make love while in another Joanna and Laura do. Each of
the Js as versions of the same self go through similar acts of anger
and love in their unique "plots" which can be seen as happening

simultaneously to the one person or in sequence to all of them. This "epic" begins *in media res* when the utopian hero Janet announces herself, for only later, near the end, do we read that it was Jael who brought Janet down to earth. And only by the very end of the book are we certain that Joanna wrote the entire text in the first place and that it was she who brought both "Janet" and "Jael" into existence. "I made that woman up," Joanna the character/author says punningly of Janet. Thus, the text cannot be reduced to one plot or time sequence. It rejects attitudes toward causality and progress that are restricted to simplified linear progression in one universal historical reality. Instead, it expresses change as a complex procedure involving many different perceptions and actions and requiring many different readings to grasp it, and even then it can never be grasped fully. The textual montage extends from plot to characters and narrative point of view, continuing the emphasis on an overall assemblage rather than a rigid whole. Shifting from third- to first-person narration and among first-person narrators (everyone but the victimized Jeannine), the text presents each of the protagonist Js both as aspects of one self and as separate members of a gender and a political movement. The text shifts in and out of focus on either the individual or collective hero. Never does the assemblage of this psychological and political montage freeze into privileging one type or one action. Never does it establish an accepted "healthy" or "correct" hierarchy of perception, privilege, or behavior. Never does it close and stop shifting. As plot and character, so also the style of the book continually changes. There are a variety of literary forms used, from internal monologue to third-person description, from novelistic to dramatic dialogue, from one-dimensional character types to complex and deep personalities, from lists to theses, from essays and lectures to dream sequences, from throwaway jokes to direct address to the reader. The text is a veritable anatomy of ways of writing about and viewing modern woman and the world she lives in.

Diverse as the montage effect makes the book, the basic literary mechanism is the science fiction narrative that establishes the premise of alternative time zones which allows the text to break out of the boundaries of restrictive realism and explore what has not happened, what could happen, and what has and is happening, from a perspective other than that privileged by male discourse. Science fiction as the primary force of creation makes possible the imaging of the utopia of Whileaway, and it also enables the presentation of the current historical situation in such a way that change becomes possible, no longer held back by the "realities" of the dominant structure. Consequently, a literary space is established wherein self-conscious utopian opposition can be asserted in the name of an authentic, multiplex opposition.

The power of the text's utopian practice is increased by the commentary in the text on its own operations. This self-reflexive commentary makes the reader more aware of what is going on and provokes a re-reading and completion of the text in her/his own perceptions and actions. This self-reflexivity is primarily carried out in the voice of the fictional author, Joanna. As McClenahan points out, Joanna – as opposed to Joanna Russ, the historical person who wrote the book – gradually emerges in her own self-awareness as the person struggling to realize herself and the text. As she becomes more aware, her references to the writing process become more pronounced. Each time Joanna considers her situation, her history in contemporary America, she discovers the "internal conflict between what she is or has been and what she wishes she could be." She becomes more and more dissatisfied and uneasy. This instability leads her to further analysis, which she then pursues by means of fantasy, particularly in the science fictional variety with its harder edge of realistic possibility. She isolates and models the four characters or aspects of her self and the worlds that produce the clearest form of each.

Thus, Joanna the character becomes Joanna the author creating first the utopian hero then the worst case victim. However, she gets caught in the binary opposition between Janet and Jeannine and is unable to move herself beyond this good and evil polarity. Consequently, she moves on to the angry and fighting character, Jael, as the necessary mediation – personally, politically, and literarily – between this static opposition. Her awareness of Jael, who can restore dynamic action to the individual woman and to the women's movement, grows slowly. The character emerges slowly into the text, coming in first as italic interruption, later as a metonymy creeping in as a pair of claws as Janet and Laura make love, and finally coming out in her own right near the end of the novel, enabling Joanna to become the female man.

The text works out a sense of female self-in-society that exists without depending on the reflections of the male gaze. The objectified and victimized female self is explored and exploded. The emancipated self is articulated in a way that does not objectify others, revealing a female protagonist who makes her own decisions about her life in a new post-industrial, post-scarcity world that goes beyond capitalism and centralized opposition: "Remember, I didn't and don't want to be a 'feminine' version or a diluted version or a special version or a subsidiary version or an ancillary version, or an adapted version of the heroes I admire. I want to be the heroes themselves" (TFM, 206). By isolating these four potentialities within herself, Russ

> pushes them to excess by gradually building up a picture of the kind of world, the kind of technological and economic state, the kind of culture which would be most likely to evoke each personality – all this in order to envision how these potentialities operate in relation to each other in "Joanna" and in "Joanna's" – our – world.[18]

From the utopian society, she moves to the utopian person, and then to an overall utopian practice.

In the process of consciousness raising the author of the text brings herself and the reader to an awareness not only of the content of this new world, new movement, and new person but also of the renewed form, the literary practice, by which this awareness is reached and ultimately expressed. Furthermore, the personal self-awareness extends to a political self-awareness that includes the realization of the use value of the utopian impulse in the process of personal and political change and in the development of the literary arsenal available to the oppositional culture of the 1970s. Thus *The Female Man* is a meditation on the role played by fantastic, visionary, indeed critical utopian, writing in the process of social revolution.

The self-reflexivity becomes apparent as Joanna's comments are re-read as comments on the text itself as well as on people and events within the text. This is most apparent in the imagined summary of the reviews that the male publishing establishment will write about this challenging feminist novel and in the closing paragraph of the book when Joanna sends it off to do its subversive work in the world, despite the reviews. The snippets of reviews that are given in Part Seven, III clearly anticipate the reception of the novel by the science fictional, male-dominated, publishing world, as it languished unprinted for four years. The fearful and condemnatory clichés batter the book with comments by male reviewers as well as by collaborationist female reviewers still operating within a male-identified world:

> Shrill . . . vituperative . . . no concern for the future of society . . . maunderings of antiquated feminism . . . selfish femlib . . . needs a good lay . . . this shapeless book . . . of course a calm and objective discussion is beyond . . . twisted, neurotic . . . some truth buried in a largely hysterical . . . of very limited interest, I should . . . another tract for the trash-can . . . burned her bra and thought that . . . really important issues are neglected while . . . hermetically sealed . . . women's limited experience . . . another of the screaming sisterhood . . . a not very appealing aggressiveness . . . could have been done with wit if the author had . . . deflowering the pretentious male . . . a man would have given his right arm to . . . hardly girlish . . . a woman's book . . . another shrill polemic which . . . feminine lack of objectivity . . . this pretense at a novel . . .

and then from the female reviews, "we 'dear ladies,' whom Russ would do away with, 'unfortunately just don't feel'" (TFM, 141). Of course, these male-oriented condemnations, if read outside of male discourse, can be perceived as appreciations of just what the book is: angry, with no concern for the continuation of this present society, healthily selfish and shapeless, beyond coopting calm and false objectivity, a "pretense" at a novel which is indeed something much more than the accepted realist or science fictional novel.

The closing paragraph sends the book off on its revolutionary assignment:

> Go little book, trot through Texas and Vermont and Alaska and Maryland and Washington and Florida and Canada and England and France; bob a curtsey at the shrines of

Friedan, Millett, Greer, Firestone, and all the rest; behave
yourself in people's living rooms, neither looking ostentatious on the coffee table nor failing to persuade due to the
dullness of your style; knock at the Christmas garland on
my husband's door in New York City and tell him that I
loved him truly and love him still (despite what anybody
may think); and take your place bravely on the book racks
of bus terminals and drugstores.   (TFM, 213)

Here, the book is seen for what it is: not a commodity item to be
placed on coffee tables, but a well-written text, incorporating the
accumulated insights of the women's movement, not putting
people off unnecessarily, open to individual males, and invading
the mass culture in places occupied by common people, doing
its work until, as Russ puts it in the closing lines, women will one
day be free.

Through the openness of the montage structure and the self-
reflexive commentary of the text, employing science fictional
creation of alternative worlds and people, the text speaks to the
emancipatory potential of the second wave of feminism. It does so
by way of re-appropriating radical utopian writing, seeing that
genre as the practice of meditating on utopian rejection and
anticipation itself and not on this or that static and cooptable
utopian system. The book opens with an illustration of utopia,
exciting in its own right as a traditional utopian expression, but in
the operations that follow Janet's speech, in the dynamism of the
characters and their conflicting worlds, and in the self-awareness
of the text itself, that initial utopian content is further radicalized
by the textual form which identifies the power of utopian expression and the potential radical impact of that expression.

The only solution *The Female Man* can be said to offer is "not
Whileaway, but the kind of interactive process which reader and
novel share – a kind of example of a process which we might learn
to enact on a social level too."[19] Utopia is not simply a *place*, it is a
practice. In *The Female Man*, the utopian place does not passively
stand as a static alternative to the present, it becomes part of the
overall movement to change that world. The utopian impulse
itself is made a part of history, particularly of women's history. As
Nadia Khouri puts it, the

introduction of a utopian component within the framework of science fiction implies first a resistance to the binding and arbitrary authority of events. It begins with the gradual consciousness of the alienating effect of these obstacles, in exposing the clashes and dysfunctions that result from the experience of them, in developing ways of dealing with them and ultimately of transcending them. Within a utopian intentionality, every alienating obstacle is conjured up inasmuch as it provokes a counter-reaction. The need for utopia arises precisely where it is negated and its realization depends on its ability to overcome contradictions.[20]

The Female Man, as the first of the critical utopias, acts on the need for utopia, inspired by the utopian element in the oppositional politics of its time. It carries itself as a text from utopian assertion to utopian praxis. It thereby rejects the false promises of the affirmative capitalist culture which offers utopia but returns only commodities and the false security of a phallocratic structure that offers utopia but returns only a pampered slavery. It rejects the narrow utopia of dogmatic, vanguard parties which restrict human energy to the narrow service of the revolutionary state, however embattled and needy that state may be as it struggles for survival against world capitalism and imperialism. Arising out of the radical politics of the late 1960s as well as out of the innovative writing of new wave science fiction, *The Female Man* from the periphery of US society challenges and condemns the dominant structure, power, and ideology of that society with a radical and angry utopian narrative. In doing so, it sets the stage and begins the institutional dialogue of the revived genre of "critical" utopian writing to be carried by others in the 1970s.

5 Ursula K. LeGuin, *The Dispossessed*

> I prefer to make things difficult, and choose both.
>
> (Shevek, in *The Dispossessed*)

Ursula LeGuin's novel, subtitled "An Ambiguous Utopia," is perhaps the best known and the most popular of the critical utopias published in the 1970s.[1] Utopian scholars, SF fans, feminists, ecologists, anarchists, and many who simply enjoy a good read have found in this ambiguous utopia a welcome alternative to bleak experimental novels or didactic tracts. To be sure, that subtitle refers the reader back to the tradition of utopian literature. LeGuin's anarcho-communism informs her narrative and recalls the radical alternatives of nineteenth century utopian writers such as William Morris and Charlotte Perkins Gilman. And yet, the "ambiguous" adjective warns the reader that the dreams of the last century are long past and that this utopia is being reasserted in a more complex and cautious way. LeGuin's realist view of the world situation with its failed revolutions and the mystical dialectic of her favored philosophy of Taoism temper her hopeful anarchism and open the novel to possibilities more suited to the 1970s than the 1890s.

Written after Joanna Russ's *The Female Man* but published before it, *The Dispossessed* is a touchstone work that has re-kindled debates about utopian literature and thought as well as cast a fresh, utopian, light on the problems and contradictions of US and world politics in the 1970s. Already a major science fiction author of both adult and children's books in the late 1960s, LeGuin published three novels previous to *The Disposses-sed* which were well received by those who would later enjoy her utopian novel.[2] *The Left Hand of Darkness* (1969) presented the world of Gethen with its biologically androgynous people as it is visited by a heterosexual male envoy from the League of All Worlds: this thought experiment allowed LeGuin to explore the experience of gender differentiation and sexism as well as the possibilities for humanity in the notion and experience of androgyny. Feminist readers praised the book for its concerns but also criticized LeGuin's use of a male protagonist and the male pronoun at the center of her narrative. *The Lathe of Heaven* (1971) explored the world of George Orr whose dreams change reality. The conflict is between George who wants to abdicate his power and Dr Haber, his psychiatrist, who greedily appropriates George's power for his own use. The novel considered the question of the individual's relationship to society, the power of dreams and the use of power, and the complications of deep social change. Coming at the end of the 1960s, the work was a medita-tion on the political currents and methods of the time: not a rejection so much as a beginning of the digestion of the intense experiences of that period. Finally, *The Word for World is Forest* (1972) dealt with the attempted extermination of a native people – a peaceful, decentralized, pastoral, tribal society whose politics are handled by the women and whose philosophy is handled by the men – by a Terran military-colonization expedition. Although the Althesheans defeat the Terrans and drive them off the planet, they do so only by learning to kill. *Word for World* recalled the genocidal destruction of the American Indian and the Vietnamese people by the US military-economic complex and the resistance of those people against it.

As John Fekete has said of *The Dispossessed*, LeGuin's "interest is in the emergence of the liberatory *novum*, of in-dividual initiative, of understanding and communication; she

92

works at the ascendant peripheries of the situation and toward the classical utopian aspirations of Western philosophy: reconciliation in the potential harmony for all."[3] *The Dispossessed* is an expression of the attitude of *détente*, of the cooperation of previously contending forces to transcend hostility, suffering, and injustice and jointly work toward a better world for all. This is not a vision which presumes simple solutions and lack of conflict; indeed, LeGuin's sense of détente is that of a goal which requires resistance and rebellion, political force and personal risk to achieve it.

The central motif of the novel is the breaking down of walls – not a simple handshake over a mended fence but the smashing of boundaries which divide and isolate. The spaceport on Anarres portrayed on the first page of the book is encircled by a wall which at the roadways is "mere geometry, a line, an idea of boundary." The wall serves to separate the utopian society from its home world, Urras. As with the isolation of the People's Republic of China from 1948 to the Nixon initiative, this spaceport wall was intended to protect the post-revolutionary society from corruption by the decadent "profiteers" of Urras. The wall becomes a necessary separation – as not only the Chinese but also sections of the minority and women's movements have required – to avoid further compromise and to build strength. However, LeGuin rejects separatism as she notes that the wall acts as limitation rather than protective separation: "Like all walls, it was ambiguous, two-faced. What was inside it and what was outside it depended upon which side you were on" (TD, 1). The wall leaves Anarres "free," but it also encloses the universe and keeps the revolution at home and consequently stifles it: "the whole planet was inside it, a great prison camp, cut off from the other worlds and other men, in quarantine" (TD, 2).

The limits of revolutionary societies, the dangers of a Gulag, the strategy of "artificial negativity" whereby a dominant power allocates a limited "free space" to the opposition are the situations exposed by LeGuin at the onset of the novel. Furthermore, her ideal of the unity and harmony of all humanity as the best way forward is the key notion behind her image of unbuilding walls. While the novel opens with the images of the wall, it closes in the transcendent act of space-flight and the breaking down of that wall by the protagonist, Shevek, who does so with the aid of that race of galactic utopians found in LeGuin's other novels, the Hainish. Created by the author as the people that first travelled the stars, the Hainish serve as the central image for LeGuin's ideal of unity and harmony of all opposites. As the ambassador from burned-out Terra – the Earth of our future presented in the novel's past – puts it, the Hainish are "older than any of us; infinitely generous. They are altruists. They are moved by a guilt we don't even understand" (TD, 304). These "meditative" people are LeGuin's quintessential Taoists: encouraging all healthy difference among the "known worlds" and reconciling every people in the Ekumen, a federation of peace and good will, a galactic UN which works.

Within the parameters of the divisive wall and the intergalactic harmony of the Ekumen, LeGuin explores the "ambiguity" of utopian ideals and dystopian denials, of rebellion and cooptation, of synchronic unity and diachronic movement toward a better world. Edged with radical values and courageous dissidence, the novel counsels humility and harmony as well as militancy and suffering as the necessary elements of social change. In the iconic register, LeGuin provides a utopian other to her own historical era as portrayed in the societies of Urras: subtly exploitive capitalism (the profiteers of A-Io), centralized authoritarian state socialism (the cadre of Thu), and endlessly suffering subordinate classes and Third World peoples (the rebels of A-Io and of Benbili). Her utopian society symbolically describes her version of the oppositional theory and practice of the late 1960s and early 1970s as well as her response to the contradictions of both capitalist and state socialist societies. In the discrete register, the protagonist, Shevek – the visitor who goes from utopia back to the original world – serves as the focus for the key ideological question of activism within the oppositional movements of the early 1970s. In the white, male, intellectual figure of Shevek, LeGuin offers her stimulating yet problematic answer. Finally, the form of the utopian text – shaped around the reconciliation of sets of binary oppositions – gives the reader a sense of how LeGuin's use of the utopian impulse connects with the prevailing historical situation of big power politics and real human needs.

94

Anarres/Urras, Terra/Hain: LeGuin's social vision

The enlistment of utopia by postwar United States society with its affluence at home and military dominance abroad is caught by LeGuin in her portrayal of the Urrasti nation of A-Io: a land of beauty and ecological wisdom with an upper class that enjoys the pleasures of sensuous consumer goods, from pleasant furnishing to erotic fashion, and a lower class that suffers in poverty and is denied political power yet used as conscripted cannon fodder in the nation's war to suppress the revolution in the Third World nation of Benbili. In the passivity of the consumers and the seething misery of the poor masked by the beauty of the land and the surface generalities of the mass media, A-Io can be recognized as an image of the America of the 1960s: a surface utopia and a hidden dystopia ready to explode. Opposed to the profiteers of A-Io are the state socialists of Thu, LeGuin's version of the Soviet state. Grim, centralist, authoritarian, and just as interested in the potential dominance of the world by means of big power politics, Thu is no more utopian than A-Io. Indeed, the utopian other to this analog of our Earth was displaced to the moon of Urras 160 years earlier when one million anarchist revolutionaries inspired by the writings and practice of their female leader, Odo, were given the moon, Anarres, in order to coopt their threat to the status quo. It is in the utopian society of Anarres that the reader finds LeGuin's oppositional images to the historical situation of her time.

The utopia on the moon is presented, as are most utopias in the literary tradition, with socio-political institutions, norms, and individual relationships spelled out in some detail. Rather than being shown to a visitor from another society, however, this utopia is described as the protagonist Shevek grows up within it and then leaves it. We also discover the flaws in the utopia as Shevek and his rebellious Odonian comrades encounter the compromise and ossification of the revolution in Anarresti society as it approaches its bicentennial. Utopia is presented both in its idealized self and in conflict with its own ideals. The result is an ambiguous utopia that avoids simple perfection and narrative boredom and serves to neutralize all existing historical alternatives except for LeGuin's mystical and harmonious anarchism, as well as her continued privileging of male activity.

LeGuin's utopian society is in many ways similar to the radical libertarianism of the American Dream which, Murray Bookchin argues, persists in the vision of the oppositional forces in the US. Indeed, Anarres is very much a frontier society which values minimal government, individual freedom, and locally exercised power, production, and consumption. It is "nonauthoritarian communist" with a decentralized economy and social system located on a dry, cold, windy planet. Providing the theoretical basis of the society are the writings of Odo. As a variety of idealist anarchism, Odo's works center on the principle of individual freedom and initiative, on one hand, and mutual aid, on the other. The philosophy recalls the work of nineteenth century anarchist Peter Kropotkin, *Mutual Aid*, and the practice of American anarcho-syndicalism, best recognized in the activity of the International Workers of the World (IWW). Furthermore, Anarresti society resonates with elements of the recent history of the People's Republic of China, Cuba, Israel, Yugoslavia, and the civil rights/anti-war/student/counter-culture movements of the 1960s.

The syndicalist economy is oriented around basic survival needs, for this is no post-scarcity world. Anarres is a desert planet with limited flora and fauna – only fish in the oceans and moonthorn and spiky holum trees on the land – set in a cold climate subject to drought and dust. It's as though LeGuin combined the Oklahoma dust bowl of the 1930s with the ecology of the high desert of the southwest and set up a utopia to scratch out its existence within this unpastoral environment. As a result of the environmental lack, the Odonian settlers are left to their own resources. Isolated from the potential abundance of a more complex ecology, they must build their lives almost solely on their human efforts. The only natural resource LeGuin allots the moon is mineral wealth in mercury, copper, bauxite, uranium, tin, and gold – a mineral wealth which Anarres trades to the Urras Council of World Governments in exchange for needed fossil fuels, machine parts, and high technology components. The mining activity serves as the material basis for the détente with Urras that allows the utopia to exist in its "artificial negativity" as a "neo-colony" of the home planet. As long as Anarres keeps its ideas to itself and ships the minerals, it is tolerated.

The "small-is-beautiful," worker-controlled economy of Anarres is a mixture of local manufacturing, small craftworks, communal agriculture, fishing, and mining. The work day is short, usually five to seven hours long, though longer during periods of harvest or famine. On one day out of ten, each Anarresti performs tasks of social maintenance: garbage detail, repairs to the infrastructure, and other boring, dirty, and routine jobs. As in Cuba and China in the 1960s, everyone, including intellectual and administrative workers, is expected to do tenth-day work. Production and distribution is administered from the major city, Abbenay, by the Production Distribution Committee (PDC), the central planning bureaucracy; while work needs and desires are coordinated by the Division of Labor (DivLab) by means of a society-wide computer network. The decentralist counterpoints to such necessary centralized planning and coordination – the anarchist corrective – are the local syndicates, "vehicles of both social action and sociability" (TD, 87). Syndicates organize people into neighborhood/living groups and work-based groups. The living and work groups then form into federations that are represented on the central committee. Ideally, initiatives and needs move from the syndicate to the center for coordination and implementation in a political structure that maximizes local democracy and minimizes central government.

Anarresti society preserves a post-industrial, urban-rural balance and relies on technology to maintain communication and a high level of civilization. The people chose not to

> regress to pre-urban, pre-technological tribalism. They knew that their anarchism was the product of a very high civilization, of a complex, highly diversified culture, of a stable economy and a highly industrialized technology that could maintain high production and rapid transportation of goods. However vast the distances separating settlements, they held to the ideal of complex organicism. They built the roads first, the houses second. The special resources of each region were interchanged continually with those of others, in an intricate process of balance: that balance of diversity

97

which is the characteristic of life, of natural and social
ecology. (TD, 77–8)

Within this complexity, then, the moral, cultural, legal systems
– the ideological apparatus – are based on the decentralized
economy but primarily on the social conscience. LeGuin recognizes the importance of ideology in modern society and avoids
a mechanical materialist subordination of superstructure to
economic base. Anarres is a community of individuals, not a
collectivity: "men and women are free – possessing nothing"
(TD, 184), living in a "culture that relied deliberately and
constantly on human solidarity, mutual aid" (TD, 164). Here,
then, is the anarcho-syndicalist vision of balance between the
liberty of the individual and the health of the community:

> with the myth of the State out of the way, the real mutuality
> and reciprocity of society and individual become clear.
> Sacrifice may be demanded of the individual, but never
> compromise: for though only the society could give security
> and stability, only the individual, the person, has the power
> of moral choice – the power of change, the essential function
> of life. The Odonian society was conceived as a permanent
> revolution, and revolution begins in the thinking mind.
>
> (TD, 267)

There are no laws, courts, or police, for "the social conscience,
the opinion of others, was the most powerful moral force" (TD,
90). Furthermore, since class, gender, race, and other differences
subject to dominance-subordination are not present in this
egalitarian society, the motivation for most crime is not present.
With "forbidden" a "non-organic word" (TD, 36), each
Anarresti is free to live as she or he pleases, given the natural
limitations of the planet. The few who do not fit in or who drop
out peacefully are allowed to leave the community and fend for
themselves; the persistently anti-social disrupters are ostracized.
For extreme cases of madness or violence there is rehabilitation
therapy or the confinement of the Asylum – an alternative which
in the course of the novel uncomfortably reflects the quite non-
utopian use of such institutions to contain dissidents in the USSR.
In this utopia, work is no longer alienated labor but freely

chosen, if also necessary and tolerated for the good of the whole. Money is not used, and goods and services are available as needed. Individuals keep very few material possessions since everything is generally available and since Odonian thought holds that "excess is excrement." Housing is based in dormitories except for bonded couples, one-night lovers, scholars, or the socially maladjusted. Meals are taken in communal cafeterias. Education is universal: individuals progress by ability in a curriculum which includes academic subjects and practical skills in an open classroom setting. Health care is also universal, and people are encouraged to stay healthy and care for themselves as much as possible. For example, Takver delivers her baby at home with Shevek's help, and the local midwife arrives later to check out the mother and child. There are no lethal weapons held by individuals, but hand-to-hand fighting is tolerated when fairly matched. Transportation is generally by foot; although there is an extensive mass transit system consisting of large busses, ships, dirigibles, bicycles, and freight trucks. Energy is available from renewable, non-polluting sources including earth-temperature differential, tidal power, solar, and wind generators, and from some imported fossil fuels. In this non-commodity, non-élitist society, the arts are integrated with the daily lives of people: many make, give, and wear personal jewelry; pottery, sculpture, weaving, and other crafts are part of daily use; poetry, dance, song, and storytelling are popular cultural forms participated in by all; the musical concert and drama are the most highly regarded of the arts.

LeGuin makes particular efforts to portray a non-sexist utopia. Children are given randomly selected, six-letter names which have no gender associations. There is no division of labor by gender: the Defence "foreman" at the spaceport is a woman, and one of the few armed members of society. Shevek's mother, Rulag, who chose work over mothering, is in a leadership position in the society. Takver, Shevek's wife, a biologist, often can find work in her field when Shevek cannot. Child care is universal and available on a twenty-four hour basis; after age 2, children are encouraged to live in dormitories and are cared for without gender discrimination.

Anarres is also a society wherein sexual activity is unfettered from childhood on and is non-exploitive. Heterosexual, homo-sexual, and bisexual preferences are recognized. No penalty or taboo applies to any sexual practice – except rape, which is regarded as an act of violence, not sex. Most Anarresti in this frontier society in which people are often on the move are promiscuous; some are celibate; a few enter partnership – although neither marriage nor prostitution exists to enslave women. Odonian partnership is a matter of commitment and free choice between equals choosing the bond: "So long as it worked, it worked, and if it didn't work, it stopped being. It was not an institution but a function. It had no sanction but that of private conscience" (TD, 197).

Such is the utopian society of Anarres: a non-sexist, ecologi-cally sound, libertarian-communist alternative to the nations of Urras that mirror LeGuin's own historical situation. However, LeGuin is beyond simple assertions of an ideal system, having seen the failure and compromises of revolutionary systems in twentieth century history in even the most well-meaning of political practices and social systems. All is not well in her utopia, because no system is ever perfect. There are always problems, always ambiguities. For LeGuin, the primary social problem is the danger of centralization of power in an élite group and the reduction of the ideals of the revolution into a dogmatic ideology that itself inhibits further emancipatory activity. In LeGuin's Anarres, the administrative bureaucracy which was to serve the society has become self-serving for the permanent bureaucrats and heads of federations located at the center in the capital city. Dissidents and non-conformists (nuchnibi) are denied desired work posting or driven to the Asylum. In the physicist, Sabul, and indeed in Rulag, Shevek's mother, we find examples of congealed personal power, self-service and resistance to change. Jealous of Shevek's work in physics, Sabul denies the young scientist a teaching post and blocks his connections with physicists in Urras. Rulag holds to the policy of isolation from Urras and votes against Shevek's Syndicate of Initiative efforts to open communication on Anarres.

The center ceases to serve and change as needed and instead holds to the status quo for the sake of the permanent élite in the bureaucracy; for although elected representatives rotate, bureaucratic civil servants do not. Indeed, the plot of the novel is motivated by Shevek's adherence to the ideals of the Odonian revolution and his need for intellectual freedom to advance the frontiers of physics conflicting with the freezing of the revolution in privilege, habit, and fear of change. As Anarres approaches its two hundredth year, Shevek, the dissident, breaks open the society, reasserts its revolutionary ideals, and thus restores the process of permanent revolution.

In describing the failure of this revolution, LeGuin exposes the rigidities of power and hegemonic ideology that are experienced in all present societies on our Earth and thus negates the cooptation of utopian values and institutions by any system, capitalist or state socialist, that claims them once and for all. She asserts the ideal of anarchist freedom and permanent rebellion over against centralized systems. She keeps the utopian impulse alive while rejecting the stasis of any utopian system, even her own.

Unfortunately, the contradictions of LeGuin's iconic images of utopia go beyond her intended ones. There is a conflict between the sexual and gender emancipation asserted and the actual words, images, and narrative produced: a conflict that calls into question the radical quality of her overall vision. By her choice of a male protagonist, use of male pronouns, and restriction of strong female characters to supporting roles, LeGuin continues to write within the rules of the male-dominated publishing game — even after being criticized by feminist readers for this tendency in her earlier works and even after she had achieved the status of a major author who could afford to risk the disapproval of the publishing and reading majority. LeGuin exhibits in at least three instances a traditional male-identified, heterosexual, monogamous nuclear family bias that undercuts her textual assertions of personal emancipation.

Samuel Delany has demonstrated how Bedap, Shevek's male lover and friend, the one who radicalizes Shevek by calling his attention to the injustices perpetrated by the Anarresti bureaucratic élite, functions as a token homosexual.[4] Bedap is seen with no other lover than Shevek, who has sex with him only to "re-establish" their friendship. There are no other gay or lesbian characters portrayed in the novel, even though LeGuin asserts the social freedom of preference. And, in a scene near the end of the novel when Bedap accompanies Shevek and his daughter to her dormitory and leaves the father and child to say their good-nights, Bedap is described as missing the joys of parenthood. As Delany notes, the implication here is that it is Bedap's homosexuality that is the cause of his misery in not being a parent. In this non-sexist, tolerant, non-nuclear-family society, such a "failing" on Bedap's part does not fit the social image LeGuin asserts. The text here betrays itself as present ideologies undercut her intended subversive vision.

Furthermore, LeGuin valorizes the nuclear family of Shevek, Takver, and their two children whom they choose to keep at home with them over against the individual and communal structure which is presented as the norm on Anarres. It is as though a nuclear family, that of a US rebel or a Soviet dissident – one which, in fact, allows the man to travel to other worlds and lead revolutions while the woman and children keep the home fires burning – were put in the middle of Anarresti society to save it from itself. Delany has also pointed out how Shevek's anger at his mother after twenty years of separation is not the typical response one would expect in a society where the entire community cares for children and the parental bond is not as strong as in current phallocratic society. Thus, while LeGuin's utopia expresses a libertarian and feminist value system, the gaps and contradictions in her text betray a privileging of male and heterosexual superiority and of the nuclear, monogamous family.

Another contradiction, less problematic and more provocative, in LeGuin's text exists in her choice of the bleak landscape as the site of a utopia. John Fekete finds that this choice of scarcity as the context for moral decisions runs counter to the notion of utopia as the place where physical and moral abundance are found, where all people benefit from the transcendence of class and property domination: "In other words, a narrowing of the objective horizons, the incorporation of the power of scarcity and survival necessity into the very structure of the situation, mark LeGuin's ambiguous utopia as less hopeful than is commonly supposed."[5] The physical parameters set by LeGuin limit the utopian logic of the book and do not pave the way for utopia as much as for individual moral excellence in the face of adversity. Nadia Khouri also picks up on this gap in the text, for she too sees

LeGuin's identification of material abundance with exploitation, selfishness, and greed: "Hence, abundance is assimilated and condemned even-handedly in all its forms, from one-dimensional consumer society to the plebian yearnings of Cockaigne. In a narrative bearing the title *Dispossessed*, material dispossession becomes the necessary condition for ethical wealth."[6] Of course, the thematic strategy of scarcity is one way to negate the ostentatious affluence of modern America, but it also serves a backward look to the "good old days" of the frontier more than it makes a serious attempt to appropriate productive surplus for the well-being of all humanity. Moral categories have replaced social-economic phenomena and political redistribution of wealth in this nostalgic emphasis on scarcity. Such limitation to the moral drama, Fekete argues, results in the failure of the text to "bring into a really strategic dynamic tension the physical and the anthropological. It fails to provide a multiplicity of technical life-support systems for a diversity of subjectivity."[7] With the novel's moral reduction and economic entropy, Khouri notes that "*The Dispossessed* is thus a classical novel in the sense that the moral denouement requires the sacrifice of the hero."[8] The underlying premise of the novel, seen in this light, is moral asceticism not utopian fulfillment.

This textual contradiction, to be sure, grows out of LeGuin's Taoism, asceticism, and ecological consciousness, not to mention her understandable revulsion over the gross consumption and waste in contemporary US culture and the false redistribution of wealth in many socialist societies. Ideologically, she is close to the ecology movement of the early 1970s, but she also senses the peaking of the US economic boom and anticipates the declining standard of living in the US of the 1970s and 1980s. She is well aware that scarcity is part of the lives of most people on the planet and has attempted to deal with the presence of scarcity in her utopia. However, in her moral idealism, in her individualism, in her simple binary oppositions, ambiguous as they are, she ends up opposing morality to post-industrial/post-scarcity materiality and does not give us dynamic images of emancipatory utopian interaction with nature. She accepts scarcity as a positive condition and not as a condition to transcend; she seems to prefer the attitudes of the realist novel or the tragedy rather than the utopia.

Another problem in the social images is the oscillating relationship between Anarres and Urras. On the surface, we learn that the Odonian revolution resulted in the migration to Anarres and the formation of the utopian state, and we see that the concrete utopian ideal of Anarres still inspires revolutionaries on Urras. Yet we do not see the utopian society subverting the world; rather, we see instead a dissident individual from utopia taking down some walls and establishing a sort of détente between the two. As Khouri points out, the binary opposition between the planets is static and not dialectic. Anarres becomes the means used by Urras to contain and coopt the Odonian revolution, and although Urras is the means used by the Syndicate of Initiative to revive the Odonian revolution the revival remains limited to the moon. Like the utopias for misfits in dystopias such as *Brave New World*, *This Perfect Day*, and *Fahrenheit 451*, Anarres is a strategic containment zone for the Urrasti hegemony. Furthermore, because of the mining trade that Anarres depends on for materials it cannot produce, the utopia becomes, in effect, a neo-colony of Urras. Finally, at the end of the novel, we do not find a social revolution caused by the utopian impulse, but a new product, a theory of physics that will revolutionize communications between star systems, and a new centralizing governmental structure, the pangalactic union of "known worlds," the Ekumen, made possible by that product. This is not, to be sure, LeGuin's intent, for Anarres is the utopia that opposes all that Urras stands for, but the dynamics of the text – or, in this case, the lack of them – contradict that apparent intent and render Anarres passive and harmless and in need of regeneration by scientific, commercial, and political events on metropolitan Urras, thereby weakening the overall critical utopian practice of the text.

The cooptation of utopia is furthered by the presence of the non-Cetian peoples (Anarres and Urras are in the system of Tau Ceti) near the novel's end: namely, the Terran ambassador and the Hainish emissary. The arrival of the Hainish on the scene might have broken the binary opposition between Anarres and Urras, dialectically mediating between the two and generating an authentic utopian moment that forced the text and the revolution onward. But this does not happen, for Hain and Terra form another binary opposition in the iconic register that reproduces the first one at a different level of galactic history and culture. Stasis is unfortunately maintained: Terra is the hell requiring salvation, a destroyed civilization that justifies a mystical and restrained super-ego, and Hain serves as just such a *deus ex machina*. As Khouri puts it, we get

> the incarnation of the author's narrative superego in the form of the unexpected appearance of the Hainish at the end of the novel. . . . This salutary conclusion allows LeGuin a way out of her own impasse. The contradictions of the writer thus become aesthetic weaknesses, as ideological perplexities intervene to channel out the production of imagination.[9]

Thus, in the preconceptual figures of the social systems presented by LeGuin in the iconic register of her text, we have an assertion of a set of utopian values that symbolically resolves the contradictions of the 1960s in both capitalist and state socialist societies and points the reader to emancipatory notions and practices that were being asserted by the social movements of the 1960s. The traditional radical ideals of freedom and mutual aid, the contemporary ideals of feminism and ecological wisdom are expressed in the content of the novel and have stimulated many readers who share such oppositional values. However, the manner in which these values are presented and the resulting textual contradictions generated in the areas of gender roles, economic scarcity, radical opposition, and centralized state and commercial power compromise LeGuin's utopian novel and render it even more ambiguous than she might herself have intended.

Shevek and the others

The contest between the images of utopia and those of the world as history finds it is confined within the iconic structure of LeGuin's text as a set of binary oppositions. When we shift our analysis from these images to the characters generated in the discrete register of the novel and the underlying ideological implications of their actions, we move to the broader historical contest between the dominant and subordinate sectors of present society. Binary closure gives way to an expansively negative conflict between prevailing ideology, which asserts that utopia has already arrived and all the human subject need do is passively cooperate with it, and oppositional vision, which states that the human subject has not yet experienced utopia and still must struggle toward that goal. Hence, the willed transformation of reality required by the oppositional forces becomes the focus of our discussion. In this question of activism, then, we again recognize the critical utopian ideologeme which resonates between the text and history. Yet, here too, textual discontinuities and compromises undercut the oppositional force of this novel.

In *The Dispossessed*, the central figure of Shevek carries most of LeGuin's reflections on the strategy and tactics of social change. Male, intellectual, and a loner in his work – both in physics and politics – Shevek is a reluctant activist. He speaks out and resists the power structure at home and in Urras long after others have done so and only when he is frustrated, meets the wall, in his own work or personal life. As presented by LeGuin, Shevek recalls the sort of intellectual-turned-dissident activist that one finds in an Einstein, a Sakharov, an Ellsberg, or even a Martin Luther King. Indeed, he is the solitary savior who acts for all humanity using tactics of non-violent confrontation toward the strategic goal of healing discord and achieving détente, harmony, and universal peace. By privileging this form of engagement, LeGuin asserts the value of prominent intellectuals serving social change, the power of non-violence, and the ideals of harmony and peace. In making her protagonist a male, a father and husband, a scholar and leader, tall and handsome, articulate and well liked, she draws on traditional qualities of the male hero in western culture to mark his activity.

With this choice of protagonist, however, other types of people and other forms of activity – for example, women or racial minorities, Third World peoples who act collectively and perhaps violently in a world less amenable to negotiation and détente – are kept at the periphery and thus rendered less important. The privileged place that the male protagonist holds in the minds of many readers overwhelmingly valorizes what Shevek represents and overshadows the other options.

Shevek's actions are presented in a binary set of chapters

alternating between those treating his development from birth to adulthood on Anarres and those concerned with his trip to Urras. The sets of chapters carry two diachronic plots running synchronously from beginning to end of the text as the younger and older Sheveks go through similar confrontations with established power and privilege and succeed in opening up the social fabric by means of work in physics and in politics. As we shall see, Shevek's breakthroughs in both areas are preceded in each instance by developments in his personal/sexual life which occur as he makes use of various women.

Although the text begins in the spaceport of Anarres, the first chapter launches the plot of Shevek's trip to Urras to further his task of breaking down walls between the utopia and its home world, within the bureaucratically rigidified utopia itself, and in his own mind as he seeks to complete his General Temporal Theory. Like Jesus entering Jerusalem to the taunts and stones of the multitude, Shevek strides unprotected to the spaceport under the shouts and stones of the Anarresti who feel that as a leader of the opposition's Syndicate of Initiative he has betrayed them and gone over to the enemy. On Urras, he is welcomed as the "man in the moon," as a prize-winning theoretical physicist, and sought after as the one who can deliver the scientific theory necessary for faster-than-light travel and communication to the nation of A-Io and thus give it an edge in the major power confrontations between A-Io and Thu. He gradually realizes that he is kept there by agents of the government and connects with the anarchist and social resistance movements in the slums of the capital city. He arrives at his General Temporal Theory and sparks a general strike as he casts off his alien/academic celebrity status and becomes the intellectual and political savior of the common people of Urrasti society and the galaxy.

In the Urras chapters, then, we find the protagonist on a quest for new opportunities for his people, for new ideas in physics, and for unity between planets and in the galaxy. He seeks, encounters problems rooted in the repressive aspects of Urrasti societies, and, with help from sympathetic revolutionaries and the ambassadors of Terra and Hain, achieves his various goals. Here, we find not utopian narrative but rather the pattern of quest and reward of the fairy tale and of speculation and criticism of the science fiction story. Shevek is the romance-fairy tale hero who defeats evil and establishes good. Although he has helpers, as the hero tradition-ally does, he does not work collectively with them but rather uses their help to achieve success single-handedly. He returns home as a leader who has literally unified the entire universe by making possible the instantaneous communicator, the ansible, and by breaking the power of centralized privilege on both planets and replacing it with the mystical and wise power of the Ekumen. Initiative and cooperation thus become the twin components of the new equilibrium.

Having established a context, a "real" world of present time, a point from which to observe within the process of change, in the Urras chapters, LeGuin shifts in the alternating chapters to Shevek's early life in utopia from when he first went against the grain of communal society by wanting the sunlight for his own in the nursery to the point when, as leader of the Syndicate of Initiative, he opposes the Anarresti bureaucracy and goes off to Urras. Like a young Jesus teaching the elders in the temple, Shevek proves to be brighter than his professors and rapidly makes strides in physics that break with the established Odonian sequential physics by articulating the principles of simultaneity. He supplants orthodox revolutionary linearity/progress with a radical understanding of repetition and progress that allows for a more complex and deconstructive apprehension of reality.

However, he also encounters the power that life in the metro-polis confers on the leading members of society, including his teacher, Sabul, and his mother, Rulag. Aided by the rebellious insights and experiences of his friends, especially Bedap, and the support of his wife, Takver, Shevek becomes politically active and leads the way in establishing the independent printing and radio operations of the Syndicate of Initiative as his group of young rebels act out the ideas of the revolution against its compromised administrators. Again, as in the Urras chapters, Shevek arrives at a major discovery in physics – the Principles of Simultaneity – and a major breakthrough in the political scene – the work of the Syndicate of Initiative. These achievements set up the situation wherein he must go to Urras to carry on his work in both areas. The early breaking down of walls on Anarres to continue revolu-tion and scholarship leads the way to the later breaking down of walls for the entire universe by means of the General Temporal Theory.

In the Anarres chapters, then, a different narrative pattern dominates: that of the bourgeois novel of development. Shevek grows up, learns about his world, goes through several crises, and finally takes his proper place in society. Of course, contrary to the bourgeois *Bildungsroman*, Shevek does not adjust to his world; rather, he changes it – which is what a good citizen of a utopia that advocates permanent revolution should be doing. He accepts his calling in life, albeit reluctantly. What he sets out to do on Anarres, he accomplishes finally on Urras. One might be tempted to say that he descends from heaven to hell to redeem all of humankind in an act of cosmic détente. In both cases, he is the individual hero – aided by others, but working alone.

Shevek is a compelling protagonist, a visitor from utopia who successfully transforms the universe. Yet in centering her picture of activism on such a character, LeGuin foregrounds a type of commitment that revolves around a single redeemer, a vanguard intellectual, and a dominant male. If the novel is considered in a linear manner rather than by alternating chapters, another pattern emerges wherein Shevek experiences a sexual encounter before each one of his scientific and political accomplishments. As a young man, he copulates with his first lover, Beshun, while on reforestation work (TD, 45); from there he returns to the Regional Institute and performs so well in physics that he is sent to study with Sabul in Abbenay; he also learns about the power that "inheres in a center" like the capital and thus begins his political education. Later, in Abbenay, after some years of fruit-less work in his field, having his publications used by Sabul to further the senior professor's own career, he reconnects with his friend Bedap and enters into a brief sexual relationship with him – although "the pleasure of it would be mostly for Bedap" (TD, 145). After this encounter, in the year 168, Shevek is politicized through conversations with Bedap and the other disaffected youth around the university, learning more examples of the abuse of privilege by the administrators and their refusal to reward truly creative or dissenting work by branding it non-functional or counter-revolutionary.

Next, his relationships with Takver on Anarres and with Vea

on Urras are intertwined over four chapters (TD, chapters 6, 7, 8, 9) as he becomes partners with Takver, has a drunken encounter with Vea, arrives at the Principles of Simultaneity on Anarres and decides to publish his work under Sabul's name in an act of political realism, and arrives at the General Temporal Theory on Urras and decides to escape and join the Iotic revolutionaries and release the theory to the Ekumen in an act of political idealism. In this pattern of sexual potency and theoretical/political break-through, LeGuin reveals a deeper valorization of the "creative potency" of the male, aided by lovers who are not equal co-workers and partners but rather stimuli for the solitary activity of the hero. Her attitude is echoed in a passing description of male animals in rut that Shevek observes on Urras: "In a pen by himself the herd sire, ram or bull or stallion, heavy-necked, stood potent as a thundercloud, charged with generation" (TD, 181).

Shevek, the "herd sire" of the novel, generates the entire action of the text, and his form of activism stands out as one type of willed transformation considered necessary to achieve utopia and universal harmony. The "heroism" of the two sub-narratives – fairy tale and bourgeois novel of development – displaces the apparent major role of the utopian visitor and subversive; consequently, this formulation has more in common with the phallocratic/capitalist/bureaucratic status quo which places the male, heterosexual, bourgeois hero at the center of its culture than it does with the forces of opposition coded around 1968. Indeed, this privileging of male, intellectual, solitary heroics within the new left was criticized by the emerging women's movement of the late 1960s.

To be sure, other radical forms of activism are represented in *The Dispossessed*, but they are pushed to the margins of the narrative and serve only as helpers for the central hero. We have seen above how LeGuin presents Bedap as a token homosexual who serves as a foil for the "healthy and whole" Shevek. Yet it is Bedap who, as a "functions analyst" trying to reform the teaching of science on Anarres, encounters the power in the center of the supposedly decentralized society; he sees the central administration for what it has become: "an anarchistic bureaucracy" (TD, 145). It is Bedap who tells Shevek about the wasted lives of many creative citizens on Anarres and who asserts that "change is freedom, change is life," and that they have let "cooperation become obedience" as the bureaucracy has seized power for itself over the years (TD, 146–7). It is Bedap who challenges Shevek to think critically and to join with the rebels in that year of 168. It is Bedap – homosexual, teacher, rebel – who stimulates Shevek into action and who catalyzes the plot toward its next stage. However, Bedap remains only a supporting character and is further devalued later as a gay man who regrets his choice of not parenting, when indeed he is probably more typical of the average movement activist in 1968 than is the élite figure of Shevek.

So too with Takver. Also portrayed as an activist who shares Bedap's convictions and joins in the discussions and actions of the rebels, Takver is the one who urges Shevek to publish his book with Sabul as a tactic of political survival so he can fight another day. She is also the one who urges Shevek to continue with his physics, to fight the university establishment, to publish his next work independently in the Syndicate of Initiative, and who encourages him to take the risky trip to Urras. A biologist, Takver represents ecological consciousness most directly in the novel:

> Her concern with landscapes and living creatures was passionate. This concern, feebly called "love of nature," seemed to Shevek to be something much broader than love. These are souls, he thought, whose umbilicus has never been cut. They never get weaned from the universe. They do not understand death as an enemy; they look forward to rotting and turning into humus. It was strange to see Takver take a leaf into her hand, or even a rock. She became an extension of it, it of her.   (TD, 162)

Yet even in this evocative description of her ecological awareness, Takver is described from the point of view of the scholarly male Shevek who is somehow above such earthy, female matters, who is an adult rather than an eternal fetus, who faces the "harder realities" of death and separation. Consequently, Takver – yet another typical example of a 1968 activist – is reduced to the role of the "good woman" behind the "great man": she bears the children, cares for them through famine and revolution, keeps the home fire burning and her own body warm for her man who is off saving the world.

111

Bedap and Takver are more complex and common examples of the activism of the 1960s than Shevek – as are other, more marginal, characters such as the playwright Tirin who is committed to the Asylum for the one satiric drama he wrote. Yet these Anarresti rebels fade to the periphery as the hero takes center stage. Furthermore, on Urras the collective heroism of the Ioti revolutionaries is dealt with in just a few pages. They are summed up quickly as non-violent libertarians (which LeGuin prefers) in the person of the older male, Tuio Maedda, as violent socialists (which LeGuin does not prefer) in the person of an unnamed "girl," and as the common working class – in the person of Shevek's servant, Efor. The power of this united front which resists the war against the Third World revolutionaries of Benbili is expressed in their ability to amass a hundred thousand people at a demonstration and shut down the capital city in a general strike. Even this power is effaced as Shevek, the lone anarchist from the moon, the hoped-for savior, speaks to the assembled demonstrators. As he speaks, military helicopters arrive and the demonstration is dispersed: Shevek, not the people, has the last word, and the collective resistance is crushed. The Benbili revolutionaries receive even less emphasis and become simply a distant threat to the nation of A-Io, even though they are an oppressed people who also espouse the teachings of Odo.

The two characters who help Shevek at the end of the novel – and who mirror Takver and Bedap – are the Terran ambassador and the Hainish representative, Ketho. The oriental woman from Terra saves Shevek from the pursuing Iotic security forces by granting him asylum in the Terran embassy, and she is the one who first mentions to Shevek that a federation of worlds would be made possible with the instantaneous communicator. Thus she is again the supporting, nurturing woman, and she is the direct conduit for the effects of Shevek's work to move out to the galaxy. On the other hand, Ketho, the first mate of the Hainish vessel that is Shevek's vehicle of re-entry to Anarres, is the one who effectively reunites Shevek with his political voyage to break down walls and keep the utopian ideal alive. Indeed, Ketho – whose mission is to "explore and investigate" new worlds – is the disciple, the active male, who most directly carries on Shevek's work by his decision to go to Anarres and continue the process of communication and extension of utopian ideals. He is the link between Shevek's action and the pan-galactic Ekumen. In these two helpers, we find the most textually important of the marginalized activists, serving as they do to complete the narrative. It is interesting to note, however, that they are the most "alien" – coming from the burned-out Terra, the ultimate dystopia, and the mystical and ancient Hain, the ultimate utopia – and that they are the most élite – holding the rank of ambassador, one officially, one by choice of his mission. Therefore, the "activists" most privileged by LeGuin's text are the highest ranked and least immersed in the daily life and social systems of the two Cetian worlds: yet their narrative roles are those of a passive female conduit/protectress and an active male disciple.

Thus, the activists in the novel who might most reflect the various movements of the late 1960s – anti-war activists, ecologists, school reformers, anarchists, socialists, working-class and poor, Third World revolutionaries – are displaced to the margins. Interestingly, the loudest silence in this array of movements is the women's movement. Women are present in the novel but denied their own political activism: Odo was a woman, but an anarchist not a feminist; Takver is a woman but she primarily represents ecology; the "girl" on Urras is a socialist who advocates violence; the Terran ambassador is a woman who is simply relieved that her people are still alive on that burned-out planet. There are no female characters who are activists in any type of directly feminist movement. In fact, the one character who mentions the emancipation of women is the male-identified Vea, and she argues against it and proves later to be a spy working for the imperialist A-Io government. LeGuin weaves many aspects of a post-sexist society into her utopian society and asserts the quality of gender in interesting ways, but her text is silent at the level of the ideologeme, at the level of the expression of how to transform society actively, when it comes to feminist activism.

LeGuin's contribution in this critical utopia to the ideologically oppositional notion of activism is one that more clearly resembles that of the dominant system of male supremacy, the success of individual leaders, and, paradoxically, the wise use of centralized power and privilege. Despite her images of utopian society with all its libertarian, ecological, and feminist elements, such emancipatory imagery remains contained within the figures of the text; while at the ideological level of contestation with the contradictions and changes in history itself, the text reveals a message of male, individual, intellectual, élitist leadership rather than one of collective resistance and common victory. In particular, the power of the women's movement of the late 1960s and early 1970s is silenced in favor of the limits of mainstream male discourse.

Ambiguous utopia/static history

When we turn from the content of *The Dispossessed*, its social images and activist characters, to a consideration of the utopian form as an ideological response to the contradictions and possibilities in history, we discover yet another dimension of compromise with the status quo. Although LeGuin's novel is an important revival of utopian discourse, with content that has stimulated many readers, the work is more of a nostalgic look to the older ideological message of the genre that emphasized the perfect utopian system than it is a breakthrough to a critical expression of an open-ended utopian imagination. The utopian matter is locked into a series of binary oppositions that result in one system converging with another in an act of premature literary détente rather than in a radical exposure of all systems, even utopia, to the pull of the not yet realized emancipatory future. What we are left with is an apparently critical text which asserts utopia and radical activism but which actually expresses the continued closure of the current social formation of male supremacy, world capitalism, and bureaucratic hierarchy, coded in a narrative of convergence and individual transformation of reality.

The presentation of utopia in this novel turns on the word "ambiguous" as LeGuin examines how the two worlds of Anarres and Urras look on each other in the double vision of dangerous enemy and utopian hope: "The wall separating the two worlds is ambiguous, two-faced." (TD, 1). Shevek and his comrades see Urras as a possible source of reviving the revolution which has closed in on itself in puritanical isolation. Both the dominant powers of Urras and the downtrodden seek "revolution" from Anarres: the first in the form of a breakthrough in physics that would allow faster than light travel and communications, and thus allow for military advance and open the planet to the commerce of other worlds; the second in the form of a social revolution to complete the aborted Odonian revolution that took refuge in one place. Rather than achieving a transcendent breakthrough for any of these forces, the novel ends up circling around in binary oppositions that mirror and enclose each other.

Urras and Anarres, Terra and Hain, young Shevek and old Shevek, Takver and the Terran ambassador, Takver and Vea, Bedap and Ketho, Bedap and Pei, the list of opposing elements could go on. The general movement of the novel is in epicycles of opposition that dissolve into the next circle without the closure being broken. Indeed, Shevek's General Temporal Theory is a textual analog for the motion of the novel as it synthesizes forward motion of time/history with repetition in endless cycle, diachrony with synchronicity, becoming with being, the arrow and circle of time:

> So then time has two aspects. There is the arrow, the running river, without which there is no change, no progress, or direction, or creation. And there is the circle or the cycle, without which there is chaos, meaningless succession of instants, a world without clocks or seasons or promises.
>
> (TD, 196)

Such a theoretical solution, Shevek argues, leads to a "true chronosophy" which clarifies moral behavior:

> seeing the difference between now and not now, we can make the connection. And there morality enters in. . . . If time and reason are functions of each other, if we are creatures of time, then we had better know it, and try to make the best of it. To act responsibly. (TD, 197)

To be sure, LeGuin's creation of the General Temporal Theory is an interesting attempt along with others in the 1970s to reconcile the synchronic and diachronic, the repetition of evil and the struggle against it as she might phrase it in ethical terms. And Shevek's statement, that "You can go home again, the General Temporal Theory asserts, so long as you understand that home is

115

a place where you have never been" (TD, 48), is an echo of Ernst Bloch's notion of *Heimat* and the forward pull of history. However, despite the implied suggestion of a spiral of repetition with forward motion that breaks beyond a given circle, the structure of the novel goes in a compensating circle rather than a revolutionary spiral. We read at the end of the novel that Shevek has gone *back* home, the voyage is completed. We read of no changes on Anarres due to his trip, no victory of the strikers in NioEssea or the revolutionaries in Benbili, no downfall of the governments of A-Io or Thu. We do read of Terra and Hain, but the alien societies cancel out each other as do Anarres and Urras. Indeed, the only evident breakthrough is Shevek's theory and the new product that is made possible by that knowledge, the instantaneous communicator, the ansible. We are left with a product that leads not to a radical negation of the opposites but rather to a convergence of all of them as it makes possible the unity of known worlds. The prime achievement of the action of the novel is the production of knowledge and the development of an electronic commodity that makes possible a galactic détente. Thus, rather than a breakthrough beyond prevailing contradictions of history, LeGuin gives us a resolution of the present contradictions – west against east, haves against have nots, peace against war – that does not negate but rather eliminates all the oppositions. The post-industrial/cybernetic production of the transnational world system dependent on various technocratic intellectuals and state bureaucracies, capitalist or state socialist, for the creativity and infrastructure necessary for continued growth is the final analog for the form of this novel. We are left not with a vision that goes beyond world capitalism in a formal expression of discontinuity and openness but rather one based on information technology and the collapse of oppositions in a unified system.

Within this narrative and historical closure, the radical ideas embodied in the imagery of Anarres and the creativity of its marginal activists are restricted to a set of artificially negative reforms that can accommodate an emerging world economy: one where the experience of personal scarcity continues despite corporate surplus; where developments in child care and changes in gender roles serve the needs of new work patterns and markets; where productivity and leisure coexist in a post-industrial system that requires fewer work hours and passive citizens. The changes suggested by LeGuin could be incorporated into a radical anti-corporate and anti-bureaucratic praxis, but as they are entrapped in her narrative they end up being stimulants for the continuance of the prevailing system instead.

Indeed, as the narrative is structured, it is Anarres, the utopia, that precedes the world in time: thus it is the Edenic utopia that allows for the reform of Urras, the development of the ansible, and the establishment of the galactic federation – not in the interest of increased autonomy and social justice but in the interest of increased organization and communication for various world systems. Utopia is appropriated for the reform of the present system rather than for its overthrow. The frontier nostalgia provoked by Anarres is an anticipation of the use of traditional American values at the time of the bicentennial not actually to revive the historic revolution but to use that ideology to contain further the recent "revolutions" of the 1960s. Utopia, then, is a message from the past preached to Urras, Terra, and Hain by the revivalist/physicist Shevek who ends up not being a radical activist who changes the world and opens up closed systems but rather a dissident who breaks from one system to unify all the systems prematurely before autonomy and justice is secured for the common people of Anarres, of A-Io, of Benbili, of Terra. The redeemer brings not a graceful new life to all people but rather a useful new product to benefit the hierarchy, the bureaucratic leadership of all the known worlds who can now set up a meta-bureaucracy of centralized power for the universe. "True voyage is return," it says on Odo's gravestone, and Shevek accomplishes such a circular trip as he returns to utopia with nothing but his theoretical work once again used by the hierarchy, his political work once again compromised, and with the radical alternative of Anarres once again limited to the moon – with a Hainish explorer now "studying" it as an ethnologist collects cultures or a biologist collects species for a zoo or conservatory.

What more can be expected of a lone individual attempting social revolution than such a cooptation in the very name of that revolution back into the service of the status quo, indeed improving and extending the profit of that given system? In the closure

117

of the opposing systems and in the plot of Shevek's apparent activism, we find not the radical praxis of the late 1960s but rather the cooptation of that energy by the forces of transnational capital, the very forces which influenced LeGuin to write within the double limits of male discourse and hope for the salvation of détente in the first place. The circle keeps closing in on itself.

Nowhere in the novel does the text call attention to its own obsession with such cyclic closure. Nowhere does the text call attention to the limitations of utopian systematizing, for even the Syndicate of Initiative is a revival of the Anarresti system, not a negation and transformation of it. The relativity of vision that perpetuates the cyclic motion of the text is echoed by the Terran ambassador when she informs Shevek that her people see Urras as utopia: "To me, and to all my fellow Terrans who have seen the planet, Urras is the kindliest, most various, most beautiful of all the inhabited worlds. It is the world that comes as close as any could to Paradise" (TD, 303). Speaking from a scarcity that is far beyond that of Anarres, the Terran woman explains that Urras for all its evils is "full of good, of beauty, vitality, achievement. It is what a world should be! It is *alive*, tremendously alive – alive, despite all of its evils, with hope' (TD, 303). Like a refugee from Eastern Europe who praises the United States to an American socialist, the Terran praises the enemy world to the utopian Shevek and thus reconfirms the nostalgic ambiguity which persists throughout the novel. Furthermore, the other alien, Ketho, who comes from the ultimate post-scarcity utopia, Hain, sees Anarres as stimulating just for its lean, scarcity-limited, yet moral and pure, system and behavior. Drawn to Anarres by the radical ideas of Odo's writings, Ketho wants to try "something new" for his own individual self coming from a race which has generally known and experienced everything. Like an adolescent of the affluent 1960s going off to a kibbutz or a sated suburban consumer in search of a new treat, Ketho seeks utopia in the scarcity and raw freedom his own world has transcended. The deprived Terran seeks utopia in Urrasti abundance; the communal and bored Hainish seeks utopia in individual experience and deprivation. Utopia is relative: pluralism of ideals and desires reigns. These oppositions are not brought together in a new society that enables the freedom of all humanity; rather, they become endlessly repeating options in the unified galactic cultural supermarket. The world system of passive consumption in a well-ordered society is nowhere transcended in *The Dispossessed*.

To be sure, *The Dispossessed* was well received when it was published in 1974 because it crystallized some of the major ideas and practices of the movements of the 1960s as well as revived utopian narrative itself. Its valorization of morality and voluntary action reflects some of the best aspects of the new left, and its portrayal of ecological, feminist, and pacifist practice touches the nerve of activism that carried on into the 1970s and 1980s. Accessible to many readers, the text can serve as an excellent introduction to the emerging oppositional consciousness in the 1970s, but as Samuel Delany put it in the conclusion to his essay on *The Dispossessed*, the novel

> will excite young and generous readers – indeed, will excite any reader beginning to look at our world and us in it. And it will excite for a long time. Nevertheless, some of these excited readers who return to the book a handful of years later will find themselves disillusioned: what excited them, they will see, was the book's ambition more than its precise accomplishments. But hopefully – a year or so after that – they will reach another stage where they will be able to acknowledge that ambition for what it was and value it; and know how important, in any changing society, such ambition is.[10]

Ambitious and well-meaning, *The Dispossessed* finally falls victim to the historical situation it opposes. Because it does not sufficiently break with the limits of the phallocratic-capitalist system in its own formal practices, the novel ensures that the enclosure of life by the dominant system is preserved more than it is negated. The narrative choices made within the traditional ideology of male privilege and world capitalism undermine LeGuin's radical desire to express a vision that would critique and transcend that ideology. Exciting oppositional prefigurations of an authentic utopian alternative are frustrated by a narrative form that does not successfully resist the compromises of the dominant system and its consumer market. Ideological expression of appropriate activism reinforces individual enterprise

119

and male supremacy at the expense of collective resistance, particularly by women. LeGuin pushes against the barriers, but in the final analysis she remains ambiguously within present boundaries of the status quo. *The Dispossessed* does not break down the wall, but – as Delany noted – it does blow the trumpets of alternative ideas and change and valiantly charges against it. And for that, and for its stimulation of the writing of utopian literature in the 1970s, it deserves recognition as an important, if flawed, critical utopia.

6 Marge Piercy, *Woman on the Edge of Time*

> The anger of the weak never goes away, Professor, it just gets a little moldy. It molds like a beautiful blue cheese in the dark, growing stronger and more interesting. The poor and the weak die with all their anger intact and probably those angers go on growing in the dark of the grave like the hair and the nails.　　(Connie, in *Woman on the Edge of Time*)

Utopian vision and an awareness of the denial of that vision in the everyday life of American society have been present in Marge Piercy's writing and politics since her first book of poetry, *Breaking Camp* (1968). In that collection, her poem, "The Peacable Kingdom," speaks to the contradiction between the images of pastoral utopia evoked by Edward Hicks's painting of the same name and the destruction of humanity and nature by the United States at home and in Vietnam. Her closing lines reveal her awareness of the utopian dream promised in the new world and the dystopian nightmare actually delivered: "This nation is founded on blood like a city on swamps / yet its dream has been beautiful and sometimes just / that now grows brutal and heavy as a burned out star."[1] The belief in a beautiful and just world and

121

the anger at the denial of it by the dominant power structure have persisted in all of Piercy's writings. These attitudes have been strengthened and deepened by her political activism beginning with the anti-war movement, continuing through her early involvement with the women's movement growing out of the new left, her involvement in ecological, mental health and community-control movements, and on to her primarily feminist politics in the 1980s. Her many volumes of poetry and her novels are the transformation of that activism and imagination into a tough and dreamy tendentious literature.[2]

Unlike that of other writers of critical utopias, Piercy's fiction did not develop directly within the world of science fiction publishing and fandom. Her second novel, *Dance the Eagle to Sleep* (1970), however, is a science fiction extrapolation on the anti-war/anti-draft, civil rights, and student movements of the 1960s in which she gives form to the dreams of revolution which sustained many in that time and weaves a tale of guerilla warfare and communes in the Catskills and the mountains of Colorado and New Mexico. She next turned to realism in her novel, *Small Changes* (1972), as she dealt not with the dreams but with the realities of sexism in the new left and the feminism that re-awakened in the struggle against it. With *Woman on the Edge of Time* (1976) she combined realism and utopian science fiction to produce what many consider to be her best novel. Piercy's work comes much more directly, then, out of the left political culture of the 1960s. To be sure, LeGuin, Russ, and Delany all developed their utopian vision in the same matrix of events and political outlook, but they did so within the artistic activism of progressive science fiction culture whereas Piercy worked within the political activism of radical, socialist, feminist politics. While *Woman on the Edge of Time* is a major work in the revival of utopias in the 1970s, it has an overt political edge to it that leads the book to be more concerned with the process of revolution itself.

Piercy's utopian novel arrives more by way of critical realism and traditional utopian literature than from science fiction or experimental fiction. In style she is closer to LeGuin. In anger and engagement more like Russ. *Woman on the Edge of Time* juxta-poses a realist narrative centering on Connie Ramos, a Chicana living on welfare in New York City, who has suffered the oppression and exploitation of the American system in an over-whelming variety of forms, with utopian images of the future society of Mattapoisett, a decentralized and democratic, anarcho-communist, feminist, ecologically aware village. Pamela Annas notes that in Piercy's novel, "the possibilities of human freedom are located not so much within the individual characters as within the social structure and the relations between the individual and that social structure."[3] The generic possibilities of a utopian science fiction that breaks open realist narrative allow for the development of a radical utopian activism in the text that offers a serious oppositional challenge to the historical status quo.

Woman on the Edge of Time weaves together a narrative of collective struggle with imagery of utopia, with one interpenetrating and influencing the other. Connie is oppressed because she is a woman, Mexican, poor, unemployed, a single parent, and branded by the medical establishment as psychotic. After migrating from her village in Mexico, eking out two years of college, losing lovers to death and poverty, she ends up in New York City with her child, Angelina, and her lover, Claud. While coping with Claud's death and surviving in the face of enforced poverty, she beats her child once in the frustration parents sometimes feel toward their frightened and demanding children in times of emotional, intellectual, and physical deprivation. Rather than getting support and assistance from the state, she is labeled a child abuser, committed to Bellevue and Rockover State Mental Hospital, and loses custody of her child to a middle-class family in Westchester. In short, Connie is a sane woman labelled insane, a survivor reduced to a victim. When the novel begins, she is back in the city, released from the hospital. Her niece comes to her for refuge from the pimp who is beating her, and, while defending Dolly from the violence of a beating, Connie herself, in an all too typical twist of bureaucratic/racist injustice, is recommitted for beating up her niece's "lover." Dolly defends Geraldo's version of the story to save herself from further violence, and Connie, the victim, is blamed for the "crime." From the chaotic violence of the streets Connie is transported to the institutional violence of the mental ward – which, as in Ken Kesey's *One Flew Over the Cuckoo's Nest*, functions as a microcosm of the

123

bureaucratic/capitalist system, with its attendant racism, sexism, and violence.

Among Connie's gifts is a mental sensitivity that enables her to be open to telepathic possibilities which extend to possible futures that could emerge from the present situation. This is the science fiction premise that informs the novel. For on page one the reader discovers that Connie is being contacted by someone from somewhere else: "Either I saw him or I didn't and I'm crazy for real this time," she says as the shadowy figure departs, leaving behind a warm chair.[4] Driven by the psychiatric power structure to doubt her abilities and perceptions, she is unsure whether she is hallucinating or really being visited by someone. It becomes clear when Connie is back on the mental ward that she is in communication with a person from the future. As in Joanna Russ's *The Female Man*, the utopian visitor is exploring the past to enlist help in the ongoing revolution to assure that a progressive line of history prevails.

Piercy's novel, appearing as it does in the year of the United States bicentennial, pits revolutionary ideals and praxis against the hierarchical rule imposed by contemporary society. With ideas and images arising from the oppositional politics of the late 1960s, Piercy employs the utopian genre to express those radical possibilities in the images of the future society of Mattapoisett and sets that utopia off against both the realist images of present day oppression and the dystopian images of a future in which the forces of profit and power prevail. The iconic figures give shape to 1960s dreams and practices not by presenting them as a static and secure utopian system but rather as still engaged in a life and death struggle in Connie's time, as she fights the psychiatric control of the dominant class, and in Mattapoisett's time, as its citizens militarily battle against the remaining forces of that class and ideologically contest the tendencies toward centralized power within the new society.

Hence, as we move to the discrete register and the consideration of the ideological message of Piercy's text regarding the ideologeme of activism, we find a much more engaged and open-ended sense of what must be done than was found in LeGuin. Like Russ, Piercy has a notion of the work necessary for the willed transformation of the present to open the way for a utopian

124

future that centers not on the redeeming quest of a single leader but on the collective struggle of a people across cultures and time. That struggle is represented not by a white, male, professional leader but by an alliance of common people of all races and cultures, connected across past, present, and future by the continuing history of the social revolution, and focused on two women of Hispanic/Indian origins – one a victim of the present system who turns revolutionary, the other the utopian example of the blossoming of the person that can occur in a truly free and just society.

While Piercy's overall strategy is one of class/gender/racial alliance, with an important focus on the autonomy of humanity and of nature, her tactics in *Woman on the Edge of Time* center not only on the ongoing effort to shed centralized power within the revolution but also on the necessity for violent struggle to achieve the social revolution given the overwhelming power of the phallocratic/capitalist/bureaucratic structure both in its ideological manipulation and its raw violence. Thus, the male violence of Dolly's pimp inflicted on Connie's vulnerable niece, the bureaucratic violence imposed on the "psychotic" patients in Rockover State Hospital, and the male and bureaucratic violence shaping Gildina's life in the dystopian New York are countered by the guerilla action that Connie carries out as she poisons the hospital staff in a deed that paves the way for the society of the future. The ongoing military and police violence of the present powers in Third World countries and American cities as well as the war still waged by those forces against Mattapoisett from bases on the moon and Antarctica are countered by the overt air war that the people of the utopia must carry out as they slowly defeat the forces of domination.

Piercy's version of the ideologeme of activism, then, is one that focuses on the strategic necessity of the alliance of the all oppositional forces and the tactical need for both ideological and violent struggle as well as personal transformation. Reflecting an awareness of the debilitating in-fighting and splits of the opposition forces in the early 1970s, her novel is a call for cooperation and coordination as she traces the common history and agenda of that opposition. Also she enunciates a radical ecological politics as part of the overall strategy as the people of Mattapoisett work to heal previous environmental damage and achieve a new partnership with a nature respected for its own existence. Reflecting the move from non-violent tactics in US radical politics to urban guerilla violence, found in the Weathermen and in various minority groups such as the Black Panthers, her novel adopts the tactics of Third World struggles in their insistence on sabotage and guerilla war to achieve the revolution. On the other hand, she also calls for personal transformation of each individual beyond the male-dominant, heterosexist, authoritarian structures of the present; here then she adopts the tactics of the feminist and male movements against the structures of institutional and personal sexism. With Piercy, we are at another pole from LeGuin's non-violent, mystically harmonious emphasis on détente and self-sacrificing (male) leadership.

As we move to the consideration of the ideology of the form of the novel, we also discover a politics of literary engagement that goes beyond the ambiguous binaries of LeGuin's noble effort. Piercy employs utopia as a literary weapon just as Connie uses the Parathion to poison the doctors of the hospital. By countering realism, with its tendency to reinforce the limits of the status quo, with utopian discourse, Piercy subverts realism from within by her use of a female and revolutionary protagonist and defeats it from without as the power of utopian imagination breaks open the realist text to a radically alternative future. In the same manner, she defeats the dystopian narrative, found in chapter 15, with the same power of the utopian impulse. Learning from the mistakes of past political dogmatism and the limits of the traditional utopian text, Piercy also demonstrates within her text a self-reflexive sense of the limits and real ambiguities of utopian discourse so that the text leaves itself open to question and varying reader responses rather than tying everything up in a closed binary circle. In her literary form, Piercy counters the totalizing closure of the status quo and expresses an open political praxis in the operations of the text that reproduces the strategy and tactics imaged in that text.

Pastoral utopia/urban dystopia

Piercy's image of the United States is not nearly so distant as LeGuin's, for the setting of Rockover State Mental Hospital is a direct realist version of present-day society in one of its more extreme and overt manifestations of power and control. Connie and the other patients – non-white, female, aged, young, gay, of various non-rational bents – are second-class citizens and victims of an establishment of white, middle-class, male doctors and psychologists with a complement of non-white and generally female helpers who are coopted into this system by their need to survive economically. The violence of the street represented in the incident with Dolly's pimp, the cooptation of middle-class success represented by Connie's suburban-based brother who refuses to help her, and the oppression and direct violence within the hospital itself convey in their critically realist images an angry picture of life in modern America. Thus, Piercy's utopia of a liberated future society is very non-ambiguously set against this present-day hell.

The utopia in *Woman on the Edge of Time* motivates Connie and the text itself: for the possibility of a better place enables both the protagonist and the realist narrative to move beyond the restrictions of the time-bound present. Elaine Hoffman Baruch notes that Piercy draws on many cultures – Third World, peasant, Native American and counter-cultural – to create an anti-racist and anti-sexist vision of the future which fuses utopia and its pursuit of civilization with a pastoral arcadia, the place of personal pleasure. It is a vision based on what Baruch calls the "equality of androgyny, that is, an equality of interchangeable differences whereby temperaments and roles traditionally assigned to one sex or another are open to both."[5]

The iconic images of the utopia begin in the second chapter of the novel with the arrival of Luciente on a New York street – thereby establishing Piercy's emphasis on the personal and the realm of everyday life as the focal point of her utopia. Connie, assuming her own cultural stereotypes, sees the person who appears as a young Indio male, but atypically not very macho; only later, when the narrative roles are reversed and the visitor to her world becomes the guide taking her as visitor around utopia, does she realize Luciente's gender. Connie is transported mentally to utopia by means of the time-travelling telepathy and matter transformation which allows her to be reconstituted in that future place. Luciente as a "sender" telepathically reaches across time to link with Connie, a natural "catcher," with the link occurring more easily at those times when – drunk, high, just waking, or simply at peace – Connie is most relaxed and receptive. Connie, the visitor, is taken from the "Age of Greed and Waste" to visit the land of the "people of the rainbow with its end fixed in earth."

The utopian village of Mattapoisett near Buzzards Bay in what was once Massachusetts is near Connie in space but not in time. The year is 2137. The forces of male supremacy and capitalism have been almost defeated in the closing years of a thirty-year war which devastated the major population centers, rendered many areas uninhabitable, and reduced the population, yet did not result in nuclear devastation. The war culminated in a revolution that created the new society, with the enemy driven back to orbiting space stations, the moon, and Antarctica. Looking over the village, Connie sees

> a river, little no-account buildings, strange structures like long legged birds that turned in the wind, a few large terracotta and yellow buildings and one blue dome, irregular buildings, none bigger than a supermarket of her day. . . . A few lumpy freeform structures overrun with green vines. No skyscrapers, no spaceports, no traffic jam in the sky. (WET, 62)

Buildings are small and randomly scattered, made of recycled material; land is under cultivation, used for grazing, or left wild. People travel on foot or bicycles and use hovercraft "floaters" for long distance travel. Personal living space is private: every adult from puberty on has a separate room. Personal freedom and tribal togetherness mark the social ambience of the village. As Luciente puts it, "We're all peasants" (WET, 64), but they are peasants who enjoy great individual freedom.

The economy of Mattapoisett is a steady-state, decentralized, anarcho-communist one with a biological-based high technology used in appropriate ways to render work less onerous but not to eliminate it. Every geographical region is "ownfed" and produces all the items it needs to survive and live a good life. Beyond that, each region produces and trades what it excels in with others. In this non-monetary economy, the necessities of life are guaranteed and the few luxuries are shared equally. The work day is short, and more like the workday of the peasant than of the factory worker:

> How many hours does it take to grow and make useful objects? Beyond that we care for our brooder, cook in our cooker, care for animals, do basic routines like cleaning, politic, and meet. That leaves hours to talk, to study, to play, to love, to enjoy the river,

says Jackrabbit, echoing Marx (WET, 120). Work is shared by all, including the elderly and the children. The non-productive jobs have been eliminated with the revolution: "telling people what to do, counting money, and moving it about, making people do what they don't want or bashing them for doing what they want" (WET, 121). With everyone working part time nobody works many hours: perhaps four hours one month, sixteen another, and continuously during harvest, catastrophes, or military duty.

High technology and sophisticated science is appropriately mixed with the ecologically balanced, non-growth economy. The use of computers allows for automation of difficult and dangerous work, but where labor can be humanly productive and fulfilling, as in child care, gardening, or cooking, automation is not used. The energy technology of Mattapoisett allows for the use of natural, non-polluting, renewable energy sources: solar, methane gas from human waste and compost, windpower, waterpower, tidal power, and wood. The science of this utopia is so advanced in areas such as genetics that plants and animals can be bred for the best use possible while preserving the genetic diversity of the ecosystem; for example, single-celled creatures called 'spinners' have been developed to serve in colonies as fences and barriers and to mend themselves as needed. Medicine makes use of advanced science in the repair of vision by cell manipulation, microsurgery for severed limbs, and extrauterine reproduction; for example, body damage is repaired by regrowing cells, a reversing of the negative energy of cancer. Yet folk medicine, ranging from voodoo to Native American to herbal and mental healing, is used as well. Science and technology, then, in production, in medicine, in all aspects of everyday life, are used appropriately to ease the human burden and improve the quality of life

129

without destroying the ecosystem or human initiative. Profit and power do not determine the use of the advanced knowledge of this culture.

While the economy is communist and steady-state, the government is a decentralized, community-based anarchism. Connie wants to see the government during one of her visits, but she is told that "nobody's working there today." On a day when it is working, she finds a representative town-hall form based at the village level; beyond that, there is a grand council of the villages in a given region. Governing is a process wherein the needs of each village are determined and scarce resources are justly divided after debate and consensus. Village reps are chosen by lot and serve for one year. This leadership is not only rotated, but restricted to avoid the accumulation of privilege: "After we've served in a way that seems important, we serve in a job usually done by young people waiting to begin an apprenticeship or crossers atoning for a crime" (WET, 244).

The social unit of Mattapoisett is dual: the self and the community or tribe. In a clear reversal of the reproductive machinery of Huxley's *Brave New World*, parenting is entered into by three friends who agree to parent and then apply to the "brooder," where conception – genetically engineered to preserve optimal diversity – occurs in a lab and fetuses are developed until birth. The "comothers" may be any combination of genders, and are seldom lovers: "So the child will not get caught in love misunderstandings" (WET, 68). Parenting is shared by the three until the child reaches puberty and goes through her or his initiation rite of a week's ordeal alone in the wilderness, where a vision quest occurs and the child enters adulthood by surviving and then choosing a name based on that experience. After this rite, the 12- or 13-year-old is a full adult, eligible to participate in government, serve in the military, or seek an apprenticeship. For three months after naming, parents may not speak to their former child, "lest we forget we aren't mothers anymore and person is an equal member" (WET, 109). So the "mothers" who nurtured and raised the child give way to three "aunts" selected at naming; the aunts of either gender serve as advisers for the years of early adulthood.

Education is a life-long process that from the early years seeks to develop the whole person: "We educate the senses, the imagination, the social being, the muscles, the nervous system, the intuition, the sense of beauty – as well as memory and intellect. . . . We want to root the forebrain back into a net of connecting" (WET, 132). Children are integrated into the life of the community: they are cared for in a nursery by those who have a gift for child care, carried about, taken to work, encouraged to help, and taught by the entire community as well as by their teachers and comothers. They are allowed to live full lives and are not kept in a separate building all day. By age 4, children are taught reading, as well as meditation and the yogin arts of body control; they are also allowed to be sexually expressive. Even into adulthood, learning goes on: "We never leave school and go to work. We're always working, always studying. We think that what person thinks person knows has to be tried out all the time. Placed against what people need. We care a lot *how* things are done" (WET, 123).

The ambience of life in Mattapoisett is easygoing but marked by hard work and hard play, and assisted by appropriate rituals. Celebrations are an important part of life, where the usual long-wearing practical clothes are set aside for costumes and "flimsies," "a once-garment for festival." There are eighteen regular holidays, another ten minor ones, and feasts when a decision is won or lost or when production norms are broken. In the course of the novel, two death rituals are described – one of a very old person, one of a young person who died in battle. Both exhibit the naturalness and community flavor that mark the rest of Mattapoisett life:

> The family, the lovers, the closest friends sit with the body to loosen their first grief. After supper everybody in the village will gather for a wake in the [fooder]. . . . All night we stay up together speaking of [the dead one]. Then at dawn we dig a grave and lay the body in. Then we plant the mulberry tree. . . . Then before we go to bed, we visit the brooder and signal the intent to begin a baby.   (WET, 154)

Rather than extend life with their advanced science for a privileged few, the people of Mattapoisett choose to accept death: "I think it comes down to the fact we're still reducing population.

Longer people live, less often we can replace them. But most every lug wants the chance to mother. Therefore, we have to give back. We have to die" (WET, 269).

With an emphasis on the quality of everyday life, communication is important. Each person wears a wrist-watch-like device, a "kenner," which links the person at all times to the central computer and communications system. An image of the utopian other to the monitoring device implanted in the patients of Rockover, the device is part personal memory, part telephone, part analytical tool; people feel lost without it because it does so much so efficiently. Also, inter-personal communications are highly stressed, with every person trained in verbal and non-verbal expression, including telepathy. With such intra- and inter-personal communications skills, the community effectively works. When necessary, it deals with conflict in criticism/self-criticism sessions. When conflict between people gets especially out of hand, the community holds a "worming" wherein the conflict is opened up and dealt with so that the "social fabric" is preserved. Appropriately in a society in partnership with nature, communications skills are also extended to animals; for in Matta-poisett higher animals, such as cows, cats, and dolphins, have either been bred to talk or people have taken time to learn the language of the particular species. Washoe Day is a major holi-day, commemorating the chimpanzee who was the first animal to learn to sign between species. Throughout the society, songs, operas, hologram, film, dance, and mixed media "rituals" make up the artistic forms whereby people express themselves and communicate with each other.

Unrepressed sexuality is regarded as a natural part of life. Parenting is separated from sexual activity, and a free and sometimes complex sexuality is part of each person's life. "Fa-sure, we couple. Not for money, not for a living. For love, for pleasure, for relief, out of habit, out of curiosity and lust" (WET, 58). One has "pillow friends," who are lovers, and "hand friends," who are not, longer-term lovers become "sweet friends" and deal with all the joys and problems of such arrangements. Some people couple monogamously for a time, some are celibate, most are sexually active with several people, of whatever genders they prefer. Not only are there positive images of liberated women of all sexual preferences and many skills and interests, but Piercy also provides male characters – such as Bee, Jackrabbit, Bolivar, and others – who are beyond the personality formations of male supremacist socialization.

To be sure, there are misfits in this utopia, people who are lazy and do not want to do their share of work or do not take care to get along with others. These people are asked to leave and may wander from village to village. And though there are no courts, no police force, no jails, there is conflict, which is worked out in community meetings with a chosen referee. There is little theft with so little private property. Like cannibalism, rape is a thing of the past. However, assault and murder occasionally happen. People get angry and strike out, but the violator is worked with, helped so that the act will not be repeated. If the act is done willfully, the person is given a sentence: "Maybe exile, remote labor. Shepherding. Life on shipboard. Space service. Sometimes crossers cook good ideas about how to atone" (WET, 201). The assaulter, the victim, and the referee work it out with the community. One murder is allowed to be atoned for, but capital punishment in this imperfect utopia is declared for a second deadly offense.

The utopian ideology of Mattapoisett is based on the dual values of personal freedom and community responsibility and on a sense of the unity of humanity and the rest of nature. All are free to act. "Person must not do what person cannot do" (WET, 92) expresses the fundamental belief in freedom shared by all the villagers. Yet this freedom is balanced by the needs of the community: everyone is expected to do their share of work, to contribute to the political and military needs of the community, to care for the natural environment. The maintenance of freedom for all means community work and meetings: "How can people control their lives without spending a lot of time in meetings?" (WET, 146). A social faith binds all together, and people express this physically: "Touching, and caressing, hugging and fingering, they handled each other constantly" (WET, 70). Happiness is not based in objects, in fetishes, but in the self and in relationships with others. Such happiness, however, occurs within a deep sense of place and connection with the local "web of nature." "Place matters to us. . . . A sense of land, of village, and base and family.

133

We're strongly rooted" (WET, 116). The entire community works on repairing the ravages of war and the earlier exploitation of nature, and the diversity of the gene pool is protected: "think of every patch of woods as a bank of wild genes. In your time thousands of species were disappearing. We need that wild genetic material to breed with" (WET, 265). For while a stable community is valued, change is accepted as a healthy given: "We're always changing things around. As they say, what isn't living dies" (WET, 64). Evil in this society is what goes against these values: "Power and greed – taking from other people their food, their liberty, their health, their land, their customs, their pride" (WET, 131). The good envisioned by all is best illustrated by the image of a mixed-media hologram produced by Bolivar:

> Two androgynes stood: one lithe with black skin and blue eyes and red hair, who bent down to touch with her/his hands the earth; the other, stocky, with light brown skin and black hair and brown eyes, spread his/her arms wide to the trees and sky and a hawk perched on the wrist.
>
> (WET, 173)

Such is the utopia of Mattapoisett developed by Piercy: democratic, anarchist, communist, environmentalist, feminist, non-racist – where freedom and responsibility are balanced in a steady-state economy and non-repressive value system. As Baruch notes,

> It is a world which keeps alive the spirit of play in adulthood. But it is also a world that allows its children to grow up. . . . Piercy's is a world that transcends the lust for power, whether over humans or things. The only power it seeks is power over the self.[6]

To be sure, elements in this utopia that mark it off from the others of its time are the use of extrauterine reproduction and the changes in the language, both revealing the radical feminist basis of Piercy's vision. Connie visits the "brooder," sees the fetuses each in their own sacs, and is understandably upset at this brave new world that has eliminated pregnancy and childbirth. Luciente explains in an argument that recalls Shulamith Firestone's argument for such a revolution in reproduction in her *Dialectic of Sex*:[7]

> It was part of women's long revolution. When we were breaking all the old hierarchies. Finally there was that one thing we had to give up too, the only power we ever had, in return for no more power for anyone. The original production: the power to give birth. 'Cause as long as we were biologically enchained, we'd never be equal. And males would never be humanized to be loving and tender. To break the nuclear bonding. (WET, 98)

If this new form of reproduction, with the attendant change of being able to adapt males for breast feeding so that all share everything, establishes equality at the beginning of life, a re-formed, non-sexist language continues to sustain such equality throughout life. *He* and *she* are replaced by the general pronoun *per*; *man* and *woman* by the general noun *person*. To sustain this change in the language, argued for by political and scholarly compatriots of Piercy's such as Nancy Henly, other changes in the language suggest the overall cultural change that had occurred by 2137. Words from telepathy have entered this language – *intersee, redding, inknowing, grasp* – as have words expressive of the life style and politics: *ownfed, suck patience, comothers, worming*. And some purely pleasurable slang has evolved from the culture: *feathers me fasure, painting the bones, running hard, barge on*, and *zo*. Language alone does not change reality, but it does sustain the reality one prefers. In the novel's dialogue Piercy shows the reader how this can work in the everyday life of a culture. The names of the people also accomplish this. Names are given to the newborn by the comothers, but chosen by the initiated after their ordeal and changed whenever one feels the need. Generally, the names come from two categories that also serve to sum up the overall vision of this utopia: nature – Jackrabbit, Dawn, Otter, Bee, Rose, Morningstar, Peony, Hawk, White Oak, Aspen, Orion, Blackfish, Corolla – and politics, primarily from the historical line of notable women or notable revolutionary nationalists and leftists of all ethnic groups – Diana, Sappho, Deborah, Sojourner, Susan B, Neruda, Sacco-Vanzetti, Luxembourg, Red Star, Bolivar, Tecumseh, Parra,

Selma, Crazy Horse. A few names come from Spanish: Luciente, Innocente, Magdalena. The reader gets a good sense of Piercy's sensibilities and ideological stance from these names, and such sensibility and stance is what informs her utopian vision.

Piercy, then, draws on history and everyday life for the material of her vision. She draws clues for the dream of utopia, as Nadia Khouri points out, from the "progressive historical continuity" (what Ernst Bloch terms the "red line of history"), from Third World and Native American cultures and from "subcultures of poverty." Those cultures not destroyed by mass culture maintain for their people "a powerful means of immediate gratification: a cultural identity, . . . a sense of community, a certain intensity of life, food, sex, the explosion of song, dance, play, contrasting sharply with the larger culture and its marginalizing influence."[8] Perhaps Connie puts it most simply when she observes the villagers: "They are not like Anglos; they were more like Chicanos or Puerto Ricans in the touching, the children in the middle of things, the feeling of community and fiesta" (WET, 119–20). To be sure, Piercy's utopia and Delany's are two that significantly incorporate anti-racist sensibilities and efforts into the utopian effort.

This utopia is a thriving community, but in the overall plot Mattapoisett is not an inevitable outcome of history. The science fictional gambit of time travel and Piercy's new left concept of the important role of human choice in the determination of the historical process within the material limits of the given situation combine to make Mattapoisett only one potential future among many. There are other possibilities: indeed Piercy devotes one chapter to a dystopian society, which Connie projects into as the possibility of Mattapoisett temporarily fades. In chapter 15, the reader encounters a totalitarian future in which the forces of phallocratic capitalism have remained dominant and produced a hierarchical society that is overpopulated, polluted, sexist, and racist. Rather than the lightbearer, Luciente, Connie meets Gildina, gold-covered, and again is a visitor in another land. Gildina 547-921-45-822-KB is a kept woman, who has been physically adapted to please the man in a way that recalls Chinese footbinding and other forms of mutilation of the female body by male society to establish and mark ownership and control. In this nightmare society, women are subservient to men: some eke out a living as one-nighters, some succeed with a longer contract. Those who can't make it, whether male or female, end up as "walking organ banks," selling off their body parts and dying at age forty, while the "richies" – Rockmellons, Morganfords, Duke-Ponts who can afford the transplants – live two hundred years. Furthermore, the richies live in space platforms to avoid the ravaged and polluted earth; while those of lower income levels have to be conditioned just to live in the polluted urban atmosphere. Here, in the other future, an Age of Uprising also occurred; here too the enemy lives on space platforms and fights with cyborgs. But here the enemy has won; plenty for all has been traded for luxury and long life for a few; the masses are used to run the social machinery and serve as surplus body parts and prostitutes for the rich. Furthermore, the masses are constantly monitored by security forces through implanted devices like those used on Connie and her friends. This dystopia is run by the "multis," the multinational corporations such as the "Chase-ITT" that have divided up the world and eliminated nation states and self-government.

Piercy's utopian and dystopian images provide contrasting symbolic resolutions of the contradictions in modern US society. Although she favors the utopian alternative, by describing both future societies she makes clear to the reader that the future is not a matter of inevitable victory for the oppressed of the world and that the present structures of power are immense and require careful, courageous, and collective work by all the forces of opposition to shape history in favor of the social revolution. Like those of the other writers, her utopia is an amalgam of values based on the principles of liberation, feminism, socialism, and ecological cooperation with nature. But this utopia is not a perfect system, for it is still subject to regressive behavior within its very human, and frail, ranks and to continuing attacks by the counter-revolutionary forces beyond its borders. Jealousy and murder, the temptation to centralize power and control nature technologically persist in utopia and must be countered by mechanisms of decentralized decision-making, criticism-self-criticism, and worming sessions, and even capital punishment if need be. And the external military threat creates the continued

137

need for universal, though voluntary, military service in the citizens' army and means that death and destruction are still a part of the reality of this struggling utopia. Piercy identifies the enemy as multinational capitalism, bureaucratic and military power, and male and white supremacy; and she stresses its power to disrupt utopia. Consequently she recognizes the need for utopian citizens to be vigilant and militant both internally and externally. Utopia could grow out of the victory of the allied oppositional forces, with the utopian impulse itself being a major motivating force in the commitment of those forces; or the dream could be crushed by the centralized power – ideological and military – of the present social formation. The outcome, as Piercy presents it, hinges not on the inevitability of material conditions or the innate goodness of powerful ideas but on human choice and engagement, on collective resistance, on the willed transformation of history by those subordinate to the present system.

Luciente and Connie/organizing and violence

The question of activism, the key ideological notion generated in the discrete register, is put quite directly by Piercy: social change requires not only a radical vision but also a radical practice so that history can be moved forward. In *Woman on the Edge of Time* the science fictional possibility of different possible time continua allows for the major conflict of the novel and establishes the context for the text's meditation on the necessary strategy and tactics for radical change. As one of the utopians haltingly explains to Connie, "at certain cruxes of history forces are in conflict. Technology is imbalanced. Too few have too much power. Alternate futures are equally or almost equally probable . . . and that affects the . . . shape of time" (WET, 189). Or, as Luciente puts it, Mattapoisett is "not inevitable grasp? Those of your time who fought hard for change, often they had myths that a revolution was inevitable. But nothing is! All things interlock. We are only one possible future" (WET, 189).

Connie lives in one of those historical conjunctures that could break the present open and set in motion events that will lead to either the blue skies of Mattapoisett or the yellow skies of New

York. Luciente in 2137 is at another crucial point wherein the revolution is on the verge of victory and could finally close out the possibility of these yellow skies. As developed in the discrete register, the plot turns on Luciente contacting and radicalizing Connie, to demonstrate qualities of a good political organizer, and Connie throwing off her victimhood and deciding to join in the revolution, to demonstrate the personal commitment that must occur whatever the persuasion of the organizer inspires. As Connie is told,

> you of your time. You individually may fail to understand us or to struggle in your own life and time. You of your time may fail to struggle together. . . . We must fight to come to exist, to remain in existence, to be the future that happens. That's why we reached you.   (WET, 189–90)

Thus, as Piercy sets up the situation: the revolution requires the praxis of both Luciente, struggling to keep utopia in existence and serving as an organizer, and Connie, struggling to pave the way of utopia and becoming a terrorist. Both women – actually versions of the same character with one being shaped by the violence of the present and the other being shaped by the nurturing of utopia – choose to help realize the future based on those principles of autonomy, feminism, and ecology shared by the various forces opposed to the status quo. The ideologeme common to the critical utopia in Piercy's novel is more radical, sharper, and less subject to cooptation than is the version that emerges from LeGuin's text, and closer in strategy and tactics to Russ's novel, although not separatist in its basic outlook.

Piercy describes the way to the alternative society of the utopian future as one paved by collective action, within which the activity of strong individuals is the essential element. The personal commitment that was the hallmark of the new left vision of the 1960s is at the heart of Piercy's ideological concern. As Luciente challenges Connie, so Piercy challenges her readers. The organizer wonders

> why it took so long for you lugs to get started? Grasp, it seems sometimes like you would put up with anything, anything at all, and pay for it through the teeth. How come

you took so long to get together and start fighting for what
was yours?   (WET, 169)

Luciente encourages Connie to get in touch with her experience
of victimization and her anger and to believe in herself and her
power to fight back. When Connie objects that she is a nobody
without power, Luciente replies:

> The powerful don't make revolutions. . . . It's the people
> who worked out the labor-and-land intensive farming we
> do. It's all the people who changed how people bought food,
> raised children, went to school . . . who made new unions,
> witheld rent, refused to go to wars, wrote and educated and
> made speeches.   (WET, 190)

Here, the variety of work engaged in by the activists of the 1960s
and after is recognized and presented in an alliance of opposition.
In the narrative gambit of differing time probabilities, the choices
that lead to either social revolution or male, white corporate
domination are made the central ideological concern of the
text.

Within this context of willed transformation, then, the actions
of both Luciente and Connie are key to the progress of the novel.
Luciente is a healthy and intelligent person nurtured by the free
and provident society of Mattapoisett. In the daily work of that
society, she is a plant geneticist who can develop new species that
either add to the ecological diversity of the natural environment
or serve to improve human existence further without damaging
nature. She shows off one of her products to Connie, a variety of
rose, named Diana after a former lover: "big, sturdy white with
dark red markings and an intense musk fragrance," popular in
Maine and New Hampshire because it is "subzero hardy" and a
good climber. Although Luciente has her own living space, she
also has two current lovers, "sweet friends": Bee, an older,
stocky, black male, who works in the brooder nurturing the
developing fetuses, and Jackrabbit, a 19-year-old male, who is an
artist but who in the course of the novel volunteers for military
duty and is killed in action. She has also parented two children,
Neruda and Dawn, and shared that parenting with two of her
best "hand friends," Morningstar and Otter.

Within the presentation of Mattapoisett society, Luciente provides a focus for the ongoing problems of utopian existence. At the personal level, Luciente becomes embroiled in jealousy as she and Bolivar, Jackrabbit's other regular lover, compete for Jackrabbit's attention. The tensions reach a level where the community's well-being is endangered and are dealt with in a communal worming wherein Luciente and Bolivar confront their conflicting feelings directly with the help of the insights and criticisms of their comrades. Whereas before the worming both were trying to diminish the other in Jackrabbit's eyes, afterward they are helped to meet together to work out their differences.

At the political level, Luciente is active in the "Shaping Controversy," the debate between differing factions of the community on appropriate uses of genetic technology. The Shapers want to intervene genetically in human development and to breed for selected traits; whereas the Mixers hold out for random genetic mixing since they claim that no one objectively knows how people should become and that the integrity of nature itself should be respected. The debate reaches the status of a "power surge" and thus must be resolved at grand council level and put to rest. Luciente, the geneticist, holds with the mixing position – as one would expect of Piercy's protagonist – and participates in hours and hours of meetings and debate on the issue. By the novel's end the controversy is not resolved, and the utopian project remains open and uncertain on this issue.

As the revolution continues its battle for survival, Luciente is selected to be the "sender" in the trans-temporal project of seeking out "catchers" such as Connie. This political task, at once physical and ideological, becomes Luciente's primary activity in the novel. She becomes the guide in the utopian narrative and the organizer in the political development of Connie. Thus, the utopian analog of Connie – who is similar in appearance to Connie, though slimmer and healthier, who has lovers who match Connie's young husband, Eddie, and old lover, Claud, who has a daughter the age of Connie's lost daughter Angelina, who is psychologically sensitive like Connie, and who has gone on to be a scientist as Connie might have in a more just society – is also the utopian inspiration for Connie to help create the very historical conditions in which such a utopian other could

141

develop. If Luciente is important in the novel as the major character of the utopian narrative and as Connie's guide and mentor, Connie is the central character of the entire novel, the visitor to utopia and the victim of the realist narrative whose final action is the very catalyst that enables – at the symbolic level of individual action – Mattapoisett and, thus, Luciente herself to exist in the future.

Piercy's plot works out of this pattern of mutual influence that spirals like a double helix beyond binary closure to a vision of historical progress wherein the establishment of utopia further opens out to the anticipated victory of the utopian forces, with key elements still unresolved such as the resolution of the shaping controversy and the continued healing of the world. The key to the spiral is Connie herself, and the nexus between Mattapoisett and Connie is her understanding of the historical process and her role in it. Connie learns

> that past, present, and future exist inside each individual and that each individual has to take responsibility for the future and act. Passivity leads to someone else shaping a future that may be lethal to all you hold sacred – such as human freedom.[9]

Connie chooses against "technology, in the service of those who control," and for insurgency (WET, 215).

The main plot of the novel, then, opens with Connie's freedom being denied once again as she is sent to the mental hospital for acting out against the society that oppresses her and her loved ones. Driven to the hospital, she is totally cut off from her life and descends into hell to be further reduced as a person and transformed into an experimental subject. Within this hell, however, are the seeds of her resistance and resurrection as a revolutionary fighter. Piercy's plot develops in a series of episodes in which Connie or one of her friends is defeated and then a utopian visit intervenes to build up her strength so she can fight back. The pattern repeats in a widening gyre until the conflict is escalated to a level of outright violence and counter-violence, to the institutionalizing of Connie after her assassination assignment, and the consequent establishment of the utopia.

With the novel narrated in the third person from Connie's

point of view, the reader follows Connie in her imprisonment, as she meets other patients, some of whom are old friends – such as Sybil, a proud and independent woman, a witch, and a fighter who has no place in mainstream society – and new friends – such as Skip, a young gay male who has been driven to insanity and eventually to his final act of resistance by suicide with an electric carving knife in his parents' kitchen by parents and officials who would not tolerate his "deviant" sexual preference. Slowly the sides line up, with Connie, Skip, Sybil, Alice Blue Bottom, Captain Cream, and other patients learning that the medical team – Dr Argent, Dr Redding, Dr Morgan, and others – are preparing them for an experiment in the control of the "socially violent." As the patients are moved to a special ward, they learn of the experiment to be performed on them. Headed by Dr Argent of the NYNPI – never spelled out, but New York Neuropsychiatric Institute fits – the project seeks to monitor patients by means of a sending device implanted in their brains that allows for computer-directed control of their behavior by direct stimulation of brain areas when the patient "acts out." Sybil sums it up: the goal is "Control. To turn us into machines so we obey them" (WET, 192). Social justice is replaced by social control: a profitable control because the implantation method would reduce social service costs by automating the supervision process. In this situation, Piercy describes the economic mechanisms wherein profits dominate social relations. As corporate greed and military expenditure reduce the financial resources available for the social wage that all in a society are entitled to, the state must respond by cutting back services and further dehumanizing its citizens by use of cybernetic technology that makes people less able to determine their own lives and the direction of society, rendering them passive in the face of corporate domination.

When the horrible implications of the new procedure sink in, the patients begin to object and resist. But the hegemonic power is on the side of the doctors, and one by one the patients fall prey to the knife and the electrode. However, Connie's visits to Mattapoisett – as visits to post-revolutionary societies such as China, Cuba, Mozambique, Poland, and Nicaragua inspire and inform many – enlighten her to the possibilities of collective resistance and a better social system. Strengthened mentally by her visits, she is trained in the skills of revolutionary struggle and recruited to the cause that affects the village of the future and the hospital ward of the present. Consequently, Connie's first act of resistance is escape, which she does with the help of Sybil and Luciente – a revolutionary female alliance of present and future, scientist and witch, that enables her to challenge the dominant power structure. Connie flees the hospital like a runaway slave of old. With "a big red star" shining overhead, she finds the North Star and "follows the drinking gourd" to what she hopes is freedom, but her few days of freedom are reduced to savored memories when she is spotted at a bus station and returned to the hospital to face her turn in the experiment.

Back in captivity, Connie sees that those who have been operated on can no longer resist: Alice found that when she tried to fight back, the monitor turned off her rage and left her confused. The doctors force a situation wherein Connie must act decisively before they get to her. Luciente encourages her: "You're important to us, we want you to survive and break out. One attempt, one failure – you have to take that for granted. What works the first time?" (WET, 254). Before she can act, however, the operation happens. After the operation, Connie, politicized and strengthened by her utopian connections, does not give up and declares her intent to escape again. At this point in the novel, the alternating moments of oppression and utopian interlude swing to one side as the forces of oppression dominate: Connie is implanted, Skip commits suicide, two others are implanted. And as these reactionary temporal vectors move ahead and influence the future, Connie's utopian friend Jackrabbit – a future version of Skip – dies in battle, the war against the enemy goes badly, and Connie loses contact with Mattapoisett and contacts the dystopia in New York instead. At this point negation dominates the dialectics of power.

The negation of the negation begins when Connie stays in a long trance, having gotten back in touch with the village and stayed on for Jackrabbit's funeral. "Her ability to stay in the future amazed her. They had been trying to rouse her since the evening before. This time, locked into Luciente, she had not even felt them. She watched the fuss through narrowed eyes. They were scared" (WET, 314). Savoring this "first victory," Connie begins to think how she can use the extra time to "scare them again," with Luciente's help. At this point the conflict in both the utopia and the world intensifies: Connie's next visit to the future finds her on the front lines in an airship piloted by the newly adult, 12-year-old Hawk. "Communing's been harder," Luciente tells her. "Something is interfering. Probability static? Temporal vectors are only primitively grasped" (WET, 316). Connie helps with the battle and receives encouragement in turn:

> Can I give you tactics? . . . . There's always a thing you can deny an oppressor, if only your allegiance. Your belief. Your co-oping. Often even with vastly unequal power, you can find or force an opening to fight back. In your time many without power found ways to fight. Till that became a power. (WET, 317)

And so Connie's final act of resistance begins to take shape. In a twilight vision between worlds, she sees all the "flacks of power who had pushed her back and turned her off and locked her up and medicated her and tranquilized her and punished her and condemned her" (WET, 325). In response to her second extended trance, the doctors panic. Fearing they have lost her, they remove the device from her head. Another victory. But now Connie knows more about the dynamics of the situation: "The war raged outside her body now, outside her skull, but the enemy would press on and violate her frontiers again as soon as they chose their next advance. She was at war. . . . No more fantasies, no more hopes. *War*" (WET, 326–7). Awake in the hospital, she tries to encourage the others, telling them that she is biding her time to see what she can do next to strike back. In response to Sybil's dreams of a better life, Connie asserts that "we can imagine all we like. But we got to do something real" (WET, 332). Utopia is useless unless one acts toward making it real.

On a visit to her brother's suburban home over Thanksgiving weekend – the reward for her "good behavior" – Connie decides against further escape and opts for violent direct action. She prepares for her final act in the novel: to assassinate the medical team by poisoning their morning coffee – taking the revolution to the realm of everyday life. She steals the most deadly pesticide from her brother's plant nursery, pouring Parathion into a small bottle to smuggle back into the hospital: "this was a weapon, a powerful weapon that came from the same place as the electrodes and the Thorazine and the dialytrode. One of the weapons of the powerful, of those who controlled" (WET, 351). Connie has "grabbed at power" so that she can fight back, for herself and her comrades.

When she next contacts Luciente she learns that the former battle scene never occurred: "Not in my life, Connie, not in this continuum," Luciente tells her (WET, 356). Connie's resolve has already affected the temporal vectors, shifting them back in a radical direction, and she goes on to discuss with Luciente her plot to poison the team's coffee. In doing so she voices her reservations about the violence she is about to commit, but Luciente reassures her: "power *is* violence. When did it get destroyed peacefully? We all fight when we're back to the wall – or to tear down a wall" (WET, 359). Unashamed after the poisoning, Connie hardens her mind, cuts herself off from Mattapoisett, and prepares for her punishment after killing four of the six members of the team.

The last chapter of the text is titled "Excerpts from the Official History of Connie Ramos," and it details Connie's continued treatment as a "socially violent" person at Rockover State Hospital. Her life goes on as a prisoner of the state. Though she has succeeded in her guerilla action, she now faces confinement in the state hospital, doped up on Thorazine or worse, for the rest of her life. The realist text ends bleakly for Connie as an individual, but it also ends with victory for the utopian forces in the long run.

The ideological message of *Woman on the Edge of Time* is that of the need for an alliance of those seeking human emancipation informed by a feminist, socialist, ecological, libertarian, and liberation politics. It calls for collective action and cooperation among all movements in the broad oppositional left: women, gays and lesbians, members of racial, ethnic or national groups, workers, neighborhood organizers, mental health and education reformers, anti-nuclear/anti-military/anti-intervention activists, radical ecologists, and others in the diverse lot opposed to the dominant system. The organization and practices of the society in Mattapoisett and the variety of individuals involved in the struggle both in the utopia and among the hospital patients sum up this anti-hegemonic alliance. Furthermore, the activities of Luciente and Connie, while they stress the commitment and courage of individuals, do not valorize the power of isolated heroism or leadership as much as they identify the importance of personal engagement within a collective effort. For neither Luciente nor Connie acts as a solitary change agent; rather, they carry out their particular contributions as parts of an overall effort involving many types of people and a variety of actions.

If collective/alliance politics are the strategic element of the picture of activism that emerges in the novel, the tactics emphasized are basically three: *service and personal development* – as imaged in the life and work of the utopians as they carry on daily life in Mattapoisett; *ideological and political struggle* – as imaged in Luciente's explanation of the historical situation to Connie and in the support and training she gives to Connie, but also in Connie's work with the other patients, in Bolivar's art, in the debates on the Shaping Controversy carried out in the grand council, and, indeed, in the way that the history of revolution is kept alive in the culture of Mattapoisett; and finally *armed struggle* – as imaged both in the military action that the utopians wage against the cyborgs and in the sabotage and assassination carried out by Connie. Although Connie's action is at the center of the novel and receives the most emphasis – a situation no doubt influenced by Piercy's sympathy for the tactics of urban guerilla actions taken by the Weathermen and by Third World liberation groups – the revolutionary violence has to be read within the overall context of an opposition movement that also includes the service/personal and ideological/political elements as equally necessary in defeating the power of the hegemonic forces and developing the ideas and practices of the revolution. Certainly many readers might find Connie's action hard to take and might prefer that social change would come about more by way of the sort of non-violent speaking and scholarship that Shevek carries on, but Piercy's plot reminds readers that the processes of radical change are complex and occur in the face of a violent power structure.

However, what is most important in Piercy's concern with activism is the basic connection between personal action and historical change itself. The revolution is not inevitable. It is a process of change that may require appropriate conditions and happen more readily at particular historical moments, but it will not happen at all without personal commitment and struggle. As Connie's action and the many names of past revolutionary activists preserved in Mattapoisett society indicate, the actions of each person throughout the years count in the never-ending process of social revolution. The future is never certain. Utopia is never fixed once and for all. Without the activism that Piercy advocates, drawn from the practice of the movements throughout the world in the 1960s, the revolution will not come about. Without that activism, the ongoing process of human emancipation will give way to forces that seek to employ human activity for a system based on profit and order rather than on justice and freedom. That message of personal activism within collective unity, sometimes requiring great sacrifice and violence, then, is at the heart of the oppositional ideology of Piercy's novel.

Generic battles: utopia, dystopia, and realism

The literary form of *Woman on the Edge of Time* conveys a similar message of activism that Piercy develops in the images of daily life in Mattapoisett and in Connie's resistance within the hospital. Just as the content of the novel reveals the power of the utopian impulse to defeat the dominant powers of the real world – whether they are the cyborg army of the multinationals or the doctors of the state mental hospital – so too the utopian form of the novel breaks through the limits traditionally imposed by the narrative forms of literary realism or dystopian fiction. The oppositional ideology of this critical utopian form is one of combative engagement with those literary practices that, in the twentieth century at least, have tended to reinforce the ideological claim that a social alternative to what currently exists is impossible. The isolated literary genres caught within the present limits of the dominant mode of production and its attendant culture are, therefore, set free and re-engaged in a radical literary practice that artistically anticipates a new social formation. In Piercy's novel, the primary conflict is between the realist narrative which carries the account of Connie's experience in the hospital and the utopian narrative which gives us Mattapoisett, but there is also a contest between the utopian and dystopian narratives. Furthermore, the utopian narrative itself is one which is self-reflexive and thus able to comment on the traditional limits of utopian writing.

The novel begins in the realist mode set in modern day New York, but the subversion of the present by the utopian dream occurs in the second sentence of the first chapter as Connie thinks to herself, "Either I saw him or I didn't and I'm crazy for real this time" (WET, 1). Here, the basic tension between the power of the state which maintains that Connie is crazy and the utopia which liberates her is established. The stage is set for the defeat of the imposed "realism" of the status quo by the utopianism of the anti-hegemonic forces. While the narrative initially appears to be in a realist mode, the science fictional and utopian mechanisms of alternative reality and willed transformation immediately begin to subvert the text. Although the first two chapters are mainly concerned with Connie's battle with Geraldo and her re-commitment to Bellevue, an account worthy of any gritty realist text, the hints of utopia – fleeting images of Luciente, a warm chair, queasy feelings – promise a deeper confrontation that begins when Luciente establishes contact with Connie in chapter 3. By that point, the narrative power of realism has been given its due and Connie's victimization by the sort of unbeatable institution portrayed in novels such as *One Flew Over the Cuckoo's Nest* is well established. At the onset of this novel, we seem to be off on yet one more tale of victims and defeat; however, Piercy sets this up only to give the liberating power of utopia more impact when it does arrive. For Connie is not crazy and is not defeated: utopia exists and helps her to assassinate the doctors who victimize her and others. Connie is not one more realist protagonist who, bound by the limitations of the world as the reader knows it, must be done in by an overpowering system. Instead, given new narrative opportunities by the generic powers of utopian and science fiction, she can change from victim to activist. Empowered by the utopia, she turns the tables on those professionals who tell us all to stop complaining and dreaming and to adjust to the world as it is – that is, to serve the system and shut up.

By using an apparently realist form, Piercy first of all challenges that form from within its own generic limits by creating a protagonist who fights back, even within the limits of the "real world." Connie, a strong female protagonist, can be seen as a powerful figure in her own time in her escapes from the doctors' power, in her encouragement to the other patients, and in her direct resistance to the imposed treatment – similar to McMurphy's resistance in Kesey's novel. But Piercy takes the protagonist a step further than Kesey did with his male Christ-like hero and allows Connie to succeed in the poisoning even though she is then condemned to life imprisonment in the hospital. That is, even if the novel were simply a realist novel, it would be anti-hegemonic in its strong female hero who resists victimization and successfully fights back, winning not in terms of the present social system but in terms of the revolutionary effort to overthrow that system.

However, Piercy is not content with that limited literary strategy. She challenges realism, in all its associations with things as they are and "must be," from outside the limits of the genre by attacking with the fantasizing power of utopian science fiction. In the fantastic mode, Piercy can break the rules of the historical situation and posit a future society with the power to reach back in time and help one of our society's victims fight back and thereby ensure the survival of utopia. Thus, even though the last chapter of the novel is a harshly "realistic" summary of Connie's hospital record, implying her continued incarceration, the overall utopian form of the novel reveals the limits of that realistic report and places the entire text against the last chapter, asserting the power of utopian discourse to deconstruct reality as we know it and to motivate literary texts as well as real people so that they refuse the world as it is and fight for a better one. As with Russ, the weapon of the utopian impulse is contributed by Piercy to the oppositional forces of her time; indeed, she does so without the ambiguity and restraint that compromises LeGuin's novel. Piercy's work is clearly more tendentious and angry and much less willing to let the present culture retain control over the utopian impulse. It is the practice of utopian discourse itself that *Woman on the Edge of Time* ultimately celebrates. It is not the system of utopian society as seen in the admittedly exciting images of life in Mattapoisett that reveals the power of utopia but rather the impact of utopian dreams and experience on the protagonist that is the primary utopian mechanism in the text. The power of dreams to help change the historical current is the key formal message that joins with the similar message of both the ideologeme and the iconic images of the novel.

Furthermore, Piercy is not content simply to defeat the cooptation of literary realism by the dominant culture. She also goes after the dystopian form in so far as it implies that the only alternative to the present bad situation is a worse situation – a suggestion to readers that they take things as they are and not make them worse by useless revolutionary efforts, for then the repression would only be greater. The infamous chapter 15 in which Connie's dystopian analog, Gildina, describes life in a totally repressive and polluted New York under the complete control of the multinationals is as good a dystopian image as one might expect and holds its own with the writing of Huxley, Orwell, and Zamyatin. Again, rather than accept a bleak future or counsel inaction, Piercy's novel serves to defeat the one-dimensional negativity of the dystopia by articulating Connie's utopian-supported action. In poisoning the doctors and thereby sending revolutionary vectors forward in time, Connie assures that Luciente's world, not Gildina's, is the one that will prevail. Dystopia is reduced to a bad moment in the long red line of history, and the hold that the dystopian narrative has had on the genre of utopian writing in the twentieth century is seriously weakened by Piercy's narrative contest between the two forms. This time, at least, the dream defeats the nightmare.

Piercy, however, does not just employ utopia against realism and dystopian fiction and celebrate utopia in a non-critical fashion. As one of the important writers who revived utopian fiction in the 1970s, she is aware of the limitations of the genre itself: its tendency to reduce alternative visions to closed and boring perfect systems that negate the utopian impulse that generated them; as well as its cooptation by the marketing and socialization mechanisms of contemporary industrial societies. Like Russ and LeGuin, she makes sure to express the limits and problems that continue within the utopian system and utopian discourse. In her own text she uses the radical potential of utopian discourse for the emerging opposition to the present social systems.

151

Some of Piercy's commentary on the limits of utopian fulfillment comes from Connie as she reacts to life in Mattapoisett.
Echoing Engels's doubts about the efficacy of literary utopias,
Connie questions the gap between utopia and history: "What
could a man of this ridiculous Podunk future, when babies were
born from machines and people negotiated diplomatically with
cows, know about how it has been to grow up in America black or
brown?" (WET, 97). Furthermore, she observes that life is still far
from perfect in this society: "you still go crazy. You still get sick.
You grow old. You die. I thought in a hundred and fifty years
some of these problems would be solved, anyhow!" (WET, 118).
With Connie's doubts, Piercy avoids a simplistic, élitist image
of utopian perfection and links utopia more closely with the
uncertainties of history.

The antagonisms that persist in utopian life are further revealed
in the controversies that occur in Mattapoisett. At the personal
level, the jealousy between Luciente and Bolivar demonstrates the
continuing problems of insecurity and love encountered by
humanity even in the best of all possible worlds. The only
difference is that in Mattapoisett people have become more aware
of conflicts and have worked out social mechanisms to deal with
them within a more nurturing social fabric. Thus utopia is seen to
help the human situation but not to perfect it out of existence. At
the political level, the continuing war against the enemy and the
Shaping Controversy demonstrate the fragility of any better
society which attempts to improve the human condition. Both
situations indicate the possibility that a revolutionary society can
be defeated by external attack or by return of misplaced power
within its borders.

These narrative gambits serve to deny the former assumed
simplicity and totalizing tendency of utopian visions and help to
create a more realistic utopia that is more palatable to the
demanding, and jaded, reader of the 1970s and 1980s. The
resulting images make clear that any utopian alternative in this
world must fight for its existence and will continue to experience
problems and contradictions; for history is a process of contradictions that continues even after the most destructive situations
have ended.

The novel approaches self-reflexivity when in the worming

scene Luciente expresses her jealousy toward Bolivar by criticizing his art. Luciente describes Bolivar's holi as too individualistic and politically thin. She expects art to be more tendentious, getting at the deep political and economic sources of the destruction of so much of humanity and nature. Bolivar, on the other hand, defends his work by arguing that "the culture as a whole must speak the whole truth. But every object can't!" (WET, 203). He characterizes Luciente's view as a "slogan mentality . . . as if there were certain holy words that must always be named" (WET, 203). "Sometimes an image radiates many possible truths," Bolivar argues, "Luciente appears to fix too narrowly on content and apply our common politics too rigidly" (WET, 203). Here, of course, is the continuing debate about the politics of art: content against form, rational critique against non-rational insight, political correctness against artistic freedom, tendentious against more indirect but perhaps more broadly acceptable art. Neither side "wins" the debate. Both are encouraged to understand each other's point of view. Piercy thus opts for a dialectical unity of the two positions, avoiding the extremes of political hack and individualistic indulgence. The novel appears to express this unity of opposites as it seeks to be both politically engaged and aesthetically multi-dimensional. However, since Luciente is a major character second only to Connie, her comments in the structure of the text tend to carry more weight than do those of the minor character, Bolivar, and the political assertiveness of the novel itself seems to tip the balance in the direction of Luciente's position. To be sure, *Woman on the Edge of Time* is a tendentious work, uncompromising in its political assessment and alternatives, its angry tone, its direct assault on a very undisguised phallocratic/bureaucratic capitalism, and its firm commitment to armed struggle.

Perhaps the most directly self-reflexive commentary in the novel is the connection between Connie's telepathic empathy and dreams and the "actual" utopian society and its political fight. The connection between utopia and the life of this apparent victim of the present system is an assertion on Piercy's part of the beneficial effect that such dreaming, the utopian impulse as Bloch and Marcuse and others have described it, can have both on a single personal life and on history itself. In the first chapter,

Connie dreams of a better life wherein she and Dolly and Dolly's daughter could live together in comfort and peace. Even though it is just a dream in the face of actual poverty, racism, sexism, and violence, Connie values the role of such fantasy in her life: "That she knew in her heart of ashes the dream was futile did not make it less precious. Every soul needs a little sweetness" (WET, 8). Piercy connects this ability to indulge in "futile" dreams with Luciente's visit and implies that dreams do demonstrate what does not yet exist and move us beyond the insufficiency of the present. Piercy reproduces within the novel the way that the hegemonic system makes each of us doubt ourselves in our dreams and perceptions. She then attacks that imposed doubt by demonstrating the liberating power of utopian dreams, especially when they join with those of others. In the content of the book, then, she demonstrates the power of the form. In the form itself, she releases the power of the unsatisfied utopian desire from its cooptation by affirmative consumer culture and sets it free to participate in the movement toward a new society that goes beyond white, male, bureaucratic, corporate power.

Woman on the Edge of Time, then, develops an image of utopia that draws on many presently subordinate cultures, on the insights of ecology and appropriate technology, on the theory and practice of feminism and overall human liberation, on the democratic anarchist and socialist tradition, and on the grassroots work by the new left in many issue-oriented movements from school and mental health reform to cooperatives and local decision-making. She describes a collective activism that preserves the importance of the individual person. However, it is an activism that involves more risk and destruction than the travelling and negotiations of a Shevek do, as well as one that leads to a revolutionary new society rather than separatism or compromising détente. The form of the novel is itself an expression of the radical power of the utopian impulse to cut through the cooptation and denial of desire in the present dominated by white male discourse and power and by hierarchy and control in the service of profit. Though less concerned with separatism and less formally experimental than *The Female Man*, Piercy's novel shares a radical vision with that novel which goes beyond the more compromising text of LeGuin's. Both Russ and Piercy see less hope in the present situation and more in the emerging power of subordinate people.

Piercy's juxtaposition of realism and utopia, as well as her revival of dystopian writing, enlists all these forms, and the utopian impulse itself, as material forces in the ongoing conflict of history. She establishes a dialectical connection between consciousness raising and the historical situation that carries out the dynamic of power relations and social change within the literary operations of the utopian text. In both content and form, Piercy asserts the power of desire as a mechanism of the collective human subject that cannot be totally denied or coopted, as an anticipation and practice of what could be as the current historical situation is negated. Piercy does not assert utopia, she activates it.

7 Samuel R. Delany, *Triton*

> Even if we have discovered the form of a micro-flaw common to every element of our thinking, to think we have necessarily discovered the form of a macro-flaw in our larger mental structures – say our politics – is simply to fall victim to a micro-flaw again. This is not to say that macro-flaws may not relate to the micro-flaws – they usually do – but it is a mistake to assume that relation is direct and necessarily subsumed by the same verbal model.
>
> (Ashima Slade, in *Triton*)

Whereas Marge Piercy's *Woman on the Edge of Time* takes the critical utopia to the barricades, Samuel R. Delany's *Triton* takes it through a black hole in the universe of generic possibilities. In doing so, he destroys traditional utopia, preserves the impulse of the utopian dream, and creates the heterotopia. To be sure, Russ's *The Female Man* and LeGuin's *The Dispossessed* influenced his work on *Triton*, and Delany's "ambiguous heterotopia" can be read as a response to both works. That response, however, carries the critical utopia far beyond the confines of the traditional utopian genre, producing a text that confronts the

156

complexity of modern life and the potential for human emancipation in such a way that the utopian impulse toward a better life is kept alive without the static support of the familiar systematic utopia.

Triton was written in three months after the completion of Delany's massive *Dhalgren*, which he spent five years writing.[1] The work benefits not only from the critical utopias of Russ and LeGuin but also from his own work in science fiction and in literary theory. From his earliest books, Delany has been concerned with the sign systems and social structures in which humanity lives and which humanity tries to manipulate to accomplish its many purposes. Language, clothing, the social codes of various subcultures from élite ruling classes to dockside mariners, life in the streets and alleys of urban centers, music, poetry, games, sexuality, dinner parties, and many other aspects of daily life have all been dealt with in works like *Babel-17*, *The Ballad of Beta-2*, and *Nova*.

Delany has also focused on the individual not only in surviving but also in shaping life within as well as breaking beyond such systems: in *Empire Star* and *The Einstein Intersection*, and the titles mentioned above, he considers the efforts of poets, musicians, writers, criminals, shepherds, spaceship captains, heirs of fortunes, and down-and-out dock rats to intervene in the flow of existence. And he has been concerned with the nature and operation of linguistic discourse, the creative process, and the literary text itself: witness the battle by musical chords in *The Fall of the Towers*, the function of language in *Babel-17*, the non-linear narrative of *Einstein Intersection*, the exploration of myth and sign systems in *Nova*, the exploration of the narrative process and the textual web in *Dhalgren*, and the exploration of language, writing, and social systems in the later novels, *Nevèryön*, *Neveryóna*, and *Flight from Nevèryön*. These concerns are also developed in his analysis of a Thomas Disch short story in *The American Shore*, his collected essays in *The Jewel-Hinged Jaw* and *Starboard Wine* and his theoretical observations in the continuing "Some Informal Remarks toward the Modular Calculus" found in several of his works. Delany is a self-reflexive writer who brought all these topics to his venture into utopian writing: the iconic concern with social system, the discrete con-

157

cern with subjectivity and social change, and the formal concern with the writing process itself.[2]

Delany comments directly on the potential of the fantastic genres in an essay published in November 1970 in *Quark*, a quarterly of speculative fiction, which he and Marilyn Hacker edited from 1970 to 1971. In "Critical Methods: Speculative Fiction," he speaks of the "web of influence" which affects a genre like science fiction in such a complex way that one cannot trace a direct line of development from one work to the next but rather must be aware of the multiplicity of influences that come from within or without that generic tradition to expand its possibilities. Science fiction is a modern genre, rooted in humanity's concern with its technology in the complex process of history. However, Delany argues that science fiction is closer to poetry than to the novel in this concern with "thingness," for it shares with poetry an "incantatory function" which names hitherto unnamed things and invests them with reality in an alternative landscape and way of knowing the world. From the original concern, emphasis on technology itself, the genre moved to consider "the ways in which these objects might affect behavior."[3] Indeed, the influential pulp magazine editor, John Campbell, urged his writers, as Delany describes it, "to make the focus of the stories the juncture between the object and the behavior it causes," that is, in our present terminology, between the iconic and discrete registers.[4] Science fiction developed from these root tendencies into the complex and plastic web of generic possibilities that it is today:

> By much the same process that poetry expanded beyond its beginnings in ritualistic chant and incantation, to become a way to paint all that is human, and etch much that is divine, so SF become able to reflect, focus, and diffract the relations between man and his universe, as it included other men, as it included all that man could create, all he could conceive.[5]

As a privileged literary form for this century, this fantastic genre is "a way of casting a language shadow over coherent areas of imaginative space that would otherwise be largely inaccessible" to older generic forms.[6]

Within the web of possibilities of science fiction, Delany identifies the "terribly limiting argument" of "Victorian" utopian fiction and its twentieth century counterpart, dystopian fiction. As Delany sees it, the limitation of the traditional utopian genre is this: "'Regard this new society. You say it's good, but I say it's bad.' Or, 'You say it's bad, but I say it's good.'"[7] This unmediated binary opposition between good and evil society, Delany argues by quoting Auden, is not a logical division at all but merely a split in temperaments. On one hand, there are those who see hope in progress, the New Jerusalem utopia:

> In New Jerusalem, hunger and disease have been abolished through science, man is free of drudgery and pain, and from it he can explore any aspect of the physical world in any way he wishes, assured that he has the power to best it should nature demand a contest.[8]

At the polar opposite, there are those who wish to return to Eden, the Arcadia:

> In Arcadia, food is grown by individual farmers and technology never progresses beyond what one man can make with his own hands. Man is at one with nature, who strengthens him for his explorations of the inner life; thus all that he creates will be in natural good taste; and good will and camaraderie govern his relation with his fellow.[9]

The final argument for either viewpoint, he alleges, simply asserts the single preferred environment: the opposition is therefore static, between two, mutually exclusive, totalities.

Having established this dichotomy, Delany asserts that modern science fiction has gone beyond this unreconcilable conflict "to produce a more fruitful model against which to compare human development."[10] Beginning with the writers working under *Astounding* editor John Campbell in the 1940s, science fiction authors began to "cluster their new and wonderful objects into the same story, or novel. And whole new systems and syndromes of behavior began to emerge . . . where an ordered sarabande of wonders reflect and complement each other till they have produced a completely new world."[11] With these new worlds, the static oppositions of utopian fictions are surpassed, and a multiplex vision of both the possibilities and dangers of emerging society are explored without simplistic condemnation or praise. Science fiction, then, is an emancipatory literature, not through obligatory happy endings or cosmic disasters, but rather

> through the breadth of vision it affords through the complexed interweave of these multiple visions of man's origins and his destinations. Certainly such breadth of vision does not abolish tragedy. But it does make a little rarer the particular needless tragedy that comes from a certain type of narrow-mindedness.[12]

In this key essay lies the basis for Delany's rejection of utopia as a useful generic strategy for the mid-twentieth century. Consequently, science fiction, particularly that variety open to literary experiment as well as social theory, becomes the genre to work in if authentic dreams that exceed present limits are still to be expressed in print. However, the 1970s was a time when writers drew on the complex tendencies of affluence and rebellion of the 1960s and revived utopian writing as one way to articulate the revived dreams and raised expectations of those in opposition to the status quo of phallocratic corporate society. Having rejected a simple utopian/dystopian strategy, how was Delany to write a critical utopia? His answer was the "heterotopia," a term borrowed from Michel Foucault's *The Order of Things*. He quotes Foucault at the beginning of "Appendix B" of *Triton*:

> *Utopias* afford consolation: although they have no real locality there is nevertheless a fantastic, untroubled region in which they are able to unfold; they open up cities with vast avenues, superbly planted gardens, countries where life is easy, even though the road to them is chimerical. *Heterotopias* are disturbing, probably because they make it impossible to name this *and* that, because they shatter or tangle common names, because they destroy "syntax" in advance, and not only the syntax with which we construct sentences but also that less apparent syntax which causes words and things (next to and also opposite one another) to "hold together." This is why utopias permit fables and discourse: they run with the very grain of language and are part of the fundamental *fabula*; heterotopias . . . desiccate

160

speech, stop words in their tracks, contest the very possibility of grammar at its source: they dissolve our myths and sterilize the lyricism of our sentences.[13]

Delany's "heterotopia" captures the spirit of the critical utopia without becoming trapped in the drawbacks of traditional utopian writing. In *Triton*, he pushes utopia beyond itself, saving it from cooptation and limitation, ultimately carrying the utopian impulse out of the trap of bourgeois culture in which it has languished since Thomas More. In short, the heterotopia is to post-capitalist, post-modern, post-Englightenment, post-industrial society as utopia was to capitalist, bourgeois society: it preserves the utopian impulse, releases it from the traditional utopian genre, and stakes out the terrain of a radically new development in that particular discourse where our dreams and our fictions intersect.

In *Triton*, then, Delany creates iconic images of a better society and a discrete narrative of the ways in which this society is achieved and lived in, but he does so in a self-reflexive text that takes the reader beyond the limits of the traditional utopia or the realist novel. Here, then, we are back to the comments by Hacker on the ability of a science fiction text to overcome the restrictions of realism by means of shifting the ground of the text, the landscape, and episteme generated in the iconic register, to new worlds in which new lives could happen. As a science fiction text, *Triton* accomplishes this and shatters the static totalities of traditional utopias by shifting from an assertion of a perfect system to an exploration of the utopian impulse itself, especially in the "post-revolutionary" interaction between utopian society and the people who live in it.

As in *The Dispossessed*, a libertarian and egalitarian society on a peripheral moon is engaged in conflict with its still repressive, metropolitan home worlds. As in *The Female Man*, the steps taken by people to preserve that utopia are described, though in much less detail. However, the narrative goes on to explore the failure of some people successfully to live and thrive in this utopian alternative. Unlike the previous three critical utopias, the impact of the revolutionary person on the establishment and/or survival of utopia is not of central importance; rather, in *Triton*,

161

the emphasis is on the impact of the revolutionary system on the individual. Utopian society, utopian activists, and the utopian form are all decentered in this heterotopian text so that the limits of the genre can be broken through and a more radical, disruptive, open impulse toward the not yet can be valorized.

The contradictions of our present historical situation – especially as society moves into a post-capitalist, post-industrial, post-scarcity potential which could either enclose human activity and nature within a world-wide structure of production, consumption, and control in the hands of a few élite corporations or open up the possibility of human fulfillment and natural renewal in a just and liberating world – are symbolically opposed in *Triton* in the war between the old corrupt worlds of Earth and Mars and the moons from Jupiter outward on which new societies are located.

In the iconic register, one of those alternative societies, Triton, on the moon of Neptune, is described in customary utopian detail. However, this text has also abandoned utopian guides and orderly tours. In a further break from traditional utopia, the alternative society comes to the reader by way of the experiences of one of its unhappy and unreasonable residents, Bron Helstrom, a misfit in utopia. The utopian society is filtered through a negative lens as Bron misunderstands, misuses, and fails to adjust to life on Triton. As in the other critical utopias, the non-utopian societies are also presented in the iconic register, although again in much less detail: Earth is seen as a wasteland of ecological and human destruction, with most of its major population centers destroyed – whether by nuclear or other holocaust is unclear; while Mars is seen in terms of its main city Bellona, whose "red light district" named "Goebbels" sums up the capitalist/ fascist ambience of this other world. Both metropolises, former centers of human civilization, are fighting for control over the revolutionary margin of satellites which have succeeded in no longer being colonies or neo-colonies of their home worlds. Indeed, the major conflict between worlds and moons is the war for economic hegemony and for the preservation of the libertarian societies achieved by the "utopian" Outer Satellite Federation. Here the emerging potentials and conflicts of our time are set forth in conflicting images of old and new, center and periphery, oppressive and emancipatory systems.

This historical conflict is sharpened in the discrete register as the activism needed to preserve these post-revolutionary societies is described. However, the ideological expression of opposition is, like the image of the utopian society, decentered and articulated in the actions of the minor characters, primarily Sam, the one political operative in the novel, and secondarily in the opinions expressed by some of the other characters, especially The Spike and Lawrence. Indeed, the ideologeme of activism appears quite effaced in *Triton* as the principal narrative line belongs to the misadventures of Bron, the un-political anti-hero, who rather than helping to achieve or preserve the alternative of Triton resists it and remains a damaged self, a male supremacist and solipsist, unable to get beyond his early socialization on Mars. Activism in this novel is primarily dealt with in its negative, in the misfit man from Mars who fails to rise to his full potential in utopia and who indeed brings out the worst in this imperfect best of all possible worlds. Thus, in this analysis of the ideological expression of the activism, we encounter two dimensions: a personal one which is concerned with the lack of activism and which casts light on the flaws in utopia, and a political one which is concerned with the waging of a war for the very survival of utopia. Further, the complex connection between the personal and political becomes a central item of interest at this level of the reading.

With the utopian images and the ideologeme of activism already set to the side of the stage and with the matter of the realist novel – that is of a dangling anti-hero immersed in his male identity crisis at the center – the formal break with the traditional utopia in *Triton* is already quite clear. This move from consoling utopia to disruptive heterotopia is furthered by the way in which the iconic and discrete elements are developed and in the language used to challenge the reader and move her or him beyond their present limited perceptions. The opening up of the utopian impulse is also achieved in the self-reflexive elements of the text, primarily those found in the "Appendices," the "Work Notes and Omitted Pages," and the "Ashima Slade Lectures." By the end of this novel, then, traditional utopia is put to rest and the utopian impulse preserved and revived in this subversive and oppositional text that pushes the transformed genre of the critical utopia to its own limits.

Utopian lunacy, mundane insanity

The utopian society in *Triton* is the least obvious of the critical utopias we have examined. To be sure, Delany's notion of heterotopia is the major reason for this tempering of utopia so that it appears as a realistic and complex alternative rather than an unreachable heaven. Delany is not interested in utopian consolation or in clearly drawn conflicts between absolute good and evil; therefore, this social alternative is described from the distancing point of view of the non-utopian eyes and experiences of Bron. Furthermore, it is presented as the historical result of a social evolution from the corruption and oppression of the old worlds. It is a complex and living society with grimy, littered streets, strange religious sects, the destruction and death of war, and the persistence of unhappy individuals whose lives do not fully correspond with the intention of the utopian society to improve the lot of all humanity. When seen in contrast to Earth and Mars, the utopian society is quite egalitarian and free, but it is not statically perfect. Indeed, it is particularly in the dynamism that resists perfection and keeps human existence radically open even in a better place that the utopian impulse is preserved and extended in the iconic register – thus taking that impulse far beyond its limitation within the traditional utopia or within the ephemeral delights offered in our present market society.

In *Triton*, the alternative societies of the Outer Satellite Federation are located on the twenty or so moons of the larger planets from Jupiter to Pluto. Each of these enclosed city-states is an autonomous political entity yet part of the larger federation – for example, when the war begins each moon must vote whether to enter the hostilities or not, and Triton is one of the last to do so. These post-revolutionary societies, none over a hundred years old, are voluntaristic and "politically low-volatile." Economic, sexual, and philosophical oppression have all been eliminated: consequently, each person is free to be or do whatever she or he wants. Indeed, "pleasure, community, respect" are available to

164

everyone, along with the implicit trust that no one will "do anything *too* stupid" (see T, 116, 122, 148). The settlement on Triton, the moon of Neptune, is 75 years old. The major city, Tethys, is enclosed within a kilometer-high gravity and sensory shield that protects the residents from the thin atmosphere on the moon and shields them "from the reality of night" with "interpenetrating pastel mists" (T, 9 and 37). This most urban of all the critical utopias is given its ambience in such phrases as the "cindery plates" of the walkways, "air convection" breezes, "greenlit tiles," and walls covered with chalk, paint, and palimpsests of torn posters. The urban units of living accommodation, shops, and eating and drinking facilities are demarcated by large walkways, underpasses, dark alleys, and bright plazas and parks.

With a fully automated, cybernetic technology that handles most of the production, distribution, and services of the society, the economy of the satellites is highly efficient, requiring few human workers while it provides abundance for all. The Federation owns and administers most sectors of the economy – with "hegemonies" replacing the private corporation, as in the "computer hegemony" that Bron works for. A few sectors, such as the postal service, are left to "private cooperatives." In this post-industrial, post-scarcity, state-owned but mixed economy, a guaranteed level of maintenance – in food, shelter, clothing, education, health care, and transportation – is available to every citizen without taxation. However, jobs for the few who design programs, troubleshoot, provide services, or work for the government result in higher credit slots. Thus, some people working the average week of twenty hours can afford housing, services, and goods beyond the basic, and very sufficient, minimum given to all. When anyone uses goods or services, their account is directly charged, via the computer, in this moneyless system. For those who are not working, about one-fifth of the population, state-supplied credit is automatic: "if you don't have labor-credit, your tokens automatically and immediately put it on the state bill" (T, 171). Because of the efficient computer network and the commitment to the freedom and well-being of every person, the costs of the social wage are kept low and the familiar social service bureaucracy is eliminated:

> Our very efficient system costs one-tenth per person to
> support as your cheapest, national, inefficient and totally
> inadequate system here [on Earth]. Our only costs for
> housing and feeding a person on welfare is the cost of the
> food and rent itself, which is kept track against the state's
> credit by the same computer system that keeps track of
> everyone else's purchases against his or her own labor
> credit. In the Satellites, it actually costs minimally *less* to
> feed and house a person on welfare than it does to feed
> and house someone living at the same credit standard
> who's working because the bookkeeping is minimally less
> complicated. (T, 179)

Thus, a well-managed production based on providing basic needs
for everyone and an efficient mechanism for distributing whatever is needed or wanted reduces the gap between rich and basic
maintenance (for there is no poor, no underclass) to a non-
antagonistic one. Indeed, the 20 per cent of the population living
on welfare rotates on a regular basis:

> Our welfare isn't a social class who are born on it, live on it,
> and die on it, reproducing half of the next welfare genera-
> tion along the way. Practically *everyone* spends *some* time
> on it. And hardly anyone more than a few years. Our people
> on welfare live in the same co-ops as everyone else, not
> separate, economic ghettos. (T, 179)

With economic equality, class and status are eliminated. Whether
one lives in a family commune out on the luxurious Ring or in
one's own room in an urban co-op, all the amenities of life are
freely available. What one does, how one lives is a matter of
personal choice, not a coded expression of dominance of subordination.

Both Federation and local governments are elected by universal
suffrage. The age of majority begins around puberty (varying
from age 11 on Triton to 14 on some Jupiter moons, the age rising
in the older satellites closer to the Inner Worlds) and is celebrated
by a person's name-day when she or he can take an adult name,
decide whether or how to have children, join the workforce, live
on her or his own, and vote. In this age free of philosophical

oppression, there are between thirty and thirty-seven parties on Triton, and each party "wins" by representing those citizens who voted for it.

> "They all win. You're governed for the term by the governor of whichever party you vote for. They all serve office simultaneously. And you get the various benefits of the platform your party has been running on. It makes for competition between the parties which, in our sort of system, is both individualizing and stabilizing." (T, 221)

Governing boards rather than individual leaders run the system; furthermore, the government seems to work efficiently and for the people, most of the time. As Sam puts it, "I don't suppose I have any illusions about our government's being a particularly moral institution. Though it's more moral than a good many others have been in the past" (T, 142). These satellites, however, are still threatened by the Inner Worlds and maintain a highly technological military; although the individual combat soldier no longer is needed. In the war between the moons and the worlds, anti-gravity devices and undercover subversion are the main weapons. In this heterotopian future, war is "all buttons and spies and sabotage, and only civilians get killed" (T, 143).

Although the legal system is not discussed, the city is divided into a licensed and unlicensed sector, the latter an area in which any behavior is tolerated. The "licensed sector" implies that laws and law enforcement exist. To be sure, it *is* mentioned that marriage, prostitution, and money are all illegal; whereas drugs, sex, and religion are permitted. There is a police force of "e-girls," named after the original all-female force on earth: mixed gender officers who are unarmed but trained in martial arts and whose duty is to patrol the city and maintain order and cleanliness; their uniform includes a black skull cap, black web shirt, black pants, shoes with open toes, with one arm sleeved in black and one bare "except for a complicated black gauntlet, aglitter with dials, knobs, small cases, finned projections" (T, 72).

With a post-scarcity economy, democratic government, and minimal laws, the "inviolable" "subjective reality" of each citizen is the primary value of the society. All divisions and discrimina-

167

tions – class, race, gender, sexual preference, political or religious belief and practice – have been eliminated. Indeed, even age discrimination has ended: childhood has been reduced to those years from birth to the age of puberty or even younger, for with an affluent and nurturing social system the years-long dependence of older children and adolescents is unnecessary. Personal life, consequently, is centered around the individual, not the family or kinship web; although many different family forms exist to meet the needs of adults and children. And regeneration treatments are available to keep one active and healthy until death. Generally, people live in their own rooms in co-ops wherein "room, food, and work arrangements were friendly but formal" (T, 139). The co-ops are organized by sexual preference, divided into mixed sex, non-specific gay and heterosexual male, non-specific gay and heterosexual female. About a fifth of the population, however, choose to live in communes as a "family," in numbers from a few to over twenty people. Some "families" are exclusively gay or heterosexual, some are for single parents, some are larger groupings of varying genders and preferences.

Roughly 20 per cent of the population chooses to have children, which keeps the birth rate just below zero population growth. Birth control is so well established that one has to go to clinics for *birth* pills to conceive a child:

> we have antibody birth control for both women and men that makes procreation a normal-off system. . . . Somewhere around name-day, you decide if you want to have children by accident or by design; if by design – which well over ninety-nine percent do – you get your injection. Then, later you have to decide that you *do* want them; and two of you go off and get the pill. (T, 132)

Further, with the sex/gender change technology available, anyone can bear a child, nurse one, or have it borne externally. Of those who choose to bear children, 70 per cent are female, but the biological limitation of childbearing to women has been broken. Here, as in Piercy, the end of male supremacy results in the liberation of men as well as women, as the positive, non-sexist characters of Sam, Philip, Windy, Lawrence, and even Alfred indicate.

Other aspects of the society emerge in bits and pieces through-out the text. Books have been replaced by easily held microfiche readers. Television carries seventy-six public channels and several private ones by subscription. Transportation in this highly urban utopia is by foot or by mass transit – interplanetary and inter-steller transport is, obviously, also well established. Medical care is available to all, and ailing people receive medical diagnosis and referrals through private computers that tie in with the central computer system. Throughout the city, "ego booster booths" provide – for a two-franq token and one's twenty-two digit government identity number – three minutes' worth of video and sound transcription of information on oneself stored in the government files, by law available only to the person in question.

Because of the climate-and-temperature-controlled environ-ment and the absence of sexual or other taboos, clothing styles in this individualist utopia depend solely on the mood and taste of the wearer and not on protection, modesty, or social status. Fashion, therefore, is completely a matter of personal preference which can change daily from nudity to full mask, cape, and gloves. Bron's friend, the 74-year-old homosexual Lawrence, prefers nudity; his friend Sam does as well, although on Earth Sam wears a sky-blue toga and black boots. Bron observes one normally dressed couple consisting of a "woman – a handsome sixty – or older if she'd had regeneration treatments – walking with one blue, high-heeled boot . . . blue lips, blue bangles on her breasts" and a "young (fourteen? sixteen?) man" with blue nails and blue breast bangles (T, 2). Bron's boss Philip comes to work in "tight pants, bare-chested (very hairy), and small grey shoulder cape" (T, 103). His other boss Audri wears a bright scarlet body-stocking with a lot of feathery things trailing from her head band" (T, 248). And to dinner one evening on Earth, Bron wears "one silver sleeve with floor-length fringe . . . a silver harness . . . and the silver briefs that matched it: a black waist pouch . . . soft black boots" with his inset gold eyebrow, the symbol of his former job as a male prostitute on Mars, painted over in black lacquer. The outfit, in Bron's obsessively self-conscious opinion, struck a proper balance of asymmetry and coherence. The Spike accompanies him barefooted and "in something sleeveless and ankle-length and black, her short hair silver now as Bron's . . .

sleeve fringe. . . . On one forearm she wore a silvery gauntlet, damasked with intricate symbols" (T, 192).

Daily life on Triton includes several types of dining, from the hegemony cafeteria with food lines ranging from vegetarian to "plain eating," to other choices of restaurants that cater to a specialized clientele, such as those for children under 10 or for generally nude men over 70. Bars are also distinguished by clientele; although as with the restaurants, one is free to use any establishment. Bron's friend Prynn prefers a bar that "catered to under-sixteen-year-old girls and fifty-five-year plus men" (T, 295); although she occasionally goes to a bar that attracts 20- to 30-year-old men when she feels like being a "child-molester." After she becomes a woman, Bron goes to a bar specializing as a meeting place for sexualizationships, a place that was "pleasantly plasticky (which meant there was no attempt to make the plastic look like either stone, ice, or wood), with a decent-enough-looking clientele, who, Bron decided, probably liked to get things settled early" (T, 306). Games from chess to vlet – a computer-based, hologrammatic game that is a combination of Dungeons and Dragons, war games and cards – are also a popular form of entertainment. Due to philosophical emancipation, religions of an uncountable number of sects exist and can be freely entered and left: Neo-Christians, the Poor Children of the Avestal Light and Changing Secret Name, the Rampant Order of Dumb Beasts are only a few.

Obviously Delany is concerned with the ambience and politics of everyday life, and he goes into great detail in this area. A major feature is the unlicensed sector, one of the primary emblems of his libertarian milieu:

> At founding, each Outer Satellite city had set aside a city sector where no law officially held – since, as the Mars sociologist who first advocated it has pointed out, most cities develop, of necessity, such a neighborhood anyway. These sectors fulfilled a complex range of functions in the cities' psychological, political, and economic ecology. Problems a few conservative Earth-bound thinkers feared must come, didn't: the interface between official law and official lawlessness produced some remarkable stable *un*official

170

laws throughout the no-law sector. Minor criminals were not likely to retreat there: enforcement agents could enter the u-1 sector as could anyone else; and in the u-1 there were no legal curbs on apprehension methods, use of weapons, or technological battery. Those major criminals whose crimes – through the contractual freedom of the place – existed mainly on paper, found it convenient, while there, to keep life on the streets fairly safe and minor crime at a minimum.
(T, 9–10)

There is a unique feel to the u-1 streets, and many chose to live there while others never entered the sector and others "chose to walk there only occasionally, when they feel their identity threatened by the redundant formality of the orderly, licensed world" (T, 10). Throughout his social vision, but especially in his treatment of the unlicensed sectors, Delany approaches utopia from the underside, from urban streets rather than university towers, from the margins of even the distant utopian center.

Sexuality on Triton is unfettered by taboos other than lack of consent. The society guarantees total personal emancipation and equality with no division of status of labor by gender or preference. Complete sexual freedom, the absence of connection between sex and procreation or between sex and marriage or prostitution, and full psychological therapy and physical rearrangement of the mind and body for anything from minor dysfunction or depression to total sex or gender change, all combine to allow a variety of guilt-free sexual activities. Some of the major sexual types in this society are "homosexuality, one out of five; bisexuality, three out of five; sadism and masochism, one out of nine; the varieties of fetishism, one out of eight" (T, 254). The silences of the remaining fractions make the reader speculate on the other possibilities. Furthermore, a clear-cut code for the initiation of "sexualizationships" exists in custom:

> she sat down on the bed beside him . . . and placed her hand affectionately on his leg, little and ring fingers together, middle and forefingers together, with a V between, which on Earth and the Moon, and Mars, and Europa and Ganymede, and Callisto, and Iapetus, and Galileo, and Neriad and Triton, in co-op and commune, park, bar,

171

> public walk and private source, was the socially acceptable
> way for men, women, children, and several of the genetical-
> ly engineered higher animals to indicate: "I am sexually
> interested." (T, 76–7)

If a person is sexually unhappy, unsatisfied, or bored, she or he
can change the situation; as The Spike puts it in one conversation,

> I mean if, one) he isn't happy with it, and two) he keeps
> going around pushing his affections on people who don't
> reciprocate, I just wonder why he doesn't do something
> about it? I mean not only do we live in an age of regeneration
> treatments; there *are* refixation treatments too. He can have
> his sexuality refixed on someone, or thing, that can get it up
> for him. (T, 90)

Gone is the factor of internal, hereditary, or moralistic repression
or guilt – arrived is a society with the economic/technological/
ideological/psychic freedom to distribute the surplus capital,
labor, and libidinal energy among all the people for maximum
human fulfillment.

In general, then, life on Triton and the other satellites is marked
by a high degree of subjective freedom in a nurturing or at least
protective environment. As The Spike tells Bron, "I mean, when
you have forty or fifty sexes, and twice as many religions,
however you arrange them, you're bound to have a place it's
fairly easy to have a giggle at" (T, 117). Delany makes clear
his vision of the relationship between the economic/political/
ideological system and non-coercive, subjective freedom in the
words of the sex therapist who speaks to Bron before his sex
change:

> The point is, with life enclosed between two vast parenthe-
> ses of nonbeing and straited on either side by inevitable
> suffering, there is no *logical* reason ever to try to improve
> any situation. There are, however, many reasons of *other*
> types for making as many improvements as you reasonably
> can . . . we have the technology – downstairs, in the west
> wing – to produce illusions, involving both relief and
> knowledge of those beliefs as true, far more complicated
> than either, by working directly on the brain. What are your

172

social responsibilities when you have a technology like that available? The answer that the satellites seem to have come up with is to try and make the subjective reality of each of its citizens as politically inviolable as possible, to the point of destructive distress – and the destruction must be complained about by another citizen; and *you* must complain about the distress. Indeed, there are those who believe down to the bottom of their subjective hearts, that the war we just ... won this afternoon was fought to preserve that inviolability ... basically our culture allows, supports, and encourages behavior that, simply in the streets of both unlicensed and licensed sectors, would have produced some encounter with some restraining institution if they were indulged in on Earth a hundred years ago.   (T, 268–9)

In this description of state-supported, personally chosen socialization, lies the basic opposition between this utopia and the author's empirical environment.

The healthy, libertarian "lunacy" nurtured by the socialist, libertarian, egalitarian, feminist satellite societies is put into clearer light as the older worlds of Earth and Mars, with their colonized moon, Luna, are briefly described. The old, old world of Earth is almost completely destroyed: its major population centers, such as Boston, no longer exist; its air is "grey-pink" and full of foul odors; its people are grim and still caught in economic, sexual, and philosophical oppression. Whether the damage was nuclear or ecological is never made clear, but the result is a dying planet that is further destroyed by the attacks of the Outer Satellites in their war to achieve economic independence. The only scientific activity on Earth that is mentioned, archaeology, is itself emblematic of the degree of destruction suffered by the original planetary home. Also, the only military activity described, the torture and interrogation of Bron, is emblematic of the police state that still governs the dying society.

Mars is characterized by its city of Bellona with its "red light" district, Goebbels. The primary image of Mars with its wealthy, upper-class women buying the services of male prostitutes, its early immigrant population from Earth that sent its children on to the better societies of the satellites, and its infamously named "sin

173

center" is one of unleashed capitalism with a fascist tinge. Earth and Mars, then, are the old center of the solar system, now emblematic of capitalism, fascism, oppression, and ecological destruction as well as of the imperialistic effort to keep the Outer Satellites under their economic hegemony. However, this center no longer holds, the revolution of the periphery is too far along. By the end of the text only a few remnants of the old worlds, namely the unchanging male supremacist Bron, exist to contrast with the new, yet imperfect, utopian satellites – separated from the corrupt center of the system by the delineation of the asteroid belt.

The iconic register in *Triton* provides a societal image quite different from the other three critical utopias. Though sharing similar political and social values such as socialism, feminism, autonomy, tolerance for all racial/ethnic/national/sexual groupings, and (at least negatively in the images of a burned-out Earth) ecological sanity, the utopia in *Triton* is less focused on the struggle toward utopia, more focused on the struggle to preserve it and live in it once it "arrives." Further, it is an urban utopia that is more concerned with personal relationships between individuals than with collectives and community – even though collective life holds the society together. The focus is on personal awareness and responsibility rather than the broad sweep of political activism and the social revolution. In many ways, the utopia in *Triton* is the most "realistic" of the critical utopias in that it is the closest to our own emerging, post-industrial, post-capitalist, post-modernist society in all its contradictions, promises, and problems.

Activism: the personal and the political

The symbolic opposition between the oppressive metropolis and the emancipated periphery developed in the iconic register of *Triton* is heightened in the ideological expression of oppositional activism developed in the discrete register. Unlike the direct political focus of this ideologeme in the other three critical utopias, however, the movement in *Triton* from the pages of the text to current questions of historical confrontation is, like the presentation of the utopian society, decentered. The question of activism is primarily covered in the plot centered on the apolitical protagonist, the misfit Bron Helstrom. The failure of Bron to adapt to utopian society is itself a decentered meditation on the political values and structures of the post-revolutionary society. In the personal microstructure of Bron's life is embedded an examination of the political macrostructure of the utopian alternative. The question of activism is secondarily dealt with in the supporting character of Sam, who as a political operative is the sign of direct political action in the novel; even here, however, Sam is described more in his private, personal existence rather than in his public role as a political activist. Whereas with Bron personal life is examined in the larger context of post-revolutionary political possibilities, with Sam political life is presented in the context of post-revolutionary personal possibilities.

The exploration of activism in *Triton* revolves around the connection made by 1970s feminism that the personal is political and vice versa. The novel is not concerned with revolutionary activism on the way to the better society, as in *The Female Man* and *Woman on the Edge of Time*; rather it considers the process of change after the revolution, as does *The Dispossessed*. Where in LeGuin's novel Shevek keeps the utopian ideals alive in the face of a compromised society, in Delany's the society remains revolutionary but one misfit male is unable to adapt to these better conditions. From LeGuin's concern with the political in the personal life of Shevek, we move to Delany's concern with the personal in the political context of Triton society. The "political" is the absent subject of the novel, brought to the reader by way of the similar but not identical dimension of the "personal."

Delany is not content with connecting the personal and political. He does, in the theater metaphors used by The Spike, assert that the macrostructure of society, the political, is comprised of many microstructures at the personal level. Yet, in the fuller statement on the matter given by the "theorist" Ashima Slade, the connection between these two dimensions is described not as one of identity but rather a mutually influential and mediated relationship between two verbal models of existence (see T, 290 and 358). Bron's personal difficulty is the result of his previous socialization on the old worlds and his failure to come to terms with the new conditions and opportunities on the moon. His personal angst is rooted in deep political conflict and practice. Sam's complex and satisfying personal life is thus a foil to Bron's as well as a sidelong entry into the actual political activity of the novel, an activity taken not by this or that character but by the collective subject of the entire Satellite Federation as it fights for survival so that it may continue to offer full subjective freedom to its citizens.

The narrative spine of Delany's novel, generated in the discrete register, is the story of Bron's attempt to be "reasonably happy." Bron's identity crisis, his quest for happiness, is an exploration of the failure of a person socialized within the ideological web of Earth and Mars to cast off his male-supremacist, self-deluding behavior and become a new person in an emancipated society that allows individual freedom to everyone without the need to dominate anyone else. Though the "plot" traces a personal journey that runs in a tedious circle, the larger ideological significance of the story is its comment on the deep political structures of society and their expansive impact on personal lives.

The immediate source for this anti-hero, as the author has acknowledged, is the protagonist in the Joanna Russ short story, "Nobody's Home."[14] In the Russ story Leslie Smith comes to live in the Komarov family commune on a future utopian earth, but Leslie is socially inept, stupid, without important or interesting skills. She has little to say, little to do, and is abandoned by one family commune after another; she is someone who "in her own person ... represented all the defects of the bad old days."[15] At the end of the story, the head of the family, Jannina, is searching for a tactful way to get rid of her, for as Jannina muses,

> Miss Smith was as normal as could be. Miss Smith was stupid. Not even very stupid. It was too damned bad. They'd probably have enough of Leslie Smith in a week, the Komarovs; yes, we'll have enough of her (Jannina thought), never able to catch a joke or a tone of voice, always clumsy, however willing, but never happy, never at ease. You can get a job for her, but what else can you get for her? Jannina glanced down at the dossier, already bored.[16]

Like Leslie, Bron is someone who represents the defects of the bad old days. He is a pre-revolutionary personality seeking refuge in a post-revolutionary society. Although there are many of his "type" still shaped by the symbolic order back on Earth and Mars, he is isolated on Triton. His dorm-mate, Lawrence, characterizes him as "hardhearted, insensitive, ungenerous, and pignoli-brained" (T, 44), but also as physically beautiful, dashing and mysterious. An émigré from Mars, where he worked as a prostitute for wealthy women, Bron is still caught up in the ideology and personality structure of a market system with its emphasis on status and exploitation, on image and impression – whereas another character who also worked as a Martian prostitute, Windy, is portrayed as having cast off that attitude and behavior and blossomed as a performing acrobat in The Spike's theater troupe. Bron, unable to see himself critically despite what his friends tell him, does not change and consequently prolongs his emigration as he undergoes a gender and sex change from a dominant male to a submissive female. Rather than facing his situation, rather than tuning into the values and social structures of the new society, Bron simply uses the advanced technology of that society to escape one more time.

As Lawrence explains, Bron is a "logically sadistic male seeking a logically masochistic female" (T, 254). Although the worlds still produce such men, the non-sexist, egalitarian moons no longer produce such women: "Your problem, you see, is that essentially you are a logical pervert, looking for a woman with a mutually compatible logical perversion. The fact is, the mutual perversion you are looking for is very, very rare – if not non-existent" (T, 253). For in the satellites, women "have only recently been treated, by that bizarre Durkheimian abstraction, 'society,' as human beings for the last – oh say, sixty-five years," and are therefore not willing in their new political and personal freedom "to put up with certain kinds of shit" (T, 252–3). Unable to find the one woman in five thousand who might be passive and self-denying enough to worship him as he would like, Bron escapes his male frustration by changing his physical and psychological gender and sexual preference and becoming that very type of logically masochistic woman. But the change only traps Bron once more, for now the subject who gazes has become the object of the gaze. There is no longer a dominant male subject to observe and consume that object. Moving from dominant master to subordinate victim, Bron is still alone, a transsexual caught in the closed circle of his solipsistic desire.

The main plot of the novel runs in a circle from the first page with Bron "at four o'clock, as he strolled from the hegemony lobby onto the crowded Plaza of Light [on the] thirty-seventh day of the fifteenth paramonth of the second year$_N$," to page 285 as she strolls out of the lobby "onto the crowded Plaza of Light" on "the fourteenth day of the nineteenth paramonth of the second year$_N$ at four o'clock." However, although Bron's story runs in circles, the other characters in this utopian society continue to struggle and grow, in spite of hard personal and political times. Bron's failure is contrasted with the successful lives of the supporting characters. Indeed, in these decentered residents of Triton, the connection between the personal and political is brought out as Delany describes how a nurturing and tolerant society provides for the subjective happiness of its many personalities – from the most unsettled, self-centered 17-year-olds to well-adjusted, horny 74-year-olds, from computer analysts to artists and political operatives.

Bron's dormitory friend, the 74-year-old gay male, Lawrence, in the wisdom of his years and motivated by a crush he has on Bron, tries to help him understand himself and change. As they play the game of vlet together, Lawrence attempts to support Bron in his struggle to be happy, but Bron backs away from Lawrence's assistance – partly out of pride and partly out of a repressed homophobia, both of which are inappropriate attitudes in this cooperative and emancipated society. It is Lawrence who points out Bron's passivity: how he lets people come to him and befriend him, how he does not take an active, responsible role in relationships. It is Lawrence who calls Bron on his male supremacist attitudes. It is also Lawrence who accepts Bron when she returns to the dorm as a woman and tries to help her adjust to her new body. However, Bron again rejects this caring friend. In contrast to Bron's vicious circle, Lawrence continues to grow and develop his life, and by the end of the novel he has gone off to the further moons of Pluto as a singer in an aleatory music commune with his new lover, Wiffles.

Also in his dormitories, both as a male and as a female, Bron gets to know younger people just starting out in life, full of self and insecurities. Green-eyed Alfred in the Serpent's house trusts Bron to be his friend, confides in Bron about his periodic impotency, and sends Bron for ointments to relieve his condition. Alfred, like Bron's other friends, came to him, sought him out, chose to trust him, but Bron avoids this trust and friendship that so nearly humanizes him. An emigrant "from some minor moon of Uranus" at age 14, Alfred is an example of the freedom and support provided by the alternative society. He is not oppressed: indeed he is well cared for in this social structure, but, typical for his age, he is still searching for a fuller sense of himself. In the meantime, he enjoys the sexual freedom of the society and continues to struggle to become a person. Unfortunately, Alfred becomes a victim of the war when part of the building falls and crushes him.

In the women's dormitory Prynn, a "really obnoxious fifteen-year-old" takes to confiding endlessly to Bron – "not so much because Bron encouraged her, but because she hadn't figured out yet how to discourage" (T, 294). Again Bron is sought out and trusted. Again Bron turns away from the relationship in self-absorption. Again, in contrast to Bron, Prynn though still trying to put her adult life together enjoys that life, including her penchant for 55-year-old men, in her struggling freedom and teenage vitality. Both adolescent characters challenge Bron to be human and responsive; both are emblems of the nurturing and tolerant society; both are healthier persons in their immaturity than Bron.

At work, Bron's two bosses provide additional examples of self-actualizing utopian citizens and contrasts to the "worldly" Bron. Audri, Bron's immediate boss, is another person drawn to him and willing to be his friend. After Bron becomes a woman Audri is interested in a sexual relationship with her and offers her a place to live. A single parent and lesbian who lives in a family co-op, Audri is well adjusted to life on Triton. She is a fair boss to Bron, encourages him in his work, is tolerant of his failures, and is supportive to her after the gender-sex change. Audri is attracted to Bron-as-woman because she is "not the threatening type" (T, 103), but Bron is not attracted because Audri is neither sadistic nor masochistic. Thus, Audri is another successful utopian citizen and another source of criticism of Bron. She describes Bron as a "very ordinary – or special, depending on how you look at it – combination of well-intentioned and emotionally lazy, perhaps a little too self-centered for some people's liking" (T, 108). In a typical refusal to face up to his own problems, Bron rejects Audri as a friend and later as a lover (homophobia again) because Audri "doesn't understand" him/her. Philip, Audri's boss, is another foil to Bron: he is rich, successful, a member of a wealthy family commune, mother of some children, father of others, and wet-nurse to more. Large, effusive, teasing, Philip is another example of the potential for human development made possible by the post-sexist society. Bron resents Philip because of his happiness and success. For all of Bron's failings, Philip supports him in his work and in his changes; again Bron rejects such critical support.

Bron's greatest personal conflict in utopia occurs in his relationship with The Spike. The Spike, Gene Trimbell, is a noted director of "ice opera" epics and micro-theater, for which she is supported by a Government Arts Endowment. She is a thriving avantgarde artist known throughout the Solar System, a theoretician and lecturer, and a strong and independent person. She lives a full life, is politically conscious, and is an effective artist. She, like Sam, is an example of the creative potential that the utopian society can nurture. As Bron's lover, she is also his confidante; and when she breaks the relationship off she becomes his enemy, threatening to "kick him in the balls" – ironic, for now Bron is a woman – if Bron approaches her. Bron's relationship with The Spike most directly shows his personal and political failure to cope with the demands and possibilities of life on Triton.

The Spike overwhelms and challenges Bron. He desires her because she broke through his defenses during the micro-theater performance and because she resists his attempts to dominate her. Because she has penetrated his defenses and touched him he wants her to be subject to him and desires/hates her when she refuses. Telling Lawrence about the micro-theater experience, he admits that The Spike

> gave me one of the most marvelous experiences of my life. At first I only thought she'd lead me to it. Then suddenly I

found out she'd conceived, created, produced, and
directed. . . . She took my hand, you see. She took my hand
and led me. (T, 45)

She opened up life to Bron: coming out of the performance he is
imprinted with her and yearns for more. Ultimately, he still
regards her in the instrumental manner with which he deals with
others, but at first he believes he is in love with her.

Like the others, The Spike sees the potential good side of Bron:
"there was just something engaging about your personality" (T,
89). When in later conversation she disagrees with him, she
arouses his usual desire to control and experience the world on his
terms alone; in response to her, Bron calls her "cold and in-
human" (T, 91). After that conflict, however, Bron returns to
confiding in her and admits that he is "not happy in the world" he
lives in: "They make it so easy for you," he tells her, "all you have
to do is know what you want: no twenty-first-century-style
philosophical oppression; no twentieth-century-style sexual
oppression; no nineteenth-century-style economic oppression"
(T, 116). Here Bron reveals himself to The Spike and to the reader
as he demonstrates his inability to grasp the degree of personal
emancipation made possible by the political reality created by the
Outer Satellites. The Spike notes that these oppressions are
generally eliminated but that remnants of them linger and that the
new society is still nowhere near the best. She tries to ease his fears
by illuminating the multiplexity of the society and thereby taking
some of the pressure off him so that he can feel free to trust others
and grow. Bron refuses her advice and only succeeds in again
feeling sorry for himself. The openness, availability, and generosity of Triton society wherein *anyone* can be happy grinds against
Bron's obsession with being unique and dominant. He does not
know how to be himself and part of the community at the same
time.

The Spike responds by noting that Bron finally seemed to be
working emotionally and getting at his unhappiness, but then he
backed off and took refuge in the instrumentally logical:

you seem to be using some sort of logical system where,
when you get near any explanation, you say: "By definition
my problem is insoluble. Now that explanation over there

181

would solve it. But since I've defined my problem as
insoluble, then by definition that solution doesn't apply."
(T, 123)

Bron, in short, lives in a shallow binary world where there is only
his self as it exists and nothing else, and as long as he stays in that
framework he cannot live in the new society that surrounds him.
Not only does he suffer because of this, The Spike tells him, but he
harms other people: "I think your confusion hurts other people"
(T, 125). Again, Bron responds by begging The Spike to save him:
"Help me. Take me. Make me whole" (T, 126). However, when
The Spike demands that he should help himself, he withdraws and
attacks her for being cold and uncaring. The Spike moves from
foil and confidante to antagonist when she begins to identify the
source of Bron's problem as his early socialization in the capitalist, male-dominant, oppressive ideology of Mars. As Bron tells
her, "I'm from another world – a world you're at war with. And
yes, we did things differently there" (T, 125). Indeed, The Spike
and Bron are, in the literal speech of science fiction as well as in
the metaphors of realism, "worlds apart." The antagonist from
utopia challenges the protagonist from the old world in this
inverted and twisted Möbius strip of narrative.

After their few days together on Triton, Bron and The Spike go
separate ways until they meet at the archaeological dig in Outer
Mongolia on Earth. The closeness of their earlier meeting has
faded, and Bron treats The Spike in an objectified, instrumental
way: he plays the old world role of client, imposing on The Spike
the role of prostitute. His defenses are up, and at the end of
dinner, with little regard for her life or her work, he declares his
"love" for her and begs her to "throw up the theater. Join your
life to mine. Become one with me. *Be* mine. Let me possess you
wholly" (T, 209). These archaic, twentieth-century, male
chauvinist attitudes do not appeal to this emancipated utopian
woman, and The Spike turns him down. She tries to explain her
rejection by telling Bron about herself, her need to be free to live
her own life and do her own work, but Bron withdraws and tunes
her out: "What she had been telling him was important to her, he
realized. Probably very important. But it *had* been unclear. And
what's more dull" (T, 214). Unable to see beyond his self-

obsessed, binary consciousness, he has no interest in The Spike
for her own sake.

The Spike finally breaks up with Bron by sending him a letter,
which he receives upon getting back to Triton. She tells him that
she doesn't "like the type of person" he is, that she "is angry at the
Universe for producing a person" like him, that he is too "emotionally lazy" "to put people at ease, to make them feel better, to
promote social communion." She elaborates with a reflection on
the non-utopian society he grew up in:

> Maybe you weren't cuddled enough as a baby. Maybe you
> simply never had people around to set an example of *how* to
> care. Maybe because you quote feel you love me unquote
> you feel I should take you on as a case. I'm not going to.
> Because there are other people, some of whom I love and
> some of whom I don't, who need help too and, when I give
> it, it seems to accomplish something the results of which I
> can see. Not to mention things I need help in. In terms of the
> emotional energies I have, you look hopeless.   (T, 228–9)

She tells him that if he wants to help her, he should stay out of her
life. Bron responds by withdrawing and attacking, calling her a
"crazy lesbian."

At this point, the personal and political crises converge as
Triton is attacked. The gravity shield is damaged, houses are
destroyed, and Bron, before he has a chance to think about
himself, rushes to his dorm to help Lawrence and then to Audri's
dorm to help her. In the frenzy of the war, he seeks out the friends
he has stayed away from, but in the aftermath of his "heroism" he
convinces himself that he has been "enlightened" by an awareness of the necessity for strong male leadership in crises. After the
crises of war and The Spike's rejection, he takes refuge in his
male-dominant, logically sadistic ideology. Bron tells Lawrence
his position on male bravery and heroism and isolation in a
hostile world:

> in a time of social crisis, *some*body's got to have that kind of
> ingenuity, if just to protect the species, the women, the
> children – yes, even the aged. And that ingenuity comes out
> of the aloneness, that particular male aloneness. . . . I just

guess women, or people with large female components to their personalities, are *too social* to have that necessary aloneness to *act outside society*.

(T, 257, my emphasis)

In this burst of narrow individualism, male supremacy and authoritarian dominance, Bron becomes immersed in the isolation of his pathological ideology. Lawrence responds by calling him a fool.

In the heat of his obsession, Bron undergoes the gender-sex change to become the logically masochistic, subordinate women he desires. He becomes a woman not out of positive self-criticism and growth but out of pathological self-immersion in his constricted view of the world. As he ironically reveals to Lawrence after the operation, "There are certain things that have to be done. And when you come to them, if you're a man . . . you have to do them" (T, 275). As a reified woman, Bron believes she will be better able to serve the reified maleness she worships: "I'll know how to leave it [male aloneness] alone enough not to destroy it, and at the same time to know what I *can* do. I've had the first-hand experience, don't you see?" (T, 275). Thus, Bron no longer has to "be modest" about male supremacy; she is free to serve "real manhood." Bron has destroyed his male personality in order to serve it.

By the end of the narrative, Bron has become "a woman made *by* a man . . . a woman made *for* a man" (T, 302), in an ironic reversal of *The Female Man*. As a "male woman" in a post-sexist, post-male-supremacist society, Bron cannot find a man who will love her on *her* terms. In her inability to love others in a multiplex way, she rejects the love of Audri and Lawrence and expects sadistic love from Sam. Bron's story ends with her caught within the moment of her own self-obsession with all of utopia flourishing around her.

Unlike the other three critical utopias that focus on characters who are political activists in the front lines of social change, *Triton* focuses on ordinary people who are able to be free because of the political context. In Bron and the others the political is expressed through the personal. The most political activity in the novel is the war to "make the subjective reality of each of its citizens as politically inviolable as possible" (T, 269). In resisting the attack by Earth and Mars to reassert economic hegemony and to reimpose an authoritarian order, the satellites preserve their emancipatory society, a society which "extends instruction on how to conform" to the utopian possibility, as well as the "materials with which to destroy themselves, both psychological-ly and physically – all under the same label, Freedom" (T, 357). The social macrostructure radically guarantees freedom with all the inherent trust and risks it places on the individual. However, that macrostructure does not directly determine how the personal microstructures of each life will work out. Bron is an example of how un-political and destructive such a personal response within the emancipatory political structure can be; whereas Sam is the counter-example of how politically constructive and fulfilling a personal response can be.

Sam is the antithesis of Bron: the sign of the personal and political potential of the new society. Black, with an "amazing mind" and a "large, magnificent body," Sam is the "good-looking, friendly, intelligent guy" that Bron could be if he let himself develop. Furthermore, Sam is the one political activist in the novel; significantly, he works in the ideological/informational sphere as

> *the* head of the Political Liaison Department between the Outer Satellite Diplomatic Corps and Outer Satellite Intelli-gence; [he] had all the privileges [and training] of both: he had governmental immunity in practically every political dominion of the inhabited Solar System. Far from being "oppressed" by the system, Sam had about as much power as a person could have, in anything short of an elected position. (T, 30–1)

Sam, then, is a political cadre who works for a healthy political system, not a totalitarian agent or a damaged self seeking satisfac-tion on a powerless citizenry. Indeed, his personal life is, like others in this social alternative, a happy and fulfilled one.

Furthermore, this other immigrant to utopia is in his own person a symbol of the collective unity of humanity made possible by a society that has ended oppression and made personal freedom its objective. Sam describes himself before he came to live on Triton and work for the government:

I was a rather unhappy, sallow-faced blonde, blue-eyed (and terribly myopic) waitress at Lux on Iapetus, with a penchant for other sallow, blonde, blue-eyed waitresses, who, as the young and immature me could make out then, were all just gaga over the six-foot-plus Wallunda and Katanga emigrants who had absolutely infested the neighborhood: I had this very high, very useless IQ and was working in a very uninspiring grease-trough. But then I got this operation, see –   (T, 149)

From female to male, white to black, lesbian to heterosexual, Sam changed successfully within the social ambience of utopia and became a self-actualized person, with a private life that included his own individual freedom as well as membership in both an extended family commune and a non-specific male dormitory and a public life that made a powerful contribution to the continuing well-being of the Federation. Sam is a direct contrast to Bron: the new person who works well and flourishes within the utopian society rather than the old person who rejects the freedom and responsibility of that alternative. If Bron's character exposes the gap between utopian society and "realistic" individual life, Sam's joins the political and personal in a fresh utopian potential – and, typically for this heterotopian narrative, does so as a decentered "minor" character.

The meditation on political activism in *Triton*, then, is quite different from that contained in the other critical utopian texts. In the investigations of the relationship between the personal and the political, Delany takes the ideological consideration of appropriate oppositional politics to levels not dealt with in the more directly activist texts such as *The Female Man* or *Woman on the Edge of Time*, which are concerned with the road taken *to* the social revolution. More like *The Dispossessed, Triton* considers the complexity of the social reality *after* the revolution. Like the LeGuin novel, Delany's explores the personal and political interface, but from the point of view of a character who rejects the utopian potential. In this negative and decentering move, Delany casts new light on the macro- and microstructure relationship. Bron may be the protagonist, the anti-hero, of the novel, but both The Spike and Sam – antagonist and foil to Bron, off to the side of the main plot – provide the ideological models of activism and personal fulfillment expressed in this non-dogmatic heterotopia.

As ideological cadre, Sam serves in the key position of mediating the flow of information between overt and covert political activity and as such is able to contribute to the survival of his post-revolutionary society. Like an omniscient narrator, he is in a political position that allows him to know everything, with the consequent power to affect the outcome of the revolutionary "plot." As part of the artistic vanguard, The Spike serves in a similar key position in the cultural life of the new society. Through her micro-theater she is able to make the already-free citizens more aware of their individual existence and potential. Since she is funded by the government itself, she too is a creative part of the post-revolutionary ideological state apparatus which helps the growth of the society, but without the limitations of either market-oriented stimulation or state-directed dogma.

In these two characters, highlighted by the foreground failure of Bron caught between them, the union of the artistic and political vanguard, the personal and political dimensions, is valorized as the type and style of activism required, at the very least in a post-revolutionary context but also in the American society of 1976 with its own bicentennial blues and political and personal struggles. In Sam and The Spike are encoded the power of those intellectual and artistic activists who can appropriate, interpret, and communicate information for the betterment of the entire population rather than for the service of the current dominant system which limits the flow of such information to technocratic channels that serve the narrow interests of the status quo. What is needed in the post-industrial, information society is not so much the utopian diplomat or the dystopian terrorist but the self-actualized person doing political or artistic work who participates in history and opens the way forward to a better world. In exploring the mutual dynamism between the personal and political, Delany identifies the political not only as a macro-structural end in itself but also as a means to personal fulfillment in the microstructures of daily life. He reveals the personal as a microstructural part of the larger political reality, shaped by and shaping that macrostructure no matter how much the given

187

individual may try to evade or deny that connection. In his heterotopian narrative, Delany brings a radical utopian impulse to bear on both dimensions and thereby deepens the self-understanding of oppositional culture and politics of the mid-1970s.

Heterotopia: utopia as praxis

Science fiction is a way of casting a language shadow over coherent areas of imaginative space that would otherwise be largely inaccessible.   (Samuel R. Delany, "Shadows")

The formal operation of the text of *Triton* is a highly self-conscious ideological intervention into the historical conflict between the forces of domination and the anti-hegemonic alliance. Like *The Female Man, Triton* is as much an exploration of its own workings as a science fictional and utopian text as it is an expression of utopian alternatives or political activism. Delany brings the power of contemporary science fiction, enriched by the self-reflexive tendencies of postmodern experimental fiction, to bear in destroying the limits of the traditional literary utopia – especially as it has been coopted and contained within the present ideological matrix – and reviving the radical utopian impulse to hold open an imaginary space in which oppositional ideology and practice can be articulated and received. He juxtaposes a utopian iconic text – albeit one full of the grime and crime, the indecision and inhumanity of real life – against a realist discrete text – dominated by a protagonist whose retrograde behavior is a sign of the present system in its denial of authentic utopian praxis. Thus, he creates a heterotopian text suitable for the task of breaking through the totalizing system of post-industrial, phallocratic capitalism and expressing a radical vision of human emancipation.

The self-reflexive commentary in "Appendix A" and "Appendix B" sharpens the text as a weapon of cultural opposition. By calling attention to its own literary practice, the text informs and challenges the reader to look beyond the limits of the present in assessing the possibilities explored in its content and form. With "Appendix A: From the *Triton* Journal: Work Notes and Omitted Pages," Delany shatters the illusion of the closed, representational novel and identifies *Triton* as an open text. The reader is supplied with what is "not in" the traditional narrative that supposedly ends on page 330 and is thus able to apprehend what the text says about itself in the so-called appendices which exist on the border between what is the text and the *textus* – Delany's term for the "language and language functions upon which the text itself is embedded" (T, 333). The appendices provide the reader with a helpful bridge by which the reading that completes and continues the text can be done. With this self-reflexivity, the reader becomes aware not only of the radical content of *Triton* but more so of its radical form.

In these appendices Delany describes the operations of the science fiction genre that render it a privileged form for breaking through the stasis of the dominant ideology. He also maps the limits of utopian fiction and points out what must be done to liberate the utopian impulse from those limits. In "Appendix A," he identifies the alternate world, the landscape created by the author in the iconic register, as the primary "hero" of the science fiction text – that is, as the literary element which motivates the entire text, for without the alternate world there would be no science fiction. So too, the episteme, the summary of how a given society understands itself in a given historical moment, is "*always* the secondary hero of the s-f novel*" (T, 333). Delany goes on to describe how the alternative landscape and episteme generate the conditions for the transformations of language and perception that science fiction is capable of and that provide the genre with its radical distancing power. Thus, not only the content of science fiction opens up new perceptions to the reader, but also the language of the text does so in a more complex manner: "old words are drawn from the cultural lexicon to name the new entity (or to rename an old one), as well as to render it (whether old or new) part of the present culture" (T, 334). Science fiction "redeems" language from the "merely metaphorical, or even the meaningless," in order to construct a fictional foreground that casts a "language shadow" over new areas of imaginative, critical space. For example, the alternative landscape of a Solar System in which Earth and Mars are politically opposed to utopian Outer Satellites provides a way of describing the sexual politics that are mapped in the relationship betweeen Bron and The Spike such that the phrase "they were worlds apart" no longer has a merely metaphorical meaning: it now signifies the (imaginary) existence of two societies, one which is still as oppressive as our own and one which embodies the values and behavior of those people and movements opposed to our present system.

In science fiction, the relationship between foreground – plot and characters, the discrete – and background – setting and episteme, the iconic – is radically different from the fiction of realism in any of its manifestations from the eighteenth century to the present. For the alternative world and episteme allow for a different social context than the one we know; this alternative can then be the site of solutions to present contradictions not possible in the present system. For example, placing a twentieth-century male supremacist, who is the typical confused dangling man of many contemporary realist narratives, against the background of a society based on principles and structures of equality and freedom rather than of profit and power "exposes" that character type – and the political reality signified by it – under a critical light which reveals that character as no longer a "hero" but rather a sad and fading figure of a dying social system. In this sense the science fictional operation of the text subverts the overall ideology of the present system of domination as well as the realist, mundane literature that helps maintain it. The generic expectations of the realist novel that express either adjustment to the status quo or, at the worst, destruction or dropping out are broken through by the portrayal of a possible social system that allows for freer, more equal, cooperative, and fulfilling behavior for everyone, not just handsome, white males. Contrary to the modern realist novel, in *Triton* the protagonist is the problem and the society is the solution.

Delany argues that the "science-fictional enterprise is richer than the enterprise of mundane fiction" because of its "extended repertoire of sentences, its consequent greater range of possible incident, and through its more varied field of rhetorical and syntagmatic organization" (T, 340). The surface "simple-mindedness" of science fiction allows for the "far wider web of possibilities such works can set resonating" (T, 340). In this self-reflexive discussion, Delany challenges the reader to think about what is going on in the text and how it transcends the limits of the mundane or realist novel and, indeed, of the episteme and the politics that inform it.

The analysis of science fiction continues into "Appendix B: Ashima Slade and the Harbin-Y Lectures: Some Informal Remarks toward the Modular Calculus, Part Two." On an immediate content level, Slade – whose name is a broken acronym for "Sam Delany" – is, like Sam and The Spike, another utopian foil for the character of Bron – another "Minor Character" whose role is more important than the "Major Character", as in the "ice opera epics" described on pages 342–3. At the self-reflexive level, Slade's lectures refer back to Delany's own essays on the literary theory of science fiction. The title of Slade's Harbin-Y lecture is "Shadows," and it was published in issues six and seven/eight of *Foundation*: Delany's own essay entitled "Shadows," which covers the same material but in a "different context," first appeared in the science fiction journal *Foundation*, issues six and seven/eight. Indeed, we learn that Slade took the title for his lecture from a "nonfiction piece written in the twentieth century by a writer of light, popular fictions" (T, 357). In these convoluted connections between Delany and Slade, the self-reflexive discussion of science fiction in *Triton* comes to the reader both in what is said and how it is said – that is, how it is expressed in the fictional account of the theoretical work of Ashima Slade. Again, the reader is prevented from passively consuming the novel as a "light, popular fiction," but is led to view it rather as a critical exploration of the current historical situation.

In the commentary on Slade, Delany goes on to discuss the relationship between micro- and macrostructures which informed our reading of the discrete register and the ideologeme of activism. But the commentary develops that discussion into a fuller exploration of "modeling" and its relationship to the science fiction text. This discussion allows the reader to see the work of science fiction as a form of modeling that creates an alternative to the world in which the author lives. The shift in meaning that occurs when certain "attitudes, objects, and various aspects of a relation between them" are used to stand for the "objects, attitudes, and relations we wish to model" (T, 367) allows for that distanced and critical perspective that makes science fiction the privileged genre for our time, able to crack the code of one-dimensional market ideology. The present situation is recast into a revealing model. For example, the shift of language in Triton society forces the reader to see how language and attitudes work in the present reality: "e-girls" as a term for police officers who are both male and female; women named Brian, George, and John; "ovular" as a replacement for "seminal" are science fictional reworkings of our present language and sexist ideology which call attention to that sexism not by way of theoretical analysis but by the playful shock of language being used in a different model.

Another example of distancing occurs in the footnote on page 349: "To all who have helped in the preparation of this appendix the *editor* extends *her* thanks" (T, 349, my emphasis). What is interesting about this example is that not only is there a shift signified in sexual politics wherein women are more able to be editors, but further, the fictional voice that has overseen the entire text of which the reader is nearing the end is now identified as female. At the most "authoritative" point of the text – the footnote that signifies the "scholarship" of the text – the author/editor is identified as a woman: thereby challenging the reader's unexamined sexist attitudes as well as continuing the textual game of gender reversal begun in the content of the utopian narrative and now continued to the formal operations, as this novel written by a "male" is given an editorial voice that is "female." The radical ideological challenge of the book occurs not only in its mind-bending content but in its form as well, in the way the text is continued and completed by the reader. The utopian shift in power from a phallocratic society to a non-sexist one – coded here by who does what work – is asserted by a female voice that, if we backread the entire text, *controls* the text from the beginning. This powerful female voice is a linguistic emblem for the utopian alternative – identifying utopian discourse not as a systematic model of a better society but as a practice informed by a theoretical understanding of its own operation and power which occurs here and now in the current reality.

Science fiction, then, is described as the genre capable of examining and subverting the present ideological context. As Delany says in his actual essay, "Shadows": "Much science fiction inadvertently reflects the context's failure. The best science fiction explores the attack."[17] The attack waged by *Triton*, in its use of the narrative techniques of popular science fiction and avantgarde self-reflexive fiction, is carried on especially in the specific historical context of the revival of utopian writing in the 1970s. Delany begins his challenge to the traditional utopia in the subtitle of the novel as he pits his "ambiguous heterotopia" against LeGuin's "ambiguous utopia." He joins in the critical revival of utopian writing by striving to eliminate the dull, systematic, totalizing quality of the genre in favor of a more radically creative "ambiguity," but he goes yet a step further as he writes a "heterotopia." By way of the Foucault quotation, Delany tells the reader that his text is one that seeks not to console by way of untroubled, fantastic societies that have no "real locality" "where life is easy, even though the road to them is chimerical." Rather, the utopian impulse in *Triton* is kept alive by a text that "destroys" the consoling syntax of the traditional utopia, that "desiccates speech, stops words in their tracks," as Bron's sentences trail off into uncomprehending confusion, that "contests the very possibility" of utopia and dissolves the myth in favor of the practice of imagining a radical other to what is. The heterotopia asserts the possibility of what is not yet in images and narration that should not be taken as a blueprint or a party line but rather as a disturbing meditation on what could be if people made an effort to change the present reality. By including Foucault within his text, Delany guards against the text being read as a systematic, totalizing utopia.

More than the other three critical utopias, *Triton* negates and transforms utopian writing and creates a qualitatively new form which avoids the authoritarian tendency of the classical utopia. *Triton* is not top-heavy with abstract ideas or systems. In a narration deceptively realistic, it describes the experience of life in a society better than our own, that implicitly critiques our own. Whereas LeGuin asserts utopia in a form close to the traditional one, Delany makes the existential operation of the utopian impulse available in the formal activity of the text. Thus, he meets Nadia Khouri's requirement for an authentically utopian text which gears utopian energy towards the explosion of established limits. As Khouri notes, "the need for utopia arises precisely

193

where it is negated and its realization depends on its ability to overcome contradictions."[18]

In our present situation, wherein utopian expression has been instrumentally confined in the false promises of post-industrial capitalism, the form of utopia itself must be exposed and transcended so that it can be revived as a practice of radical opposition. It cannot be left in its traditional form, for then it will either be coopted or ignored. It must be negated to insure the future-bearing impulse. The dialectic between a radical consciousness and the historical situation necessary to radical utopian discourse is found in *Triton* not only in its *presence* in the alternative society and in the characters of Sam, The Spike, Slade, and the others but also in its *absence* in Bron and his failure to thrive in that utopian alternative. The dialectic is also found in the disruptive form of the text itself: both in the jarring juxtaposition of a utopian alternative with a dystopian protagonist and plot and in the commentary on science fiction, which generates the utopian text, and utopia/heterotopia itself. The dialectic is thus present in the heterotopian form which activates utopia and breaks it open, which writes and deconstructs utopia on each page.

It is no accident that this renewal and transcendence of utopian discourse in critical utopias that arise out of the radical political and social ruptures of the late 1960s was achieved by means of the generic possibilities of modern science fiction. For science fiction's ability to posit alternative landscape and episteme, to shift the way we see and understand the present, coupled with the open form and self-reflexivity of experimental fiction supplies the literary mechanism by which the utopian impulse is liberated from its denial and cooptation by the totalizing structures and ideologies of the twentieth century.

Of all the critical utopias *Triton* is the most extreme, for it flatly denies utopian writing in order to set free the impulse that breaks through our perceptions and satisfactions toward a future fulfillment that is not yet achieved but yearned for. After the critical utopias, the utopian impulse must be seen for the practice that it is: neither the blueprint or idealized heaven it once was, nor the commodity packaged and sold in the present market. Revived in the politics and the art of the late 1960s, utopian hope is the expression of the tendency of human beings to resist exploitation

and oppression and to desire and work for freedom and fulfillment. The radical utopian impulse is part of the historical process
of social struggle and change. It is the dream that moves us on.

8 Conclusion

> We need to make the creation of prefigurative forms an
> explicit part of our movement against capitalism. I do not
> mean that we try to hold an imaginary future in the present,
> straining against the boundaries of the possible until we
> collapse in exhaustion and despair. This would be utopian.
> Instead such forms would seek both to consolidate existing
> practice and release the imagination of what could be.
>
> (Sheila Rowbotham)

No literary text can be read so as to achieve a full understanding
of its unique place in the world, for the web of relations and forces
in which text and reader are situated is complex and shifting and
prevents a final and complete reduction. "The thing itself always
escapes," says Derrida. What we are left with is a reading of a
certain group of novels done at a particular time with a particular
analytical/interpretive grid from the perspective of a particular
historical and personal sensibility. The utopian novels discussed
in the previous pages could have been approached separately in
terms of the *oeuvre* of each author; they could have been read
generically in more limited terms as science fiction, *or* feminist

fiction, *or* fantasy; some would be tempted to read them as examples of the "commie-fag-braburning-hippie decadence" of the 1960s that threatens the moral majority of modern-day America. That I chose to look at them from within the changing tides of a literary genre which seemed to have gone out of business in the twentieth century and from within the oppositional theory and practice of the last twenty or so years was certainly not an isolated idiosyncratic act but a deliberate move to widen the current understanding of utopian impulses and anti-hegemonic politics and culture in order to see the historical situation a bit more clearly and a bit more militantly.

Utopian writing has so often been a boring and totalizing literature – often written by those few privileged individuals who have had the time and money to speculate while others struggle just to survive. Thus, it might seem surprising when radical writers and readers have a go at the genre. Identifications with the rise of capitalism, warnings of the authoritarian tendencies of closed systematizing, realizations of the distance between ideal worlds and political activity – all these aside, through the past few centuries we have been given the forward-looking and challenging radical utopian visions of the likes of Rabelais, Fourier, Morris, Gilman and most recently the critical utopian writers of the last decade.

Engels did have a point in his criticism of the utopian socialists when he stressed the danger of distracting readers from the current struggle. Delany has one too as he warns us, via Foucault, of the soporific limits of neat and totalized utopian narratives that serve to lull us further into the artificial dreams of the present social formation. And yet, Russ has been highly important for the development of feminist writing and politics because of her utopian and activist visions and her radically open literary practice; LeGuin has attracted many readers and stimulated new interest in utopian discourse as well as in ecology and anarchism; Piercy has crystallized the experience of new left, feminist, ecological, and liberation movements in a novel that reached many in its mass-marketed publication; and Delany himself had to venture into the utopian genre in order to transcend it.

Despite the denials and the cautions, we have available to us a group of texts – and we have not examined important companion

197

examples such as Callenbach's *Ecotopia*, Gearhardt's *Wanderground*, or Charnas's *Motherlines* – that are critically utopian and play their part in anti-hegemonic politics. As revivals and transformations of utopian writing, these works have added to the ways in which we perceive the dissatisfaction of the present and tune into the pull of future possibilities. They contribute to the wider utopian dialogue of speculation about the emancipatory society and share in the reassessment of activism going on since the 1960s. The recognition of the interrelation of the personal and political as well as the implicit critique of the vanguard party with its master discourse have led to a fresh understanding of oppositional politics as a pluralistic alliance of forces which does not rely on central leadership or parliamentary politics. Finally, in the form of the critical utopian text, the open and self-reflexive operations common to these novels break utopian discourse out of its petrified systematizing as well as its denial and cooptation by market and state structures which have restricted utopian desire to the affirmative culture. Thus, the critical utopian impulse itself becomes the primary message of these texts. Utopian imagination is valorized as a seditious practice that helps carry the project of emancipation beyond any limit it reaches.

Figures of hope

> Utopian dialogue in all its existentiality must infuse the abstractions of social theory. My concern is not with utopistic "blueprints" (which can rigidify thinking as surely as more recent governmental "plans") but with the dialogue itself as a public event.   (Murray Bookchin)

The utopias which Russ, LeGuin, Piercy, and Delany have created are not blueprints or plans to be imposed by one author or by a central authority; rather they are a diverse series of preconceptual images which express the dreams behind that political activity and anticipate the social alternatives that many are still working for. Michael Albert and Robin Hahnel stress the necessity to articulate a broad vision of an egalitarian, just, and liberating society, for without such a vision the battle for survival alone will not be sufficient to sustain people in their ongoing political work:

If our organizations of opposition, our consciousness and
culture of resistance and our newly elaborated values are to
move us toward socialism, then we must have a reasonable
vision of the new society here and now, even as we begin to
nurture socialism's roots in the present.[1]

Indeed, the social imagery of the four authors under consideration contributes to an expanding force field of political life that,
as Murray Bookchin notes, "places America's corporate future at
odds with the country's most lofty traditional ideals."[2] He
reminds us that radicalism in the United States has since the last
century drawn on two traditions which include strong utopian
elements: European socialism with roots in the struggle against
quasi-feudal contexts as well as industrial capitalist ones, and
American populism with roots in the libertarian context of the
American revolution and frontier as well as in the radical
opposition after the Civil War. In the 1960s, that vision of justice
and economic democracy as well as minimal government, individual and group freedom, decentralist ideals, and localist
claims has been expressed in documents such as the *Port Huron
Statement*, the founding manifesto of the Students for a Democratic Society, and Martin Luther King's "I Have a Dream"
speech. Furthermore, the rejection of the cybernetic, robotic,
centralized, rationalized corporate society has been deepened in
the theory and practice of contemporary feminism and radical
ecology as well as in racial and ethnic liberation movements. As
Bookchin puts it:

We have produced the contours of a counter-culture – not
only in lifestyle but in ecology, feminism, gay rights and
lesbian rights movements, and the claims of ethnic identity.
This counter-culture, mixed and lacking as it may be in
many respects, forms the underpinnings of major movements in Europe today, notably the German Greens. What
we must now help the American people create – in some
respects revive – are the decentralized and confederal coun-
terinstitutions that will provide this counter-culture with
political tangibility.[3]

The social imagery contributed by the four authors is part of
the oppositional dialogue that informs contemporary radical

politics. This dialogue also includes the work of radical theorists such as Shulamith Firestone, Wendell Berry, André Gorz, and Murray Bookchin. Utopian imagery plays a key role in expressing the general sensibility of their proposals. The utopia outlined by Firestone in *The Dialectic of Sex* is in many ways a direct reply to the dystopia of Huxley's *Brave New World*, and elements of her vision can be found in the novels of Russ, Piercy, and Delany. In the conclusion to her 1970 study, she describes the "ultimate revolution" in utopian terms. Firestone's vision to "create a paradise on earth anew" rests on four demands: (1) "The freeing of women from the tyranny of their biology by any means available, and the diffusion of the childbearing and childrearing role to the society as a whole, to men and children as well as women." (2) "The economic independence and self-determination of all." (3) "The total integration of women and children into the larger society." (4) "Sexual freedom, love, etc."[4] As one of the first syntheses of traditional socialism with contemporary feminism and the movements for autonomy and libidinal freedom, Firestone's utopia may seem dated by now, but her analysis and subsequent utopian vision played an important role in radical political life in the early 1970s. Her rejection of the traditional nuclear family, her willingness to advocate extrauterine reproduction as the last break in the chain binding women to their biological and social subordination, her support of the liberation of children, together with the emancipatory benefits of democratic socialism and ecological politics combine to provide an example of strategic utopian discourse that, as in the four novels, helps people desire a social structure beyond the one that shapes their lives and limits their freedom.

Wendell Berry's suggestions in the last pages of *The Unsettling of America* are the expression of a Jeffersonian, small farmer populism that resonates with LeGuin's scarcity utopia. Berry's vision departs from the present corporate and consumer culture and describes an autonomous existence based on a clear social morality. He calls for the "withdrawal of confidence from the league of specialists, officials, and corporation executives who for at least a generation have had almost exclusive charge of the problem and who have enormously enriched and empowered themselves by making it worse."[5] He calls for a revival of human energy, "not as something to be saved, but as something to be used and to be enjoyed . . . in useful, decent, satisfying, comely work." He calls for an egalitarian redistribution of wealth by heavy taxation of "people of wealth and corporations" for low-interest loans to enable people to buy family-size farms, for a system of "production and/or price controls that would tend to adjust production both to need and to the carrying capacities of farms," for local self-sufficiency in food by means of growers' and consumers' cooperatives, for a revised policy on waste production and disposal in a series of economic/social moves to reorient America toward a decentralized, small farming-based society valuing human wholeness and health, and production and consumption for need rather than for growth or profit. He closes his chapter entitled "Margins" with a call for "the greatest possible technological and genetic diversity" to preserve the ecological health of the biosphere and to explode the one-dimensionality of industrial society. As Berry puts it, "the world has room for many people who are content to live as humans, but only for a relative few intent upon living as giants or as gods." Like LeGuin, Berry provides an agenda based on a morality of restraint, appropriateness, and balance that draws on a populist wisdom. Berry's work challenges those who take up more "forward-looking" positions too easily without first checking out the accumulated wisdom of past, pre-corporate social values and structures.

André Gorz ends both *Ecology as Politics* and *Farewell to the Working Class* with his utopia for post-industrial society. Gorz's suggestions, like Bookchin's, are rooted in the triple alliance of feminism, ecology, and libertarian socialism that informs all four novels. In describing the "new morning" that French citizens wake up to after the utopian revolution, Gorz paints a picture of a society that has restored personal autonomy, that has stopped economic growth and reoriented production toward basic human needs, that has reduced the work week to twenty-four hours for everyone but also provided studios and workshops in all living units for the renewal of "free creative work," that redefines education as a life-long project which seeks to develop the whole person and not just the mind, that encourages regional self-sufficiency, and that imagines the utopian prime minister forbidding television programs on Fridays and Saturdays "in order to encourage the exercise of the imagination and the greater exchange of ideas."[6]

Bookchin's utopian description at the end of his monumental study, *The Ecology of Freedom*, revolves around the "re-empowerment" of every individual and the creation of an "ecological society" based on cooperation with nature, "usufruct" or the unrestricted and unquestioned sharing of all things, the non-hierarchical "equality of unequals," and "complementarity" or the world-wide interdependency of all individuals and social systems. The basic shape of the new society revolves around the relationship of people based no longer on blood ties but on "a simple affinity of tastes, cultural similarities, emotional compatibilities, sexual preferences, and intellectual interests."[7] These relationships would be located in "the commune – freely created, human in scale, and intimate in its consciously cultivated relationships – rather than clan or tribal forms that are often fairly sizable and anchored in the imperatives of blood and the notion of a common ancestry." On a larger scale, he envisions regional communes, networks of smaller units organized confederally by ecosystems, bioregions, and biomes that are "artistically tailored to their natural surroundings." He calls for decentralization, ecological economy, the return of craft at the expense of centralized industry, and the consequent reduction of society to a face-to-face human scale "where the fetishization of needs would give way to the freedom to choose needs, quantity to quality, mean-spirited egoism to generosity, and indifference to love." He closes with a call for an ecological ethics, "whose concept of 'good' takes its point of departure from our concepts of diversity, wholeness, and a nature rendered self-conscious – an ethics whose 'evil' is rooted in homogeneity, hierarchy, and a society whose sensibilities have been deadened beyond resurrection."

Gorz's and Bookchin's alternatives are readily recognizable in the societies portrayed by all four writers. Furthermore, Bookchin's call for social organization by way of bioregions rather than by kinship or nation is suggestive of a change in the conception of social space that also has its utopian-inspired driving force. The calls for revival of healthy neighborhoods; for the expansion of decision-making at the town hall level; for autonomous regions as in the Basque and Catalonian situations; for the shift of social conceptualization of space from the limits of state and national boundaries to organic areas determined by the watersheds of major rivers and their consequent bioregions; as well as the more tactical call for geographical areas designated as nuclear-free zones – as for example, the Scandinavian or Balkan peninsulas or the Republic of Ireland – are all examples of a radically new geographical perception that begins in the utopian impulse to envision a world other than the one now mapped by the dominant system.

These preconceptual figures of hope, whether in novels or in theoretical works, go far beyond the instrumentally rational planning undertaken by that creation of corporate think-tanks – or their state socialist counterparts – known as futurism or futurology. As Bookchin notes, radical utopian alternatives

> at least come to mean revolutionary change in the status quo and a radical critique of its abuses. Futurism, at its core, holds no such promise at all . . . futurism is essentially an extrapolation of the present into the century ahead. . . . It does not challenge existing social relationships and institutions, but seeks to adapt them to seemingly new technological imperatives and possibilities – thereby redeeming rather than critiquing them. . . . Futurism, in effect, does not enlarge the future but annihilates it by absorbing it into the present. What makes this trend so insidious is that it also annihilates the imagination itself by constraining it to the present, thereby reducing our vision – even our prophetic abilities – to mere extrapolation.[8]

This multiplex utopian polylogue moves beyond the present historical situation in a series of suggestions and images that often differ from and contradict each other. As Michael Ryan puts it, the potential emancipatory society cannot be reduced to the product of one paradigm. It "would not be conceived as an integrated system with a central nervous system, a homogeneous whole whose unity and self-identity excludes all diversity and difference, but rather as a social collectivity, a heterogeneous aggregate."[9] The contribution which the utopian dialogue makes to this oppositional project, therefore, must be self-consciously diverse and disruptive as it offers multiple strategies, scenarios, and images based on anti-hegemonic principles of the allocation of resources for basic human needs and the expansion of social structures for the nurturing of human emancipation. The utopian dialogue must be an ongoing participatory one that does not give way to the dictates of technocratic experts, political leaders, or any achieved situation.

The critical utopian novels have been part of this dialogue for the past decade or more. In alternative societies located at peripheries still in conflict with the metropolitan center, these marginal images of a better life have challenged many readers. Whileaway, Anarres, Mattapoisett, and Triton are certainly not our future – much as we may long to spend a bit of time in one or another of them as befits our temperament and/or our politics. Yet they are symbolic provocations that help us to break from what is our present and to work together to create what could be our future. These utopias help to sustain us after long meetings and political defeats. They help to provoke our imaginations as we work out new strategies to meet our needs and desires. They challenge us to play with alternatives and thereby break out of the ideological chains that have restricted our socialized imaginations.

Willed transformation

The margins are at the center.   (Jacques Derrida)

The emancipated future, however, will not be reached by utopian dreaming alone. The way forward involves personal and collective effort. As we have seen in the previous chapters, at the ideological core of the critical utopian novels is a message of contestation with the current dominant forces, a set of meditations on the process of willed transformation, the activism, required for social revolution. Too often in past utopian writing have inspiring societies been described without a care given to the measures needed to move from the historical present to the new society. Engels's caution returns again as we realize that the suggestive political yearnings of this literature can absorb in wish-fulfillment the libidinal energy needed for their historical realization. Some radical utopias, however, have made the effort to include this necessary account of the revolutionary transition, as for example in William Morris's *News from Nowhere*. Just as Morris outlined the process of revolution, so too have the more recent critical utopias, for these texts are as much concerned with the discrete process of consciousness raising and political engagement as they are with iconic social images. Indeed, a powerful realism is brought to utopian fantasy as the radicalizing process at both micro/personal and macro/public levels is traced in characters who realize their oppression, find the solidarity of collective opposition, and take radical steps in their personal and political lives to destroy the realm of necessity and make way for the realm of freedom.

Each politicized character is presented initially as a divided person, marking the process of social change at its origins in each person's daily experience. In Russ, the four Js are distinct characters as well as aspects of one personality. In the course of the text the diverse personas come together in a stronger and more self-aware whole that is both a sign of greater personal fulfillment as well as of greater political, now collective and varied, effectiveness. In LeGuin, Shevek's youthful struggles in the Anarres chapters are replicated in the adult breakthroughs achieved in the adult, Urras chapters. In Piercy, Connie ceases being an isolated and oppressed victim with the help of her future double, Luciente; the person she could be in a better social structure helps to inspire her to be a self-aware person and successful guerilla in the society in which she is actually caught. In Delany, the process of radicalization is shown in a negative light as Bron goes through a series of personal emigrations between societies and genders, but for all his identity crises he never becomes the self-actualized or effective political person that Triton society allows him to be. He recycles his self-delusion and mistreatment of others in his new selves, and his low political effectiveness is measured by the passive survival of a torture session and active help in the anti-gravity attack which he later uses to his personal benefit in espousing a male supremacist ideology rather than for the benefit of the greater society. The process of radicalization is shown in a positive light, however, in Sam who undergoes a successful sex, race, and gender change in order to become a more happy individual and who makes a major political contribution to the survival of the utopian alternative in the satellites. Also, The Spike, who maintains her own integrity, continues to raise awareness in the utopian population by her art.

In each novel, then, the personal and the political are interrelated but not conflated. The interplay between social context and the personal and political dimensions of the character is explored in a variety of ways in the four texts. In linking the process of personal experience and self-actualization with the process of politicization and social change, the critical utopias reflect the experience of activism in the 1960s and 1970s and add to an understanding of revolutionary psychology that can continue to inform ongoing oppositional work.

The strategy and tactics of political activity in these novels are a further contribution to the oppositional ideology of activism. While Russ's novel claims the necessity of separatism for the survival and health of women in the face of continuing male supremacy, the other three novels describe a strategic alliance of all oppositional forces that incorporates separatist movements within its ranks. Each novel describes political activity that is primarily non-electoral, including personal change, ideological and cultural work, negotiation and organizing, and military engagement. With the exception of Shevek's battles in the administrative council and Luciente's participation in her decentralized government's Shaping Controversy, the political work described is primarily ideological/cultural, as in Joanna or Sam, or military, as in Jael or Connie. However, all four novels include non-elected revolutionary government officials in key roles which involve either organizing or negotiation: for example, Janet/Jael, Shevek, Luciente, and Sam. In the critical utopias, as well as in oppositional theoretical writing, the politics of alliance with an emphasis on extra-parliamentary work has replaced the more traditional left notion of the vanguard organization or party as the cutting edge of radical social change.

This understanding of the oppositional alliance is the result, as Stanley Aronowitz points out, of a new conception of the emancipatory project which goes beyond that provided by traditional socialism.[10] At its core is the "self-liberation of the subordinated classes" as the primary condition of a self-managed socialism. It is

206

a goal that is no longer simply consistent with the narrow aspiration to control the state by parliamentary or other means. As Aronowitz says, modern left-parliamentary politics may "aggregate desire, but it tends to suppress its extra-parliamentary expressions." Thus, he argues, the parliamentary left, "because of its claim to a master discourse," a single party line, "becomes the most indefatigable enemy of the opposition in those countries where it 'represents' the masses within the state."

To be sure, parliamentary left activity is not to be dispensed with. Parties of socialism have been and continue to be organizations which, while often compromising with the ruling hegemony of capital, seek to raise the "horizon of freedom" in various political struggles. However, Aronowitz holds that an effective master discourse of revolution articulated by such parties is no longer possible: the revolutionary party does not fully represent the subordinate classes and groups as they live out their daily lives because these very groups are divided by industry, sector, national origin, race, sex, age, and the like. Thus, the subordinate classes and groups "remain serially organized," in Sartre's terms. "Their unification depends upon the formation that can weld these disparate parts into a single force against capital as such, rather than against its segments."

Such a force is not the party, for it cannot represent this anti-hegemonic aggregate as though it were a unitary working class. The party "can only 'represent' the proletariat in its multiple interests by suppressing the emancipatory goal which, in effect, remains unrepresentable in the empirical sense." Indeed, the more the party becomes a separate institution, a bureaucracy functioning within the present social formations of capitalism and state socialism, the more distant it gets from the emancipatory agenda and the less claim it has to asserting an effective master discourse. Aronowitz argues that while the party historically represented the interests of the working class, it maintained a revolutionary role only "so long as it occupied the space for those demands that were not recuperable within the framework of specific capitalist or proto-capitalist societies." The more that capitalist and state socialist societies stabilized after the Second World War, the more the party "became only *upon occasion* oppositional, when excluded from bourgeois or bureaucratic hegemony." In recent time, the party of the left has become a party of order, helping to rule rather than to attack the dominant hegemony. In short, the revolutionary left party and its inadequate master discourse can no longer provide the moral, intellectual, and political leadership of the anti-hegemonic forces.

Thus, Aronowitz like others calls for an alliance not based in the left party but built from "a micropolitics of autonomous oppositional movements, whether derived from production relations or not." The demands of this new block include the end to male supremacy and the emancipation of women, the restoration of the autonomy of nature, the self-management of workplace and living space, and the liberation of racial, ethnic, and linguistic groups. These demands are such that the oppositional historic bloc must remain anti-hegemonic as both a political and social principle so that the deep and deserving differences are permanently guaranteed. Autonomy in all sectors would be a condition and a practice that would prevail both in the course of the ongoing struggle and in the process of living in the new society.

In this context, Gramsci's identification of the terrain of ideology and culture as the major site for contesting the dominant power describes a key strategy. Aronowitz:

> It is not only that moral and intellectual leadership of the society is a necessary concomitant to political and economic power, but it becomes its very condition. Thus the struggle over culture, rather than the struggle for economic advantage, is connected to the problematic of historical change, since under late capitalist conditions economic struggles no longer retain their subversive content.

Since ideology allows for the persistence of present domination, it is at the level of ideology and culture that the oppositional project of breaking that rule must be carried out – along with the continuing effort in the economic and political sectors. In the radical self-management, feminist, and ecology movements – and in a more contradictory manner the progressive movements in religion and nationalism – new conceptions and practices of social and natural relations are being developed to challenge those which maintain the prevailing order.

We must, then, speak of a "series of anti-hegemonies." As

self-management, feminism, and ecology redefine our relationship to each other and to nature, and as liberation theology and
other such spiritual movements and the democratic nationalism
of subordinate peoples also redefine morality and community,
these oppositional movements cluster around the common utopian desire for freedom. Furthermore, the liberation of this desire
calls for a "return to the notion of will" on the part of each and
every person which transcends the "claims of centrally-organized
political parties to *represent* desire." Although the ability of
world capitalism to destroy opposition or to render it useful to the
status quo remains startlingly powerful, the demands for "a
self-managed society on the basis of the formation of an historic
bloc that is simultaneously anti-capitalist and anti-hierarchical
remains beyond the recuperative powers of the prevailing order."
The anticipation of this historic bloc in the broad utopian
dialogue which we have been describing is quite clear. In the
critical utopian discourse the fulfillment of desire and the revival
of willed transformation are the basic shared insights throughout
all the texts. As Aronowitz says, "socialism is, now as before, a
utopian vision rather than a scientifically deduced certainty,"
but it is a utopian vision rooted in the diverse historical
experience of the entire oppositional movement.

"What is at stake, then," Michael Ryan argues,

> is a politics of multiple centers and plural strategies, less
> geared toward the restoration of a supposedly ideal
> situation held to be intact and good than to the micro-
> logical fine-tuning of questions of institutional power,
> work toward re-distribution, sexual politics demands,
> resource allocation, domination, and a broad range of
> problems whose solutions would be situationally
> and participationally defined.[11]

These solutions have their prefigurative utopian input, as what is
not yet is imagined by those seeking to engage what is. In his
discussion of "Post-leninist Marxism," Ryan, like Aronowitz,
recognizes the need for a "new organization, founded not on
guidance, leadership, a knowing elite, and an abstract set of
concepts, but instead on participation, self-activity, a diffusion of
the leadership function, differences, and radical participatory

democracy."[12] This diverse force breaks away from authoritarian, male-dominant, centralized politics that have no place in the efforts of people engaged in responsible and creative work to change their own lives. This alliance of margins without a center anticipates in both the personal and political dimensions the new values and the new society. Within this broad anti-hegemonic opposition, the critical utopian novels of Russ, LeGuin, Piercy, Delany, and others help to express the imagined and emerging social forms that pull the struggle forward. In their shared textual ideologeme they help to articulate the process of transformation which at the present moment in history characterizes that deep and necessary conflict.

Utopian praxis

> Is the unavoidability of metaphor also the unavoidability of sedition?   (Michael Ryan)

> The "lived relation of subordination" is to be contested wherever it is to be found.   (Sheila Rowbotham)

Utopia, when limited to the isolated work of an individual writer, a revolutionary organization, or a ruling parliamentary party, loses its cutting edge and slips peacefully into the affirmative culture of the prevailing ideology. That, of course, is the point of Bloch's, Engels's, and Delany's cautions about literary utopias, and it is also part of the criticism that Aronowitz and Ryan make about the master discourse of centralized revolutionary organizations. To be part of the emancipatory project, therefore, utopian writing breaks with the limits of the traditional genre and becomes a self-critical and disturbingly open form that articulates the deep tensions within the political unconscious at the present moment. The imposed totality of the single utopian text gives way to the contradictory and diverse multiplicity of a broad utopian dialogue.

We have seen how the limits and possibilities of the contemporary situation have resulted in the revival, destruction, and transformation of the literary genre of utopia. The critical utopian texts mark a shift in anti-hegemonic culture and politics away from male-dominant, capitalist, hierarchical social structures. The critical utopias give voice to an emerging radical perception and experience that emphasize process over system, autonomous and marginal activity over the imposed order of a center, human liberation over white/phallocratic control, and the interrelationships of nature over human chauvinism – and they give voice to the seditious utopian impulse itself. The critical utopias still describe alternative societies, but they are careful to consider the flaws and insufficiencies of these systems. They still draw on the provocative mode of the fantastic, but they also mix in a realism that allows for fuller exploration of the activism required to move toward the better society. But beyond self-criticism at the symbolic level and generic discontinuities which help express the common ideologeme, these texts also call attention to their own formal operations in self-reflexive gambits that identify the utopian form itself as a mechanism which makes such anticipations and activisms possible. The critical utopias refuse to be restricted by their own traditions, their own systematizing content; rather, it is their own radically hopeful activity as meaningful proto-political acts which they contribute to the current opposition.[13]

As expressions of a self-reflexive and open utopian impulse, the critical utopias go beyond that current metaphysical thinking "by binary oppositions, norms and margins, insides and outsides, instead of differences and relations" which "preserves the purity of the social system by making a decisive opposition between the good inside and the bad outside, the good, self-sufficient Brazilian bourgeoisie and the bad, parasitic marginals who come from outside."[14] By shattering the unity and perfection of their utopian societies, by rendering the relationship between home world and utopian periphery more complex than one of simple good and evil, by tracing the diversity and difficulty of revolutionary action, and by revealing the utopian process in a critical light, these texts reject the metaphysical structuring of reality that restricts perception and activity by excluding the negative and marginal. In the critical utopia, the margins are brought back into the historical situation, thus rendering the situation more complex, more conflictual, more subject to revolutionary change. Once included the contradictions must be faced, the struggle cannot be avoided. These texts privilege that oppositional way of thinking which is "negative, critical, relational, and differential, in the sense that it refuses to isolate and divide what is interrelated and interdependent."[15] The revolutionary other is kept within the situation, not denied by its expulsion: it is given new force as it explodes inside the belly of the alien beast. Put back into the process of historical change, the non-compromising utopian impulse is once again free to transcend the limits of the present and create a yearning for what has not yet been achieved.

The critical utopias, then, have restored the utopian impulse to the general oppositional movement. Therein radically hopeful figurations can become part of the collective, participatory, and non-hierarchical project of tearing down the present dominant system and meeting the historical, material, and situationally specific needs of all people rather than of the few who benefit from the current structure. As part of this oppositional project, utopian dissatisfaction helps to "de-privilege" the centrality of the logos or cogito and the work of individual writers or single organizations rationally to impose a planned society conceived as "a homogeneous whole whose unity and self-identity excludes all diversity and difference."[16] The utopian impulse which can never be satisfied or enclosed helps to preserve "the role of uncertainty, the modifications imposed by diverse situations and different contexts, the need for inclusion, rather than exclusion, of variables, the wisdom of choosing policies over monolithic programs, and the impossibility of mapping a whole reality."[17] For the utopian impulse, once separated from restraints of the utopian system in its idealist and totalizing form, continually bases its drive in the personal experience of unfulfilled human need, rather than in instrumentally rational systemic requirements. If those whose lives are oppressed and unfree are able to dream beyond the present, then the utopian impulse as a non-exclusive activity no longer limited to imposed models will play an increasingly significant role in the oppositional project. Since no perfect reality is ever achieved, in so far as human understanding and activity as well as the reality of nature push ever beyond a given "totality," that role will be a permanent one.

As Ryan suggests, there is a "necessary relationship between conceptual apparatuses and political institutions."[18] Just as coopted, enclosing utopian discourse serves the present social structure, so too critical utopian discourse connects with the politics and culture of the opposition. The critical utopias express "the continuous revolutionary displacement of power toward radical egalitarianism and plural defusion of all forms of macro- and micro-domination."[19] They help achieve a breach in the ideological and cultural structures that surround us and thus help create that oppositional public sphere in which the play of alternatives can be elaborated. In their self-reflexive and decon- structive questioning of utopian discourse they free the utopian impulse for the ongoing task of social change.[20]

In his discussion of the role of philosophical deconstruction in breaking down assumptions and conceptual apparatuses that privilege absolute meaning and absolute sovereign power, Ryan refers to Derrida's argument that metaphor, the thing that be- comes other than itself, is more fundamental than absolute meaning and identity. Metaphor names that state of things characterized by transformation, alteration, relationality, dis- placement, substitution, errancy. Metaphor holds open our perception of reality to otherness, to historical change. Thus, Ryan links metaphor and sedition as linguistic and political activities that share the challenge to the forces of containment, authority, totality. The seamless universality claimed by the present dominant system is thereby ruptured by these twin practices.

In this context, then, traditional utopias can be read as dis- courses that generate metaphysical models which have served the dominant social formation. Critical utopias can be read as metaphorical displacements arising out of current contradictions within the political unconscious. The utopian societies imaged in critical utopias ultimately refer to something other than a predict- able alternative paradigm, for at their core they identify self- critical utopian discourse itself as a process that can tear apart the dominant ideological web. Here, then, critical utopian discourse becomes a seditious expression of social change and popular sovereignty carried on in a permanently open process of envisioning what is not yet.

Notes

1 Introduction: the critical utopia

1 This introductory essay is not intended to be a full history of utopian thought and writing but rather a lead-in to the critical utopias of the 1970s. For literary histories that are much more detailed than this schematic introduction, the reader is referred to Robert C. Elliott, *The Shape of Utopia: Studies in a Literary Genre* (Chicago: University of Chicago Press, 1970); Frank E. Manuel and Fritzie P. Manuel, *Utopian Thought in the Western World* (Cambridge, Mass.: Belknap Press, 1979); and A. L. Morton, *The English Utopia* (London: Oxford University Press, 1952). Good bibliographies of utopian literature include Glenn Negley, *Utopian Literature: A Bibliography* (Lawrence: Regents Press of Kansas, 1977) and Lyman Tower Sargent, *British and American Utopian Literature, 1516–1975, An Annotated Bibliography* (New York: G. K. Hall, 1979).

2 Morton, *The English Utopia*, 49.

3 Leo Marx, *The Machine in the Garden: Technology and the Pastoral Ideal in America* (London: Oxford University Press, 1964). For other useful studies of the connection between utopia and the new world see R. W. B. Lewis, *The American Adam: Innocence, Tragedy, and Tradition in the Nineteenth Century* (Chicago: University of Chicago Press, 1952); and Henry Nash Smith, *The Virgin Land: The American West as Symbol and Myth* (Cambridge, Mass.: Harvard University

Press, 1950). See also the recent collection of essays: Kenneth Roemer, ed., *America as Utopia* (New York: Burt Franklin and Co., 1981).

4 Friedrich Engels, "Socialism: Utopian or Scientific," in Lewis S. Feuer, ed., *Marx and Engels: Basic Writings on Politics and Philosophy* (Garden City, NY: Anchor Books, 1959). For an interesting critical reading of this key essay see Darko Suvin, " 'Utopian' and 'Scientific': Two Attributes for Socialism from Engels," *Minnesota Review*, No. 6 (Spring 1976), 59–70.

5 M. H. Abendsour, *Utopias et dialectique du socialisme*, quoted in Raymond Williams, "Utopia and Science Fiction," in *Problems in Materialism and Culture* (London: Verso Books, 1980), 196–213.

6 Williams, "Utopia and Science Fiction," 203.

7 For a good discussion of the relationship between the utopian novels and radical politics of this period, see Jeanne Pfaelzer, "Utopian Fiction in America, 1888–1900: The Impact of Political Theory on Literary Forms." Dissertation: University College, London, 1975.

8 For a good discussion of this transition, see James Weinstein, *Ambiguous Legacy: The Left in American Politics* (New York: New Viewpoints Press, 1975) and *The Decline of Socialism in America, 1912–1925* (New York: Monthly Review Press, 1967).

9 Stuart Ewen, *Captains of Consciousness: Advertising and the Social Roots of Consumer Culture* (New York: McGraw Hill, 1976). For analyses of the deskilling of labor and the development of technocratic managerial power, see Harry Braverman, *Labor and Monopoly Capital: The Degradation of Work in the Twentieth Century* (New York: Monthly Review Press, 1974) and David F. Noble, *America by Design: Science, Technology, and the Rise of Corporate Capitalism* (London: Oxford University Press, 1977).

10 For a good discussion of the mechanism of "artificial negativity" in capitalist culture, see Paul Piccone, "The Crisis of One-Dimensionality," *Telos*, No. 35 (Spring 1978), 43–54; and Tim Luke, "Culture and Politics in the Age of Artificial Negativity," *Telos*, No. 35 (Spring 1978), 55–72.

11 André Gorz, *Farewell to the Working Class: An Essay on Post-Industrial Socialism* (London: Pluto Press, 1982), 81.

12 Gorz, *Farewell to the Working Class*, 85. For another discussion of the "post-instrumental" opposition, see, especially, chapter 10, "Feminism, Participatory Democracy, and Ecology: Toward a Post-Instrumental Mode of Symbolization," in Isaac D. Balbus, *Marxism and Domination: A Neo-Hegelian, Feminist, Psychoanalytic Theory of Sexual, Political and Technological Liberation* (Princeton: Princeton University Press, 1982).

2   The utopian imagination

1   Fredric Jameson, *The Political Unconscious: Narrative as a Socially Symbolic Act* (Ithaca, NY: Cornell University Press, 1981), 92.

2   Jack Zipes, *Breaking the Magic Spell: Radical Theories of Folk and Fairy Tales* (London: Heinemann, 1979), 97.

3   See Herbert Marcuse, "The Affirmative Character of Culture," *Negations* (Boston: Beacon Press, 1968).

4   Antonio Gramsci, *Selections from the Prison Notebooks* (New York: International, 1971), 258.

5   See Michel Foucault, *Madness and Civilization* (New York: Pantheon, 1965); *The Order of Things* (New York: Pantheon, 1970); *The Birth of the Clinic* (New York: Pantheon, 1973); *Discipline and Punish* (New York: Pantheon, 1977); and *The History of Sexuality* (New York: Pantheon, 1978).

6   See Harry Braverman, *Labor and Monopoly Capital: The Degradation of Work in the Twentieth Century* (New York: Monthly Review Press, 1974).

7   Althusser's theory of ideology can be found primarily in "Marxism and Humanism" in *For Marx* (New York: Vintage, 1970), and in "Ideology and Ideological State Apparatuses" in *Lenin and Philosophy* (London: New Left Books, 1971). For an important critique and expansion of this work see Teresa de Lauretis, *Alice Doesn't: Feminism, Semiotics, Cinema* (London: Macmillan, 1984), especially the chapter "Semiotics and Experience" in which de Lauretis' concept of "experience" allows for openings that a strict Althusserian analysis tends to prevent.

8   Tony Bennett, *Formalism and Marxism* (London and New York: Methuen, 1979), 118. For another discussion of ideology see Jorge Larrain, *The Concept of Ideology* (London: Hutchinson, 1983).

9   Fredric Jameson, "Reflections in Conclusion," in *Aesthetics and Politics* (London: Verso Books, 1980), 212.

10   See Karl Mannheim, *Ideology and Utopia: An Introduction to the Sociology of Knowledge* (New York: Harvest Books, 1936).

11   Jameson, *Political Unconscious*, 286.

12   Jameson, *Political Unconscious*, 287.

13   Jameson, "Reflections in Conclusion," 210.

14   Ernst Bloch, quoted in Zipes, *Breaking the Magic Spell*, 129.

15   Ernst Bloch, *On Karl Marx* (New York: Herder & Herder, 1971), 172. Selections translated from *Das Prinzip Hoffnung* (Frankfurt/ Main: Suhrkamp Verlag, 1959).

16   Fredric Jameson, *Marxism and Form: Twentieth Century Dialectical Theories of Literature* (Princeton: Princeton University Press, 1971), 129.

17   Quoted in Zipes, *Breaking the Magic Spell*, 137.
18   Bloch, *On Karl Marx*, 136.
19   Bloch, *On Karl Marx*, 172.
20   Herbert Marcuse, *Eros and Civilization* (Boston: Beacon Press, 1955), 134.
21   Stanley Aronowitz, *The Crisis in Historical Materialism: Class, Politics, and Culture in Marxist Theory* (New York: Praeger, 1981), 127–8. For further discussions of the movements comprising the oppositional historic bloc, see Arthur Hirsh, *The French New Left: An Intellectual History from Sartre to Gorz* (Boston: South End Press, 1981) and Michael Albert and Robin Hahnel, *Marxism and Socialist Theory* (Boston: South End Press, 1981), as well as Balbus cited above.
22   See Jürgen Habermas, *Toward a Rational Society* (Boston: Beacon Press, 1970); Oskar Negt and Alexander Kluge, *Öffentlichkeit und Erfahrung: Zur Organisations-analyse von burgerlicher und proletarischer Öffentlichkeit* (Frankfurt/Main: Suhrkamp, 1973); Eberhard Knödler-Bunte, "The Proletarian Public Sphere and Political Organization: An Analysis of Negt's and Kluge's *The Public Sphere and Experience*," *New German Critique*, No. 4 (Winter 1975), 51–77; and Zipes, *Breaking the Magic Spell*, 125.

3   The literary utopia

1   Fredric Jameson, *The Political Unconscious: Narrative as a Socially Symbolic Act* (Ithaca, NY: Cornell University Press, 1981), 19–20.
2   Jameson, *Political Unconscious*, 106.
3   Jameson, *Political Unconscious*, 104.
4   Northrop Frye, *Anatomy of Criticism* (Princeton: Princeton University Press, 1957), 193.
5   Frye, *Anatomy*, 187–8.
6   Glenn Negley and J. Max Patrick, *The Quest for Utopia* (New York: Schumann, 1952), 3.
7   Raymond Williams, "Utopia and Science Fiction," in *Problems in Materialism and Culture* (London: Verso Books, 1980), 203.
8   Darko Suvin, "Defining the Literary Genre of Utopia: Some Historical Semantics, Some Genealogy, a Proposal, and a Plea," *Metamorphoses of Science Fiction* (New Haven: Yale University Press, 1979), 49.
9   Suvin, "Defining the Literary Genre of Utopia," 54.
10   Jack Zipes, *Fairy Tales and the Art of Subversion* (London: Heinemann, 1983), 173.
11   Sigmund Freud, "The Uncanny," reprinted in *New Literary History*, 7 (Spring 1976), 630. See also Hélène Cixous, "Fiction and its

Phantoms: a Reading of Freud's *Das Unheimliche*," in the same issue, 525–48.

12   Ernst Bloch, *On Karl Marx* (New York, Herder & Herder, 1971), 30–1.

13   For the discussion of the iconic and discrete modes that led to my formulation, see J. M. Lotman, "The Discrete Text and the Iconic Text: Some Remarks on the Structure of Narrative," *New Literary History*, 6 (Winter 1975), 333–8. For Delany's usage of outer and inner discourse and the discourse with the world, see Samuel R. Delany, *The American Shore* (Elizabethtown, NY: Dragon Press, 1978).

14   Jameson, *Political Unconscious*, 112.

15   Jameson, *Political Unconscious*, 115.

16   Louis Marin, *Utopiques: Jeux d'Espace* (Paris: Minuit, 1973), 20–1. Translated by Eugene Hill and quoted in his review of Marin: "The Place of the Future: Louis Marin and his *Utopiques*," *Science-Fiction Studies*, 27 (July 1982), 167–80.

17   Fredric Jameson, "Of Islands and Trenches: Neutralization and the Production of Utopian Discourse" (a review of Louis Marin, *Utopiques: Jeux d'Espace*), *Diacritics*, 7, No. 2 (Summer 1977), 6.

18   Jameson, summarizing and quoting Marin, "Of Islands and Trenches," 11.

19   Jameson, "Of Islands and Trenches," 21.

20   For historical and theoretical treatments of the science fiction genre, see Samuel R. Delany, *The Jewel-Hinged Jaw: Notes on the Language of Science Fiction* (Elizabethtown, NY: Dragon Press, 1977); Patrick Parrinder, *Science Fiction: Its Criticism and Teaching* (London and New York: Methuen, 1980); Robert Scholes and Eric Rabkin, *Science Fiction: History, Science, Vision* (New York: Oxford University Press, 1977); and Darko Suvin, *Metamorphoses of Science Fiction* (New Haven: Yale University Press, 1979).

21   Fredric Jameson, "Progress Versus Utopia; or, Can We Imagine the Future?," *Science-Fiction Studies*, 27 (July 1982), 152.

22   See Ernst Bloch, "Non-Synchronism and the Obligation to Dialectics," *New German Critique*, No. 11 (Spring 1977), 22–39.

23   See Jameson, *Political Unconscious*, 144–5.

24   Jameson, *Political Unconscious*, 83.

25   Jameson, *Political Unconscious*, 76.

26   Jameson, *Political Unconscious*, 99.

4   Joanna Russ, *The Female Man*

1   Preceding *The Female Man*, there was *Picnic on Paradise* (New York: Ace Books, 1968) and *And Chaos Died* (New York: Ace Books,

1970). After TFM, and still working out the anxieties, problems, and contradictions dealt with in that central novel, came *We Who Are About To . . .* (New York: Dell, 1975) and *The Two of Them* (New York: Berkley, 1978). See also Russ's children's book, dealing with the same questions, *Kitatinny* (New York: Daughters Press, 1978).

2   Ann J. Lane, "Introduction," to Charlotte Perkins Gilman, *Herland* (New York: Pantheon Books, 1979), xxii. This is the first publication of *Herland* in book form since it was serialized in Gilman's own magazine, *The Forerunner*, in 1915.

3   Marilyn Hacker, "Science Fiction and Feminism: The Work of Joanna Russ," introduction to Joanna Russ, *The Female Man* (Boston: Gregg Press, 1977). In conversation with Samuel R. Delany in Milwaukee, Wisconsin on September 12, 1977, I was told by Delany that Russ began work on what was to be TFM as early as 1966. The novel grew out of her short story, "When It Changed," published in *Again Dangerous Visions*, ed. Harlan Ellison (New York: New American Library, 1972).

4   This information comes from Samuel R. Delany in conversation in Milwaukee, Wisconsin on September 12, 1977.

5   Joanna Russ, "Creating Positive Images of Women: A Writer's Perspective," Women Writer's Conference, Cornell University, n.d., 5.

6   Russ, "Creating Positive Images," 5.

7   Russ, "Creating Positive Images," 5.

8   Russ, "Creating Positive Images," 9.

9   See the critiques of science fiction and its male-dominated publishing establishment: Beverly Friend, "Virgin Territory: Women and Sex in Science Fiction," *Extrapolation*, 14, No. 1 (December 1972), 49–58; Joanna Russ, "The Image of Women in Science Fiction," *Vortex*, No. 1 (February 1974), 53–7; Mary Kenny Badami, "A Feminist Critique of Science Fiction," *Extrapolation*, 18, No. 1 (December 1976), 6–19; Joanna Russ, "*Amor Vincit Foeminam*: The Battle of the Sexes in SF," *Science-Fiction Studies*, No. 7 (March 1980), 2–15.

10 Russ, "*Amor Vincit Foeminam*," 15.

11 Hacker, "Science Fiction and Feminism," 68.

12 Pamela J. Annas, "New Worlds, New Words: Androgyny in Feminist Science Fiction," *Science-Fiction Studies*, No. 15 (July 1978), 145. Annas further argues that SF is "structurally suited to a role as revolutionary literature" by describing the rapid development of SF in the 1930s as the other side of the critical realist/left literature of Meridel LeSuer, Jack Conroy, Richard Wright, Mike Gold, and others. Whereas the realist works analyzed the economic, political, and social situations of the immediate present, SF was able to be tapped as a critical literature that broke beyond the "realistic" perceptions to a distanced perception – by means of its ability to work

on the problems of this world in the imagery of another – that was both critical of the present and expressive of a not yet realized future.

13　Joanna Russ, *The Female Man* (New York: Bantam Books, 1975), 6–7. Subsequent references will be coded in parentheses in the text as TFM.

14　Catherine McClenahan, "Textual Politics: the Uses of the Imagination in Joanna Russ's *The Female Man*," *Transactions of the Wisconsin Academy of Sciences, Arts, and Letters*, Vol. 70 (1982), 114–25.

15　Hacker, "Science Fiction and Feminism," 75.

16　Russ, "Creating Positive Images," 7.

17　Yves Lomax, "Montage?," *Camerawork*, 24 (March 1982), 8–12.

18　McClenahan, "Textual Politics," 120.

19　McClenahan, "Textual Politics," 120.

20　Nadia Khouri, "The Dialectics of Power: Utopia in the Science Fiction of LeGuin, Jeury, and Piercy," *Science-Fiction Studies*, 7 (March 1980), 49.

5　Ursula K. LeGuin, The Dispossessed

1　Ursula K. LeGuin, *The Dispossessed* (New York: Harper & Row, 1974). Subsequent references will be coded in parentheses in the text as TD.

2　*The Left Hand of Darkness* (New York: Walker & Company, 1969); *The Lathe of Heaven* (New York: Scribner's, 1971); *The Word for World is Forest* (New York: Berkley, 1972).

3　John Fekete, "*The Dispossessed* and *Triton*: Act and System in Utopian Science Fiction," *Science-Fiction Studies*, 18 (July 1979), 131.

4　Samuel R. Delany, "To Read *The Dispossessed*," in *The Jewel-Hinged Jaw* (Elizabethtown, NY: Dragon Press, 1977), see 292–3.

5　Fekete, "*The Dispossessed* and *Triton*," 135.

6　Khouri, "The Dialectics of Power: Utopia in the Science Fiction of LeGuin, Jeury and Piercy," *Science-Fiction Studies*, 7 (March 1980), 51.

7　Fekete, "*The Dispossessed* and *Triton*," 135.

8　Khouri, "Dialectics of Power," 52.

9　Khouri, "Dialectics of Power," 53.

10　Delany, "To Read *The Dispossessed*," 293.

6　Marge Piercy, Woman on the Edge of Time

1　Marge Piercy, "The Peaceable Kingdom," in *Breaking Camp* (Middletown, Conn.: Wesleyan University Press, 1968), pp. 68–9.

2   Piercy's poetry published in book form includes: *Breaking Camp* (Middletown, Conn.: Wesleyan University Press, 1968); *Hard Loving* (Middletown, Conn.: Wesleyan University Press, 1969); *4-Telling* (Trumanstown, NY: Crossing Press, 1971); *To Be of Use* (New York: Doubleday, 1973); *Living in the Open* (New York: Knopf, 1976); *The Twelve Spoked Wheel Flashing* (New York: Knopf, 1978); *The Moon is Always Female* (New York: Knopf, 1980). Piercy's novels include: *Going Down Fast* (New York: Trident, 1969); *Dance the Eagle to Sleep* (Garden City, NY: Doubleday, 1970); *Small Changes* (Garden City, NY: Doubleday, 1973); *Woman on the Edge of Time* (New York: Knopf, 1976); *The High Cost of Loving* (New York: Harper & Row, 1978); *Vida* (New York: Summit, 1979).

3   Pamela J. Annas, "New Worlds, New Words: Androgyny in Feminist Science Fiction," *Science-Fiction Studies*, No. 15 (July 1978), p. 154.

4   Marge Piercy, *Woman on the Edge of Time* (New York: Knopf, 1976). Subsequent references to this book will be coded in parentheses in the text as WET.

5   Elaine Hoffman Baruch, "A Natural and Necessary Monster: Women in Utopia," *Alternative Futures*, 2, No. 1 (Winter 1979), 44.

6   Baruch, "A Natural and Necessary Monster," 45.

7   Shulamith Firestone, *The Dialectic of Sex* (New York: Bantam Books, 1970).

8   Nadia Khouri, "The Dialectics of Power: Utopia in the Science Fiction of LeGuin, Jeury, and Piercy," *Science-Fiction Studies*, 7 (March 1980), 58.

9   Annas, "New Worlds, New Words," 159.

7   Samuel R. Delany, Triton

1   This information comes from a conversation with Samuel R. Delany in Milwaukee, Wisconsin on September 12, 1977.

2   See *The Jewels of Aptor* (New York: Ace Books, 1962); *The Ballad of Beta-2* (New York: Ace Books, 1965); *Empire Star* (New York: Ace Books, 1966); *Babel-17* (New York: Ace Books, 1966); *The Einstein Intersection* (New York: Ace Books, 1968); *Nova* (New York: Bantam, 1968); *Dhalgren* (New York: Bantam, 1974); *Tales of Nevèryön* (New York: Bantam, 1979); *Neveryóna* (New York: Bantam, 1983); *Flight from Nevèryön* (New York: Bantam, 1985); and the critical works, *The Jewel-Hinged Jaw* (Elizabethtown, NY: Dragon Press, 1977); *The American Shore* (Elizabethtown, NY: Dragon Press, 1978); *Starboard Wine* (Hastings-on-Hudson, NY: Dragon Press, 1984). For a "Bibliography" of the "Modular Calculus," see *Flight from Nevèryön*, 381.

3   Samuel R. Delany, "Critical Methods: Speculative Fiction," *Quark 1*,

ed. Samuel R. Delany and Marilyn Hacker (New York: Paperback Library, 1970), 191.

4   Delany, "Critical Methods," 191.

5   Delany, "Critical Methods," 191.

6   Samuel R. Delany, "Shadows," in *The Jewel-Hinged Jaw: Notes on the Language of Science Fiction* (Elizabethtown, NY: Dragon Press, 1977), 133–4. The "Shadows" essay is dated 1973–4.

7   Delany, "Critical Methods," 191.

8   Delany, "Critical Methods," 191–2.

9   Delany, "Critical Methods," 192.

10   Delany, "Critical Methods," 192.

11   Delany, "Critical Methods," 193.

12   Delany, "Critical Methods," 194.

13   Michel Foucault, quoted in Samuel R. Delany, *Triton* (New York: Bantam, 1976), 345. Subsequent references will be coded in parentheses in the text as T.

14   Conversation with Delany in Milwaukee, Wisconsin, September 12, 1977. See Joanna Russ, "Nobody's Home," in *New Dimensions*, ed. Robert Silverberg (New York: Ballantine, 1972), and in *Women of Wonder*, ed. Pamela Sargent (New York: Vintage, 1974). The 1974 edition is the one referred to in the text.

15   Russ, "Nobody's Home," 253.

16   Russ, "Nobody's Home," 252.

17   Delany, "Shadows," 99.

18   Nadia Khouri, "The Dialectics of Power: Utopia in the Science Fiction of LeGuin, Jeury, and Piercy," *Science-Fiction Studies*, 7 (March 1980), 49.

8   Conclusion

1   Michael Albert and Robin Hahnel, *Marxism and Socialist Theory* (Boston: South End Press, 1981), 3.

2   Murray Bookchin, "On Remaking the American Left," *Socialist Review*, 73 (January/February 1984), 115.

3   Bookchin, "On Remaking the American Left," 115–16.

4   Shulamith Firestone, *The Dialectic of Sex* (New York: Bantam Books, 1970), 238–40.

5   Wendell Berry, *The Unsettling of America* (New York: Avon Books, 1977); see 219–22 for all references.

6   André Gorz, *Farewell to the Working Class: An Essay on Post-Industrial Socialism* (London: Pluto Press, 1982); see 145–53 for all references.

7   Murray Bookchin, *The Ecology of Freedom* (Palo Alto, California: Cheshire Books, 1982); see 344–7 for all references.

8   Bookchin, *Ecology of Freedom*, 333.
9   Michael Ryan, *Marxism and Deconstruction: A Critical Articulation* (Baltimore and London: Johns Hopkins University Press, 1982), 187.
10   Stanley Aronowitz, *The Crisis in Historical Materialism: Class, Politics, and Culture in Marxist Theory* (New York: Praeger, 1981); see pp. 123–235 for all references.
11   Ryan, *Marxism and Deconstruction*, 116.
12   Ryan, *Marxism and Deconstruction*, 203.
13   See Fredric Jameson, *The Political Unconscious: Narrative as a Socially Symbolic Act* (Ithaca: Cornell University Press, 1981), 149.
14   Ryan, *Marxism and Deconstruction*, 127.
15   Ryan, *Marxism and Deconstruction*, 150.
16   Ryan, *Marxism and Deconstruction*, 187.
17   Ryan, *Marxism and Deconstruction*, 192.
18   Ryan, *Marxism and Deconstruction*, 8.
19   Ryan, *Marxism and Deconstruction*, 8.
20   See Sheila Rowbotham, Lynne Segal, Hilary Wainwright, *Beyond the Fragments: Feminism and the Making of Socialism* (Boston: Alyson Publications, 1979), especially 21–157. See. too, Isaac D. Balbus, *Marxism and Domination: A Neo-Hegelian, Feminist, Psychoanalytic Theory of Sexual, Political and Technological Liberation* (Princeton: University Press, 1982), and Teresa de Lauretis, *Alice Doesn't: Feminism, Semiotics, Cinema* (London: Macmillan, 1984). Rowbotham recalls for us the moment within each of our daily lives wherein "real life inequities" and desires are experienced, and she marks that moment as the basis from which the ongoing social revolution develops. This is done in the context of her critique of Leninism wherein she attacks the imposition of the external vanguard party agenda and the failure of the revolutionary party to facilitate that deeper moment of subversive self-activity. Her point is similar to Aronowitz's and was a direct influence on Ryan. Rowbotham's discussion, as well as that of Balbus and de Lauretis, pinpoints the juncture between the "personal" and "political," public/private, macro/micro, as the key location of deep change. It is at this juncture that the utopian impulse makes its most fundamental move – whether it takes the form of writing, reading, or more generally daydreaming. With this last note, the discussion of "critical utopias" ends, but the fuller exploration of that juncture, of the role of utopian desire in revolutionary psychology, has yet to happen. Another not yet.

Bibliography

Adams, Robert P. *Utopias and Social Ideals.* Seattle: University of Washington Press, 1976.

Adorno, Theodor. *Negative Dialectics.* New York: Seabury Press, 1973.

———. *Prisms.* London: Spearman, 1967.

Albert, Michael and Hahnel, Robin. *Marxism and Socialist Theory.* Boston: South End Press, 1981.

Aldiss, Brian W. *The Billion Year Spree: A History of Science Fiction.* New York: Schocken, 1974.

Althusser, Louis. *For Marx.* New York: Vintage, 1970.

———. *Lenin and Philosophy.* London: New Left Books, 1971.

Annas, Pamela J. "New Worlds, New Words: Androgyny in Feminist Science Fiction." *Science-Fiction Studies,* No. 15 (July 1978), 143–56.

Aronowitz, Stanley. *The Crisis in Historical Materialism: Class, Politics, and Culture in Marxist Theory.* New York: Praeger, 1981.

———. *False Promises: The Shaping of American Working Class Consciousness.* New York: McGraw Hill, 1973.

Astle, Richard Sharp. "Structures of Ideology in the English Gothic Novel." Dissertation, University of California-San Diego, 1977.

Badami, Mary Kenny. "A Feminist Critique of Science Fiction." *Extrapolation,* 18, No. 1 (December 1976), 6–19.

Balbus, Isaac D. *Marxism and Domination: A Neo-Hegelian, Feminist,*

Psychoanalytic Theory of Sexual, Political, and Technological Liberation. Princeton: Princeton University Press, 1982.

Baran, Paul and Sweezy, Paul M. *Monopoly Capital: An Essay on the American Economic and Social Order.* New York: Monthly Review Press, 1966.

Baruch, Elaine Hoffman. "A Natural and Necessary Monster: Women in Utopia." *Alternative Futures,* 2, No. 1 (Winter 1979), 29–49.

Baxandall, Lee and Morowski, Stephan. *Marx and Engels on Literature and Art.* St Louis: Telos Press, 1973.

Benjamin, Walter. *Illuminations.* New York: Harcourt, 1968.

Bennett, Tony. *Formalism and Marxism.* London and New York: Methuen, 1979.

Berneri, Marie Louise. *Journey Through Utopia.* New York: Shocken, 1971.

Berry, Wendell. *The Unsettling of America.* New York: Avon Books, 1977.

Bierman, Judah. "Ambiguity in Utopia: *The Dispossessed.*" *Science-Fiction Studies,* No. 7 (November 1975), 249–56.

Bloch, Ernst. "Alienation, Estrangement." *Brecht.* Erika Munk, ed. New York: Bantam, 1972.

——. *Das Prinzip Hoffnung.* 2 vols. Frankfurt/Main: Suhrkamp, 1973.

——. "Dialectic and Hope." *New German Critique,* No. 9 (Fall 1976), 3–11.

——. *Man On His Own: Essays in the Philosophy of Religion.* New York: Herder & Herder, 1971.

——. "Non-synchronism and the Obligation to Its Dialectics." *New German Critique,* No. 11 (Spring 1977), 22–39.

——. *On Karl Marx.* New York: Herder & Herder, 1970.

——. *Philosophy of the Future.* New York: Herder & Herder, 1970.

Bookchin, Murray. *The Ecology of Freedom.* Palo Alto, California: Cheshire Books, 1982.

——. "On Remaking the American Left." *Socialist Review,* 73 (January–February 1984), 113–16.

Braverman, Harry. *Labor and Monopoly Capital: The Degradation of Work in the Twentieth Century.* New York: Monthly Review Press, 1974.

Brenkman, John. "Theses on Cultural Marxism." *Social Text,* No. 7 (Spring–Summer 1983), 19–33.

Brown, Bruce. *Marx, Freud and the Critique of Everyday Life.* New York: Monthly Review Press, 1973.

Bryant, Dorothy. *The Kin of Ata Are Waiting for You.* New York: Random House, 1971.

Buber, Martin. *Paths in Utopia.* Boston: Beacon Press, 1949.

Callenbach, Ernest. *Ecotopia.* Berkeley: Banyon Books, 1975.

——. *Ecotopia Emerging.* New York: Bantam 1982.

Calverton, Victor F. *Where Angels Dare to Tread: Socialist and Communist*

Utopian Colonies in the United States. Freeport, NY: Books for Libraries Press, 1941.

Charnas, Suzy McKee. *Motherlines.* New York: Berkley, 1979.

Cixous, Hélène. "Fiction and Its Phantoms: A Reading of Freud's *Das Unheimliche*." *New Literary History*, 7 (Spring 1976), 525–48.

———. "The Laugh of the Medusa." in *New French Feminisms*, ed. Elaine Marks and Isabel de Courtivon. Brighton, Sussex: Harvester Press, 1980.

Clareson, Thomas D. *Science Fiction: The Other Side of Realism: Essays on Modern Fantasy and Science Fiction.* Bowling Green, Ohio: Bowling Green University Press, 1971.

Contoski, Victor. "Marge Piercy: A Vision of the Peaceable Kingdom." *Modern Poetry Studies*, 8, 205–16.

Delany, Samuel R. "About Five Thousand One Hundred and Seventy-five Words." *SF: The Other Side of Realism*, ed. Thomas D. Clareson. Bowling Green: Bowling Green University Press, 1971.

———. *The American Shore.* Elizabethtown, NY: Dragon Press, 1978.

———. *Babel-17.* New York: Ace Books, 1966.

———. *The Ballad of Beta-2.* New York: Ace Books, 1965.

———. "Critical Methods: Speculative Fiction." *Quark 1*, ed. Samuel R. Delany and Marilyn Hacker. New York: Paperback Library, 1970.

———. *Dhalgren.* New York: Bantam, 1974.

———. *The Einstein Intersection.* New York: Ace Books, 1968.

———. *Empire Star.* New York: Ace Books, 1966.

———. *The Fall of the Towers.* New York: Ace Books, 1966.

———. *Flight from Nevèryön.* New York: Bantam, 1985.

———. *The Jewel-Hinged Jaw: Notes on the Language of Science Fiction.* Elizabethtown, NY: Dragon Press, 1977.

———. *The Jewels of Aptor.* New York: Ace Books, 1962.

———. *Neveryóna.* New York: Bantam, 1983.

———. *Nova.* New York: Bantam, 1968.

———. *Starboard Wine.* Hastings-on-Hudson, NY: Dragon Press, 1984.

———. *Tales of Nevèryön.* New York: Bantam, 1979.

———. *Triton.* New York: Bantam, 1976.

De Lauretis, Teresa. *Alice Doesn't: Feminism, Semiotics, Cinema.* London: Macmillan, 1984.

———. "Semiotic Models, *Invisible Cities*." *Yale Italian Studies*, 2, No. 1 (Winter 1978), 13–39.

De Lauretis, Teresa, Huyssen, Andreas, and Woodward, Kathleen, eds. *The Technological Imagination: Theories and Fictions.* Madison: Coda Press, 1980.

Deleuze, Gilles and Guattari, Felix. *Anti-Oedipus: Capitalism and Schizophrenia.* New York: Viking, 1977.

Derrida, Jacques. *Of Grammatology.* Baltimore and London: Johns Hopkins University Press, 1974.

Disch, Thomas M., ed. *The New Improved Sun: An Anthology of Utopian S-F.* New York: Harper & Row, 1975.

Doig, Ivan, ed. *Utopian America: Dreams and Realities.* Rochell Park, NJ: Hayden Books, 1976.

Du Plessis, Rachel Blau. "The Feminist Apologues of Lessing, Piercy, and Russ." *Frontiers*, 4 (Spring 1979), 1–8.

Eagleton, Terry. *Criticism and Ideology.* London: New Left Books, 1976.

Elliott, Robert C. "Literature and the Good Life: A Dilemma." *Yale Review*, 65 (Autumn 1975), 24–37.

——. *The Shape of Utopia: Studies in a Literary Genre.* Chicago: University of Chicago Press, 1970.

Engels, Friedrich. "Socialism: Utopian or Scientific," in Lewis S. Feuer, ed. *Marx and Engels: Basic Writings on Politics and Philosophy.* Garden City, NY: Anchor Books, 1959.

Ewen, Stuart. *Captains of Consciousness: Advertising and the Social Roots of Consumer Culture.* New York: McGraw Hill, 1976.

Feher, Ferenc. "Is the Novel Problematic?" *Telos*, No. 15 (Spring 1973), 47–75.

Fekete, John. "*The Dispossessed* and *Triton*: Act and System in Utopian Science Fiction." *Science-Fiction Studies*, No. 18 (July 1979), 129–43.

Firestone, Shulamith. *The Dialectic of Sex.* New York: Bantam Books, 1970.

Fischer, Ernst. *Art Against Ideology.* New York: Braziller, 1969.

——. *The Necessity of Art.* Baltimore: Penguin, 1963.

Fisher, Judith L. "Trouble in Paradise: The Twentieth-Century Utopian Ideal." *Extrapolation*, 24, No. 4 (Winter 1983), 329–39.

Foucault, Michel. *The Archaeology of Knowledge.* New York: Pantheon, 1972.

——. *The Birth of the Clinic.* New York: Pantheon, 1973.

——. *Discipline and Punish.* New York: Pantheon, 1977.

——. *The History of Sexuality.* New York: Pantheon, 1978.

——. *Madness and Civilization.* New York: Pantheon, 1965.

——. *The Order of Things.* New York: Pantheon, 1970.

Frank, André Gunder. *Capitalism and Underdevelopment in Latin America.* New York: Monthly Review Press, 1967.

——. *World Accumulation.* London: Macmillan, 1978.

Franklin, H. Bruce. *Future Perfect: American Science Fiction of the Nineteenth Century.* New York: Oxford, 1978.

Friend, Beverly. "Virgin Territory: Women and Sex in Science Fiction." *Extrapolation*, 14, No. 1 (December 1972), 49–58.

Frye, Northrop. *Anatomy of Criticism: Four Essays.* Princeton: Princeton University Press, 1957.

Gearhardt, Sally Miller. *The Wanderground: Stories of the Hill Women.* Watertown, Mass.: Persephone Press, 1979.

Gendron, Bernard. *Technology and the Human Condition*. New York: St Martin's Press, 1977.

Gerber, Richard. *Utopian Fantasy*. London: Routledge & Kegan Paul, 1955.

Gilison, J. M. *The Soviet Image of Utopia*. Baltimore: Johns Hopkins University Press, 1975.

Gilman, Charlotte Perkins. *Herland*. New York: Pantheon Books, 1979.

Goodman, Paul. *Utopian Essays and Practical Proposals*. New York: Vintage Books, 1960.

Goodman, Percival, and Goodman, Paul. *Communitas: Means of Livelihood and Ways of Life*. New York: Vintage Books, 1960.

Goodwin, Barbara and Taylor, Keith. *The Politics of Utopia: A Study in Theory and Practice*. London: Hutchinson, 1982.

Gorz, André. *Ecology as Politics*. Boston: South End Press, 1980.

——. *Farewell to the Working Class: An Essay on Post-Industrial Socialism*. London: Pluto Press, 1982.

Gove, Philip Babcock. *The Imaginary Voyage in Prose Fiction*. London: Holland Press, 1961.

Gramsci, Antonio. *Selections from the Prison Notebooks*. New York: International, 1971.

Gray, Donald and Orick, Allan, eds. *Designs of Famous Utopias*. New York: Holt, Rinehart & Winston, 1959.

Habermas, Jürgen. "The Entwinement of Myth and Enlightenment: Rereading *Dialectic of Enlightenment*." *New German Critique*, No. 26 (Spring–Summer 1982), 13–54.

——. *Legitimation Crisis*. Boston: Beacon Press, 1975.

——. *Toward a Rational Society*. Boston: Beacon Press, 1970.

Hacker, Marilyn. "Science Fiction and Feminism: The Work of Joanna Russ." "Introduction" to Joanna Russ, *The Female Man*. Boston: Gregg Press, 1977.

Hansot, Elisabeth. *Perfection and Progress: Two Modes of Utopian Thought*. Cambridge, Mass.: MIT Press, 1964.

Hassan, Ihab. *The Dismemberment of Orpheus: Toward a Postmodern Literature*. New York: Oxford University Press, 1971.

——, ed. *Liberations*. Middletown, Conn.: Wesleyan University Press, 1971.

——. *Paracriticisms*. Urbana: University of Illinois Press, 1975.

——. *The Right Promethean Fire: Imagination, Science, and Cultural Change*. Urbana: University of Illinois Press, 1980.

Hauser, Arnold. *The Social History of Art*. 4 vols. New York: Vintage, 1964.

Hawkes, Terence. *Structuralism and Semiotics*. London and New York: Methuen, 1977.

Hayden, Dolores. "Communal Idealism and the American Landscape." *Landscape*, 20 (Winter 1976).

———. *Seven American Utopias: The Architecture of Communitarian Socialism, 1790–1975.* Cambridge, Mass.: MIT Press, 1976.

Hebdige, Dick. *Subculture: The Meaning of Style.* London and New York: Methuen, 1979.

Hertzler, Joyce Oramel. *The History of Utopian Thought.* New York: Macmillan, 1923.

Hillegas, Mark R. *The Future as Nightmare: H. G. Wells and the Anti-Utopians.* New York: Oxford University Press, 1967.

Hirsh, Arthur. *The French New Left: An Intellectual History from Sartre to Gorz.* Boston: South End Press, 1981.

Holland, Norman N. *The Dynamics of Literary Response.* New York: Norton, 1968.

Horkheimer, Max. *Critical Theory.* New York: Herder & Herder, 1972.

———. *Critique of Instrumental Reason.* New York: Seabury Press, 1974.

Horkheimer, Max and Adorno, Theodor W. *The Dialectic of the Enlightenment.* New York: Herder & Herder, 1972.

Howard, June. "Widening the Dialogue on Feminist Science Fiction," in *Feminist Re-visions: What Has Been and Might Be,* ed. Vivian Patraka and Louise A. Tilly. Ann Arbor, Michigan: Women's Studies Program, University of Michigan, 1983.

Huyssen, Andreas. "Critical Theory and Modernity." *New German Critique,* No. 26 (Spring–Summer 1982), 3–13.

Jackson, Rosemary. *Fantasy: The Literature of Subversion.* London and New York: Methuen, 1981.

Jameson, Fredric. "Introduction/Prospectus: to Reconsider the Relationship of Marxism to Utopian Thought." *Minnesota Review,* No. 6 (Spring 1972), 53–9.

———. "Of Islands and Trenches: Neutralization and the Production of Utopian Discourse." *Diacritics,* 7, No. 2 (Summer 1977), 2–22.

———. *Marxism and Form: Twentieth Century Dialectical Theories of Literature.* Princeton: Princeton University Press, 1971.

———. *The Political Unconscious: Narrative as a Socially Symbolic Act.* Ithaca, NY: Cornell University Press, 1981.

———. *The Prison House of Language: A Critical Account of Structuralism and Russian Formalism.* Princeton: Princeton University Press, 1972.

———. "Progress Versus Utopia; Or, Can We Imagine the Future?" *Science-Fiction Studies,* No. 27 (July 1982), 147–59.

———. "Reflections in Conclusion." in *Aesthetics and Politics.* London: Verso Books, 1977.

———. "World Reduction in LeGuin: The Emergence of Utopian Narrative," *Science-Fiction Studies,* No. 7 (November 1975), 221–31.

Jones, Howard Mumford. *O Strange New World: American Culture, The Formative Years.* New York: Viking Press, 1952.

Kahn, Herman J. and Wiener, Anthony. *The Year 2000: A Framework for Speculation on the Next Thirty-three Years*. New York: Macmillan, 1967.

Kalin, Martin G. *Utopian Flight from Unhappiness: Freud against Marx on Social Progress*. Totoway, NJ: Littlefield, Adams, 1975.

Kateb, George. *Utopia and its Enemies*. New York: Free Press, 1963.

Kellner, Douglas, and O'Hara, Harry. "Utopia and Marxism in Ernst Bloch." *New German Critique*, No. 9 (Fall 1976), 11–35.

Khouri, Nadia. "The Dialectics of Power: Utopia in the Science Fiction of LeGuin, Jeury, and Piercy." *Science-Fiction Studies*, No. 7 (March 1980), 49–61.

——. "Utopia and Epic: Ideological Confrontation in Jack London's *The Iron Heel*." *Science-Fiction Studies*, No. 9 (July 1976), 181–7.

Klare, Karl. "The Critique of Everyday Life: Marxism and the New Left." *Berkeley Journal of Sociology*, 16 (1971–2).

Knödler-Bunte, Eberhard. "The Proletarian Public Sphere and Organization: An Analysis of Negt and Kluge's *The Public Sphere and Experience*." *New German Critique*, No. 4 (Winter 1975), 51–77.

Lane, Ann J. "Introduction" to Charlotte Perkins Gilman, *Herland*. New York: Pantheon Books, 1979.

Larrain, Jorge. *The Concept of Ideology*. London: Hutchinson, 1983.

Lefebvre, Henri. *Everyday Life in the Modern World*. New York: Harper & Row, 1971.

LeGuin, Ursula K. "American SF and the Other." *Science-Fiction Studies*, No. 7 (November 1975), 208–10.

——. *The Dispossessed*. New York: Harper & Row, 1974.

——. *The Language of the Night: Essays on Fantasy and Science Fiction*. New York: Perigee, 1979.

——. *The Lathe of Heaven*. New York: Scribners, 1971.

——. *The Left Hand of Darkness*. New York: Walker, 1969.

——. *The Word for World is Forest*. New York: Berkley, 1972.

Leitenberg, Barbara. "The New Utopians." Dissertation, Indiana University, 1975.

Lewis, R. W. B. *The American Adam: Innocence, Tragedy, and Tradition in the Nineteenth Century*. Chicago: University of Chicago Press, 1955.

Lichtheim, George. *The Concept of Ideology and Other Essays*. New York: Vintage, 1963.

Lomax, Yves. "Montage?" *Camerawork*, 24 (March 1982), 8–12.

Lotman, J. M. "The Discrete Text and the Iconic Text: Some Remarks on the Structure of Narrative." *New Literary History*, 6, No. 6 (Winter 1975), 333–8.

Lukács, George. *The Historical Novel*. Boston: Beacon Press, 1963.

——. *History and Class Consciousness*. Cambridge, Mass.: MIT Press, 1971.

——. *Realism in Our Time*. New York: Harper & Row, 1964.

——. *Studies in European Realism.* New York: Grosset & Dunlap, 1964.

——. *The Theory of the Novel.* London: Merlin Press, 1971.

——. *Writer and Critic.* London: Merlin Press, 1970.

Luke, Tim. "Culture and Politics in the Age of Artificial Negativity." *Telos,* No. 35 (Spring 1978), 55–72.

McClenahan, Catherine. "Textual Politics: The Uses of the Imagination in Joanna Russ' *The Female Man.*" *Transactions of the Wisconsin Academy of Sciences, Arts, and Letters,* Vol. 70 (1982), 114–25.

Macherey, Pierre. *A Theory of Literary Production.* London: Routledge & Kegan Paul, 1978.

Mandel, Ernest. *Late Capitalism.* London: Verso Books, 1972.

Mannheim, Karl. *Ideology and Utopia: An Introduction to the Sociology of Knowledge.* New York: Harcourt, 1936.

Manuel, Frank E. *The Prophets of Paris.* Cambridge, Mass: Harvard University Press, 1962.

——., ed. *Utopias and Utopian Thought.* Boston: Houghton Mifflin, 1966.

Manuel, Frank E. and Manuel, Fritzie P. *Utopian Thought in the Western World.* Cambridge, Mass.: Belknap Press, 1979.

Marcuse, Herbert. *The Aesthetic Dimension.* Boston: Beacon Press, 1977.

——. *Counter Revolution and Revolt.* Boston: Beacon Press, 1972.

——. *Eros and Civilization.* Boston: Beacon Press, 1955.

——. *An Essay on Liberation.* Boston: Beacon Press, 1969.

——. *Five Lectures: Psychoanalysis, Politics, and Utopia.* Boston: Beacon Press, 1970.

——. *Negations.* Boston: Beacon Press, 1968.

——. *One Dimensional Man.* Boston: Beacon Press, 1964.

——. *Reason and Revolution: Hegel and the Rise of Social Theory.* Boston: Beacon Press, 1960.

Marin, Louis. "Theses on Ideology and Utopia." *Minnesota Review,* No. 6 (Spring 1976), 71–6.

——. *Utopiques: Jeux d'Espaces.* Paris: Minuit, 1973.

Marx, Leo. *The Machine in the Garden: Technology and the Pastoral Ideal in America.* London: Oxford University Press, 1964.

Mayer, Hans. *Steppenwolf and Everyman.* New York: Crowell, 1971.

Miller, Margaret. "The Ideal Woman in Two Feminist Science-Fiction Utopias." *Science-Fiction Studies,* No. 30 (July 1983), 191–8.

Morton, A. L. *The English Utopia.* London: Lawrence & Wishart, 1952.

Mumford, Lewis. *The Story of Utopias.* New York: Boni & Leverwright, 1922.

Nairn, Tom. *The Break-Up of Britain.* London: Verso Books, 1981.

Negley, Glenn. *Utopian Literature: A Bibliography.* Lawrence: Regents Press of Kansas, 1977.

Negley, Glenn and Patrick, J. Max. *The Quest for Utopia.* New York: Schuman, 1952.

231

Negt, Oscar. "Mass Media: Tools of Domination or Instruments of Emancipation? Aspects of the Frankfurt School's Communications Analysis." *Theories of Contemporary Culture*, Vol. II. Madison: Coda Press, 1978.

———. "The Non-Synchronous Heritage and the Problem of Propaganda." *New German Critique*, No. 9 (Fall 1976), 46–71.

Negt, Oskar and Kluge, Alexander. *Öffentlichkeit und Erfahrung: Zur Organisations-analyse von burgerlicher und proletarischer Öffentlichkeit*. Frankfurt/Main: Suhrkamp, 1973.

Noble, David F. *America By Design: Science, Technology, and the Rise of Corporate Capitalism*. London: Oxford University Press, 1977.

Norris, Christopher. *Deconstruction: Theory and Practice*. London and New York: Methuen, 1982.

Parrinder, Patrick. "Imagining the Future: Zamyatin and Wells." *Science-Fiction Studies*, No. 1 (Spring 1973), 37–41.

———. *Science Fiction: Its Criticism and Teaching*. London and New York: Methuen, 1980.

Parrington, Vernon Louis, Jr. *American Dreams: A Study of American Utopias*. New York: Russel & Russel, 1964.

Patai, Daphne. "Utopias." *Aphra*, 15, No. 3, 2–16.

Patrick, J. Max. "Iconoclasm, the Complement of Utopianism." *Science-Fiction Studies*, No. 9 (July 1976), 157–61.

Pfaelzer, Jean. "A State of One's Own: Feminism as Ideology in American Utopias 1880–1915." *Extrapolation*, 24, No. 4 (Winter 1983), 311–28.

———. "Utopian Fiction in America 1888–1900: The Impact of Political Theory on Literary Forms." Dissertation, University College, London, 1975.

———. *The Utopian Hypothesis*. Pittsburgh: University of Pittsburgh Press, 1984.

———. "Women in American Utopias, 1880–1900: The Impact of Political Theory on Literary Forms." Unpublished MS, 1979.

Philmus, Robert M. *Into the Unknown: The Evolution of Science Fiction from Francis Godwin to H. G. Wells*. Berkeley: University of California Press, 1970.

Piccone, Paul. "The Changing Function of Critical Theory." *New German Critique*, No. 12 (Fall 1977), 24–38.

———. "The Crisis of One-Dimensionality." *Telos*, No. 35 (Spring 1978), 43–54.

Piercy, Marge. *Breaking Camp*. Middletown, Conn.: Wesleyan University Press, 1968.

———. *Dance the Eagle to Sleep*. Garden City, NY: Doubleday, 1970.

———. *Going Down Fast*. New York: Trident, 1969.

———. *Hard Loving*. Middletown, Conn: Wesleyan University Press, 1969.

———. *Living in the Open*. New York: Knopf, 1976.

——. *To Be of Use*. New York: Doubleday, 1973.

——. *Woman on the Edge of Time*. New York: Knopf, 1976.

Porter, David L. "The Politics of LeGuin's Opus." *Science-Fiction Studies*, No. 7 (November 1975), 243–8.

Propp, Vladimir. *Morphology of the Folk Tale*. Austin: University of Texas Press, 1968.

Rabinbach, Anson. "Ernst Bloch's *Heritage of Our Times* and Fascism." *New German Critique*, No. 11 (Spring 1977), 5–22.

Rabkin, Eric. *The Fantastic in Literature*. Princeton: Princeton University Press, 1976.

Reich, Wilhelm. *Sex-Pol Essays: 1929–1934*. New York: Vintage, 1972.

Reiter, Rayna, ed. *Toward an Anthropology of Women*. New York: Monthly Review Press, 1975.

Renault, Gregory. "Speculative Porn: Aesthetic Form in Samuel R. Delany's *The Tides of Lust*." *Extrapolation*, 24, No. 2 (Summer 1983), 116–29.

Roemer, Kenneth M. *The Obsolete Necessity: America in Utopian Writings, 1888–1900*. Kent: Kent State University Press, 1976.

——. ed. *America as Utopia*. New York: Burt Franklin, 1981.

Rowbotham, Sheila and Segal, Lynne and Wainwright, Hilary. *Beyond the Fragments: Feminism and the Making of Socialism*. Boston: Alyson Publications, 1979.

Russ, Joanna. "*Amor Vincit Foeminam*: The Battle of the Sexes in SF." *Science-Fiction Studies*, No. 7 (March 1980), 2–15.

——. *And Chaos Died*. New York: Ace Books, 1970.

——. "Creating Positive Images of Women: A Writer's Perspective." Women Writer's Conference, Cornell University, n.d.

——. *The Female Man*. New York: Bantam Books, 1975.

——. "Nobody's Home." in *New Dimensions*. Robert Silverberg, ed. New York: Harper & Row, 1980.

——. *Picnic on Paradise*. New York: Ace Books, 1968.

——. "Towards an Aesthetics of Science Fiction." *Science-Fiction Studies*, 2 (1975), 112–19.

——. *The Two of Them*. New York: Berkley, 1978.

——. *We Who Are About To . . .* New York: Dell, 1975.

——. "What Can a Heroine Do? or Why Women Can't Write." In *Images of Women in Fiction: Feminist Perspectives*, ed. Susan Koppelman Cornillon. Bowling Green, Ohio: Bowling Green University Popular Press, 1972.

Ryan, Michael. *Marxism and Deconstruction: A Critical Articulation*. Baltimore and London: Johns Hopkins University Press, 1982.

Sargent, Lyman Tower. *British and American Utopian Literature, 1516–1975, An Annotated Bibliography*. New York: G. K. Hall, 1979.

——. "A Note on the Other Side of Human Nature in the Utopian Novel." *Political Theory*, 3 (February 1975), 88–97.

——. "Themes in Utopian Fiction Before Wells." *Science-Fiction Studies*, No. 10 (November 1976), 275–82.

——. "Utopia and Dystopia in Contemporary Science Fiction." *The Futurist*, 6 (June 1972), 93–8.

——. "Utopia – The Problem of Definition." *Extrapolation*, 16, No. 2 (May 1975), 137–48.

Sartre, Jean-Paul. *Critique of Dialectical Reason*. London: Verso Books, 1976.

Scholes, Robert. *The Fabulators*. New York: Oxford University Press, 1967.

——. *Fabulation and Metafiction*. Urbana: University of Illinois Press, 1979.

——. *Structural Fabulation: An Essay on the Fiction of the Future*. South Bend, Indiana: Notre Dame University Press, 1975.

Scholes, Robert and Rabkin, Eric. *Science Fiction: History, Science, Vision*. New York: Oxford University Press, 1977.

Segal, Howard P. "Life in a Technocracy: What it Might be Like." *The New Republic*, October 30, 1976, 42–4.

——. "Technological Utopianism and American Culture, 1830–1940." Dissertation, Princeton University, 1975.

——. "Utopianism As Ideology: A Defense." presented at First Annual Conference on Utopian Studies, Ann Arbor, Michigan, October, 1976.

Shorter, Edward. *The Making of the Modern Family*. New York: Basic Books, 1975.

Sibley, Mulford Q. "Apology for Utopia, II." *The Journal of Politics*, 2 (May 1949), 165–88.

Sklar, Martin J. "On the Proletarian Revolution and the End of Political-Economic Society." *Radical America*, 3, No. 3 (May–June 1969).

Smith, Henry Nash. *The Virgin Land: The American West as Symbol and Myth*. Cambridge, Mass.: Harvard University Press, 1950.

Solomon, Maynard. "Marx and Bloch: Reflections on Utopia and Art." *Telos*, No. 13 (Fall 1972), 68–86.

Spector, Judith A. "Dr. Jekyll and Mrs. Hyde: Gender-Related Conflict in the Science Fiction of Joanna Russ." *Extrapolation*, 24, No. 4 (Winter 1983), 370–9.

Strauss, Sylvia. "Women in 'Utopia.'" *South Atlantic Quarterly*, 75 (Winter 1976), 115–31.

Suvin, Darko. "The Alternate Islands: A Chapter in the History of SF: With a Bibliography on the SF of Antiquity, the Middle Ages, and the Renaissance." *Science-Fiction Studies*, No. 10 (November 1976), 239–48.

——. "Defining the Literary Genre of Utopia: Some Historical Semantics, Some Genealogy, a Proposal, and a Plea." *Studies in the Literary Imagination* (Fall 1972), 121–45.

——. *Metamorphoses of Science Fiction*. New Haven: Yale University Press, 1979.

——. "Parables of De-Alienation: LeGuin's Widdershins Dance." *Science-Fiction Studies*, No. 7 (November 1975), 265–74.

——. "On the Poetics of the Science Fiction Genre." *College English*, 34, No. 3 (December 1972), 372–82.

——. "Radical Rhapsody and Romantic Recoil in the Age of Anticipation: A Chapter in the History of SF." *Science-Fiction Studies*, No. 4 (Fall 1974), 255–69.

——. "The River Side Trees, or SF and Utopia: Degrees of Kinship." *The Minnesota Review*, Nos 2 and 3 (Spring-Fall 1974), 108–16.

——. "Science Fiction and the Genealogical Jungle." *Genre*, No. 6 (September 1973).

——. "SF Theory: Internal and External Delimitations and Utopia." *Extrapolation*, 19, No. 1 (December 1977), 13–16.

——. "'Utopian' and 'Scientific': Two Attributes for Socialism from Engels." *Minnesota Review*, No. 6 (Spring 1976), 59–70.

Swanson, Roy Arthur. "The True, the False, and the Truely False: Lucian's Philosophical Science Fiction." *Science-Fiction Studies*, No. 10 (November 1976), 228–39.

Sweezy, Paul. "Capitalism and Democracy." *Monthly Review*, 32, No. 2 (June 1980), 27–32.

Tafuri, Manfredo. *Architecture and Utopia: Design and Capitalist Development.* Cambridge, Mass.: MIT Press, 1976.

Taylor, Keith. *The Political Ideas of the Utopian Socialists.* London: Frank Cass, 1982.

Theall, Donald F. "The Art of Social-Science Fiction: The Ambiguous Utopian Dialectics of Ursula K. LeGuin." *Science-Fiction Studies*, No. 7 (November 1975), 256–65.

Urbanowicz, Victor. "Personal and Political in *The Dispossessed*." *Science-Fiction Studies*, No. 15 (July 1978), 110–18.

Vaihinger, Hans. *The Philosophy of "As If": A System of the Theoretical, Practical, and Religious Fictions of Mankind.* New York: Harcourt, 1924.

Veldhuis, R. *Realism Versus Utopianism?* Assen, Netherlands: Royal Van Gorcum, 1975.

Wallerstein, Immanuel. *The Modern World System.* New York: Academic Press, 1974.

Walsh, Chad. *From Utopia to Nightmare.* Evanston: Northwestern University Press, 1964.

Waxman, Chaim I., ed. *The End of Ideology Debate.* New York: Clarion Books, 1969.

Weinstein, James. *Ambiguous Legacy: The Left in American Politics.* New York: Monthly Review Press, 1967.

Williams, Raymond. *Keywords: A Vocabulary of Culture and Society.* London: Oxford University Press, 1976.

——. *Marxism and Literature.* London: Oxford University Press, 1977.

——. *Problems in Materialism and Culture*. London: Verso, 1980.

——. *The Sociology of Culture*. New York: Shocken, 1982.

——. "Towards Many Socialism." *Socialist Review*, No. 85 (Jan.–Feb. 1986), 45–67.

Winston, David. "Iambulus' *Islands of the Sun* and Hellenistic Literary Utopias." *Science-Fiction Studies*, No. 10 (November 1976), 219–28.

Wollheim, Donald A. *The Universe Makers: Science Fiction Today*. New York: DAW Books, 1973.

Zaretsky, Eli. *Capitalism, The Family and Personal Life*. New York: Harper & Row, 1976.

Zipes, Jack. *Breaking the Magic Spell: Radical Theories of Folk and Fairy Tales*. London: Heinemann, 1979.

——. *Fairy Tales and the Art of Subversion*. London: Heinemann, 1983.

——. "Mass Degradation of Humanity and Massive Contradictions in Bradbury's Vision of America in *Farenheit 451*." in *Explorations in Utopian/Dystopian Fiction*, Martin Greenberg, Joseph Olander, Eric Rabkin, eds. Carbondale: Southern Illinois University Press, 1982.

——. *The Trials and Tribulations of Little Red Riding Hood: Versions of the Tale in Sociocultural Context*. London: Heinemann, 1983.

Index

Abendsour, M. H., 5, 215n
Adorno, Theodor W., 25
affirmative culture, 1, 8, 16, 25, 42, 90, 198, 210
Albert, Michael and Robin Hahnel, 198, 217n, 222n
alternative society, 3, 5, 33, 36–8, 43–5, 48, 64, 65, 139, 149, 162, 164, 179, 189, 190, 194, 204, 211
Althusser, Louis, 17, 19, 20, 216n
Amazing Tales, 41
America as Utopia, 4, 20, 47, 48, 95, 96, 214n, 215n
American Shore, The, 157, 218n, 221n
Amis, Kingsley, 37
And Chaos Died, 58, 218n
Annas, Pamela J., 61, 123, 219n, 221n
anti-hegemonic bloc, 11, 27, 28, 147, 188, 197, 198, 204–13,

215n, 217n, 223n
Arcadia, 79, 159
Aronowitz, Stanley, 27, 206–10, 217n, 223n
art, 22, 25, 26, 71, 99, 132, 153, 180, 187, 194, 206, 208
artificial negativity, 93, 96, 116, 215n
Astounding, 159
Auden, W. H., 159
Augustine, 23
Aurora: Beyond Equality, 60

Babel-17, 157, 221n
Badami, Mary Kenny, 219n
Balbus, Isaac D., 215n, 217n, 223n
Ballad of Beta-2, The, 157, 221n
Bankier, Amanda, 60
Baruch, Elaine Hoffman, 127, 134, 221n
Bellamy, Edward, 6
Bennett, Tony, 18, 216n

237

Berry, Wendell, 30, 200, 201, 222n
Bildungsroman, 109–10
Black Panthers, 126
Bloch, Ernst, 20–6, 28, 35, 43, 136, 153, 210, 216n, 217n, 218n
Bogstad, Janice, 60
Bookchin, Murray, 199, 200, 202, 203, 222n, 223n
Brave New World, 9, 104, 130, 200
Braverman, Harry, 17, 215n
Breaking Camp, 121, 220n
Brecht, Bertolt, 1, 33
Bryan, William Jennings, 7
Bryant, Dorothy, 41, 60
Burke, Kenneth, 37

Callenbach, Ernest, 41, 198
Campbell, John, 158, 159
Charnas, Suzy McKee, 41, 60, 74, 198
"city on a hill," 4
Cixous, Hélène, 29, 217n
Comforter, The, 60
concrete utopia, 21, 23, 28, 55, 104
Conroy, Jack, 219n
"Creating Positive Images of Women," 57, 219n, 220n
"Critical Methods, Speculative Fiction," 158, 221n, 222n
critical utopia, 2, 10–12, 26, 30, 31, 33, 36, 41–6, 48–52, 56, 75, 83, 90, 91, 104, 106, 120, 122, 148, 156, 157, 161, 162, 164, 165, 174, 184, 186, 193, 194, 197, 198, 204–6, 209, 213, 214n, 223n

Dance the Eagle to Sleep, 122, 221n
Dawn of the Dead, 9
De Civitate Dei, 23
Delany, Samuel R., 2, 10, 30, 37, 41, 44, 56, 60, 101, 102, 119, 120, 122, 136, 156–95 *passim*, 197, 198, 200, 205, 210, 218n, 219n, 220n, 221n, 222n
de Lauretis, Teresa, 216n, 223n
Derrida, Jacques, 45, 196, 204, 213
desire, 1, 3, 4, 8, 9, 11, 22, 25, 28, 29, 31, 35, 47, 78, 79, 154, 155, 195, 198, 200, 204, 207, 209, 223n
Dhalgren, 157, 221n
Dialectic of Sex, The, 30, 135, 200, 221n, 222n
difference, 20, 27, 36, 208, 211, 212
discrete, the, 36, 38, 43, 45, 49, 50, 64, 75, 76, 83, 94, 105, 124, 138, 139, 157, 161, 163, 174, 176, 188, 190, 191, 205, 218n
Disneyland/Disneyworld, 8, 47
displacement, 31–3, 213
Dispossessed, The, 2, 41, 45, 46, 60, 91–120 *passim*, 156, 161, 175, 186, 220n
"Dreamland," 2
dystopia, 9, 10, 26, 57, 64, 73–5, 81, 83, 94, 95, 113, 121, 124–6, 136, 137, 144, 148, 149, 151, 155, 159, 160, 187, 194, 200

Ecology as Politics, 201
Ecology of Freedom, The, 202, 222n, 223n
Ecotopia, 41, 198
Einstein, Albert, 106
Einstein Intersection, 157, 221n
Elliott, Robert C., 214n
Ellsberg, Daniel, 106
Elsie Dinsmore, 55
Empire Star, 157, 221n
Engels, Friedrich, 5, 24, 197, 204, 210, 215n
English Utopia, The, 2, 214n
Eros and Civilization, 24, 217n

estrangement, 33–6, 60
Ewen, Stuart, 8, 215n

Fahrenheit 451, 104
fairy tale, the, 21, 32, 34, 107, 108, 110, 216n
Fall of the Towers, The, 157, 221n
fantastic, the, 24, 25, 31, 33, 34, 87, 150, 158, 160, 193, 211
fantasy, 1, 24, 25, 31, 34, 35, 38, 42, 79, 86, 154, 197, 205
Farewell to the Working Class, 29, 201, 215n, 222n
Fekete John, 92, 102, 103, 220n
Female Man, The, 2, 41, 46, 55–90 *passim*, 92, 124, 154, 156, 161, 175, 184, 186, 188, 218n, 219n
Firestone, Shulamith, 30, 134, 199, 221n, 222n
Flight from Nevèryön, 157, 221n
Foucault, Michel, 17, 160, 193, 197, 216n, 222n
Foundation, 191
Fourier, Charles, 5, 23, 197
Freud, Sigmund, 8, 22, 24, 25, 34, 217n, 218n
Friedan, Betty, 58
Friend, Beverly, 219n
From the Legend of Riel, 60
Frye, Northrop, 31, 33, 34, 217n
futurism, 203

Garden of Eden, 2
Gearhardt, Sally, 41, 60, 198
genre, 6, 9, 12, 29, 30–6, 42–4, 50, 51, 56, 60, 61, 63, 72, 82, 83, 89, 90, 114, 123, 124, 148, 151, 156, 158–60, 162, 164, 189–94, 197, 210, 211, 217n, 218n
Gernsbach, Hugo, 41
Gilman, Charlotte Perkins, 6, 56, 91, 197, 219n

Gold, Mike, 219n
Golden Age, 23
Gorz, André, 11, 26, 29, 200–2, 215n, 222n
Gramsci, Antonio, 17, 208, 216n
Green Party, the, 199
guide, the, 37, 38, 40, 44, 127, 141, 162

Habermas, Jürgen, 28, 217n
Hacker, Marilyn, 57, 60, 77, 158, 161, 219n, 220n
Happy Hunting Ground, 2
Heimat, 21, 34, 116
Henly, Nancy, 135
Herland, 6, 56, 219n
heterotopia, 44, 156, 160–4, 167, 186–8, 193, 194
Hicks, Edward, 121
Hirsh, Arthur, 217n
hope, 1, 2, 4, 9, 20–2, 194, 198, 203, 211
Huxley, Aldous, 9, 130, 151, 200
Hy Brasil, 2

iconic, the, 36–8, 43–5, 47, 48, 50, 61, 63–5, 73–5, 83, 94, 101, 104, 105, 124, 127, 151, 157, 161–3, 164, 174, 188–90, 205, 218n
ideologeme, 38, 44, 45, 49, 50, 75, 106, 124, 125, 139, 151, 163, 174, 191, 210, 211
ideology, 2, 6, 7, 15–20, 25, 27, 28, 33, 36, 38, 40, 48, 50, 51, 61, 66, 98, 100, 101, 106, 114, 117, 119, 125, 126, 133, 138, 140, 146, 147, 172, 176, 177, 182, 184, 187, 188, 190, 192, 194, 204, 205, 208, 213, 216n
ideology, dominant, 1, 2, 12, 17, 18, 20, 25, 27, 48, 75, 90, 189, 190, 210, 213

ideology, oppositional, 2, 11, 18, 20, 26–8, 75, 83, 87, 113, 148, 188, 192, 206, 208, 213

"I Have a Dream," 10, 199

imagination, the, 1, 5, 12, 15, 18, 20–6 *passim*, 36, 40, 42, 45, 50, 77, 83, 114, 122, 126, 196, 198, 204

International Workers of the World, 96

Iron Heel, The, 6

Jameson, Fredric, 15, 19, 22, 30, 37, 40, 42, 43, 48, 216n, 217n, 218n, 223n

Janus, 60

Jesus, 107, 108

Jewel-Hinged Jaw, The, 157, 218n, 221n, 222n

Kesey, Ken, 123, 150

Khouri, Nadia, 89, 102–5, 136, 193, 220n, 221n, 222n

Kin of Ata, The, 41, 60

King, Martin Luther, 10, 106, 199

Knödler-Bunte, Eberhard, 217n

Kropotkin, Peter, 96

"Land of Cokaygne, The," 2, 3, 32, 103

Lane, Ann J., 56, 219n

Larrain, Jorge, 216n

Lathe of Heaven, The, 92, 220n

Left Hand of Darkness, The, 92, 220n

LeGuin, Ursula K., 2, 10, 30, 41, 44, 57, 60, 91–120 *passim*, 122, 126, 139, 150, 151, 154, 156, 157, 175, 193, 197, 198, 200, 201, 205, 210, 220n, 221n, 222n

LeSuer, Meridel, 219n

Levin, Ira, 9

Lewis, R. W. B., 214n

literary utopia, the, 2–12 *passim*, 21, 23, 24, 29–52 *passim*, 41–6 *passim*, 56, 89, 95, 126, 151, 152, 155, 188, 193, 210, 213, 214n, 217n, 218n

Lomax, Yves, 82, 83, 221n

London, Jack, 6

Looking Backward, 6

Lotman, J. M., 218n

Luke, Tim, 215n

McCarthy, Gene, 10

McClenahan, Catherine, 63, 86, 220n

McIntyre, Vonda, and Susan Janice Anderson, 59

McKinley, William, 7

Mannheim, Karl, 18, 216n

Manuel, Frank E. and Fritzie P., 214n

Mao Tse Tung, 44

Marcuse, Herbert, 24–6, 153, 216n, 217n

Marin, Louis, 38, 46, 218n

Marx, Karl, 129, 215n

Marx, Leo, 4, 214n

Marxism, 23, 209

metaphor, 182, 189, 190, 210, 213, 220n

metonymy, 86

Millett, Kate, 58

Mitchell, Joni, 2

Modern Utopia, A, 6

montage, 63, 82–5, 89

More, Thomas, 2–5, 23, 33, 44, 161

Morris, William, 69, 91, 197, 205

Morton, A. L., 2, 214n

Motherlines, 41, 60, 74, 198

Mutual Aid, 96

Negley, Glenn, 214n

Negley, Glenn and J. Max Patrick,
32, 33, 217n
Negt, Oscar and Alexander Kluge,
28, 217n
Nevèryön, 157, 221n
Neveryóna, 157, 221n
New Jerusalem, 159
New Moon, 60
new world, the, 2, 4, 214n
News from Nowhere, 6, 205
1984, 9
1968, 10, 21, 110, 111
Noble, David F., 215n
"Nobody's Home," 176, 222n
Nova, 157, 221n
novum, 21, 92

One Flew Over the Cuckoo's Nest,
123, 149
O'Neill, Gerald, 41
Order of Things, The, 160, 216n
Orwell, George, 9, 151
Owen, Robert, 5

Parrinder, Patrick, 218n
Pfaelzer, Jeanne, 215n
Piccone, Paul, 215n
Picnic on Paradise, 58, 218n
Piercy, Marge, 2, 10, 30, 41, 60,
121–55 *passim*, 156, 168, 197,
198, 200, 205, 210, 220n,
221n
Plato, 2
political unconscious, the, 30, 43,
46, 210, 213
Port Huron Statement, 199
Principle of Hope, The, 20, 216n
public sphere, 28, 48, 213, 217n
Puritans, 4

Quark, 158, 221–2n

Rabelais, 197

realist novel/realism, 31, 36, 38, 45,
61, 63, 75, 85, 88, 103, 122–4,
126, 127, 142, 146, 148–51,
155, 161, 163, 182, 188–91,
211, 219n
Republic, The, 2
Roemer, Kenneth, 215n
romance, the, 31, 32, 34, 35, 36,
43, 108
Romero, George, 9
Rowbotham, Sheila, 196, 210,
223n
Rowbotham, Sheila, Lynn Segal,
Hilary Wainwright, 223n
Russ, Joanna, 2, 10, 30, 41, 55–90
passim, 92, 122, 124, 139, 150,
151, 154, 156, 157, 176, 197,
198, 200, 205, 206, 210, 218n,
219n, 220n, 222n
Russian Formalists, 33
Ryan, Michael, 203, 209, 210, 212,
213, 223n

Saint-Simon, Henri, 5
Sakharov, André, 106
Sargent, Lyman Tower, 9, 214n
Sargent, Pamela, 59, 222n
Sartre, Jean Paul, 207
Scholes, Robert and Eric Rabkin,
218n
science fiction (SF), 10, 32, 33, 35,
41, 42, 57, 59, 60, 61, 63, 65, 82,
85, 86, 88, 90–2, 107, 122–4,
136, 138, 149, 150, 157–61,
182, 188–94, 196, 218n, 219n
self-reflexive/self-critical, 31, 43–5,
51, 56, 83, 86, 87, 89, 126, 149,
152, 153, 157, 161, 163,
188–91, 193, 194, 198, 210,
211, 213
"Shadows," 188, 191, 192, 222n
Small Changes, 122, 221n
Smith, Henry Nash, 214n

"Socialism: Utopian or Scientific,"
5, 215n
Son of the Sheik, The, 55
Spicy Western Stories, 55
Staatsroman, 5
Starboard Wine, 157, 221n
Staton, Mary, 60
Students for a Democratic Society,
199
Suvin, Darko, 33, 36, 215n, 217n,
218n

This Perfect Day, 9, 104
totally administered society,
16–18, 28, 51
Triton, 2, 41, 45, 46, 60, 156–95
passim, 221n

uncanny, the, 34, 217n
unconscious, the, 16, 22, 25
Unsettling of America, The, 30,
200, 222n
Utopia, 2, 3, 33
utopian form, 39, 43, 46, 50, 51,
61, 62, 64, 82, 83, 89, 114, 116,
126, 148, 150, 154, 155, 188–94
passim, 198, 210–13
utopian impulse, the, 5, 15, 16,
18–28 *passim*, 29, 41, 42, 46,
51, 56, 87, 89, 94, 101, 126, 138,
148, 150, 151, 154, 155, 157,
161, 163, 164, 188, 189, 193–5,
198, 203, 211–13, 223n

Verne, Jules, 41
visitor, the, 36–9, 40, 43–5, 49, 63,
72, 95, 109, 124, 127, 128, 142,
143

Walk to the End of the World, 74
Wanderground, 41, 60, 198
We, 9
Weathermen, the, 126, 147
Weinstein, James, 215n
Wells, H. G., 6, 41
Western Paradise, 2
Wilde, Oscar, 29
willed transformation/activism, 32,
33, 35, 49–51, 66, 75, 78, 80–2,
94, 106, 110, 112–14, 119, 122,
124, 125, 138, 140, 147–9, 154,
163, 174, 175, 186, 187, 191,
198, 204–6, 209, 211
Williams, Raymond, 6, 32, 33,
215n, 217n
Winstanley, Gerard, 5
Wiscon, 60
Witch and the Chameleon, The,
60
Woman on the Edge of Time, 2, 41,
46, 60, 121–55 *passim*, 156,
175, 186, 221n
Women of Wonder, 59, 222n
Woolf, Virginia, 58
Word for World is Forest, The, 92,
220n
Wright, Richard, 219n

YV 88, 41

Zamyatin, Evgeny, 9, 151
Zipes, Jack, 16, 34, 216n, 217n